The Golden Age of Probation

Mission v Market

Edited by Roger Statham

With a Foreword by Alan Bennett

≋ WATERSIDE PRESS

The Golden Age of Probation
Mission v Market
Edited by Roger Statham

ISBN 978-1-909976-14-6 (Paperback)
ISBN 978-1-908162-81-6 (Epub ebook)
ISBN 978-1-908162-82-3 (Adobe ebook)

Cover design © 2014 Waterside Press. Design by www.gibgob.com.

Main UK distributor Gardners Books, 1 Whittle Drive, Eastbourne, East Sussex, BN23 6QH. Tel: +44 (0)1323 521777; sales@gardners.com; www.gardners.com

North American distribution Ingram Book Company, One Ingram Blvd, La Vergne, TN 37086, USA. Tel: (+1) 615 793 5000; inquiry@ingramcontent.com

Cataloguing-In-Publication Data A catalogue record for this book can be obtained from the British Library.

Printed by CPI Group (UK) Ltd, Croydon, CR0 4YY

e-book *The Golden Age of Probation* is available as an ebook and also to subscribers of Myilibrary, Dawsonera, ebrary, and Ebscohost.

Published 2014 by
Waterside Press
Sherfield Gables
Sherfield-on-Loddon
Hook, Hampshire
United Kingdom RG27 0JG

Telephone +44(0)1256 882250
E-mail enquiries@watersidepress.co.uk
Online catalogue WatersidePress.co.uk

Contents

Copyright and publication details   *ii*

Acknowledgements   *vi*

Foreword   *vii*

The Editor and Contributors   *viii*

The Author of the Foreword   *viii*

Dedication   *ix*

Introduction: Probation — The Beginning or End? *10*
Roger Statham

1. **A Probation Officer in Coventry** 21
Barrie Bridgeman

2. **Probation: A Journey in Caring** 25
Basil Hylton

3. **A Road Well Travelled** 37
Cedric Fullwood

4. **Probation Memories** 56
Colin Archer

5. **A Home Office Perspective** 64
David Faulkner

6. **Remembering Probation in the Sixties** 70
David Millard

7. **Probation: An Earlier Life** 79
Gordon Read

8.   A Personal Probation Journey...................................... 89
     Howard Lockwood

9.   A View of Probation in the 1960s: From the Bottom 97
     Jim Cannings

10. A Probation Memoir 1965 to 2001................................. 107
     John Harding

11. My Life in Probation... 116
     Michael Vizard

12. The Hat on the Office Door...................................... 124
     Malcolm Lacey

13. From Wales to Durham and Back: My Probation Experience........ 148
     Martin Jones

14. From San Francisco to Jordan: A Probation Journey..........153
     Mary Anne McFarlane

15. The Road From Wigan Pier 160
     Mike Worthington

16. A Probation Journey within Teesside 1975–2005: 169
     Never Far from Home, Forever Striving
     Peter Hadfield

17. My Probation Journey 181
     Peter Warburton

18. From Stoke to Middlesbrough: 185
     A Probation Journey Through Industrial and Political Wastelands
     Roger Statham

19. One Journey Across Four Decades of Probation: 1972–2010 196
Steve Collett

20. Seventies Probation 210
Sue Winfield

Index *218*

Acknowledgements

Sincere and grateful thanks to all those in these pages who have managed to contribute to the writing of this book. It is the very difference of style and approach by each of them that has helped create a real evocation of the golden age of probation, which I trust will be sensed by all those that read it. Thanks also to the many other colleagues in the Association of Retired Chief Officers and Inspectors of Probation who in different circumstances might have added richly to the text. Over time, and during a long probation career, there have been many who have provided support, advice, and inspiration; there are reflections of them all in these pages and I remain indebted to every one.

Thanks to the Probation Chiefs Association for their work on probation's legacy which provided the impetus for this book; and to Bryan Gibson for his patient counsel, in the process of putting it all together — the presentation of the book is a testimony to this.

Alan Bennett's support and contribution simply could not have been anticipated at the outset. His backing for public sector probation and his concerns about market forces are beautifully expressed. I would like to record my very grateful thanks for his help.

Finally, thanks also to Wendy for her readiness to proof read endlessly, and to all my family for their patience when the blue mist descends, and I am lost in distraction.

Roger Statham
August 2014

Foreword

Probation belongs at a local level and profit should not come into it. The satis-factions of the Probation Service are not financial ones and nor should they be; they are the rewards of dedication and service. But because such values cannot be quantified this government prefers to believe they are out-of-date, and even that they do not exist. Profit is thought to be the only trustworthy motive and thus that probation can be farmed out to whatever agency thinks it can make it pay.

The remedying of misfortune, which is what probation is about has no more to do with profit than the remedying of disease.

Alan Bennett

The Editor and Contributors

After being a probation officer in Stoke-on-Trent in 1968, Roger Statham rose through the ranks to become chief probation officer for Teesside (formerly Cleveland). He has held various positions including chair of the Adventure Playgrounds Association in Stoke; the Local Review Committee at HM Prison Durham; the North-East Prison After-Care Society (NEPACS); the Social Policy Committee of the Association of Chief Officers of Probation and Continuing Care Review Panels of the National Health Service in Yorkshire. He was a member of the Parole Board from 1996 to 2000 and has written extensively about probation including as co-author of the two works mentioned at the end of his own story in *Chapter 18*. He is Vice-President of NEPACS and joint secretary of the Association of Retired Chief Officers and Inspectors of Probation. This book contains contributions by 20 people with similar or associated backgrounds whose brief descriptions follow their own contributions.

The Author of the Foreword

Alan Bennett is one of the UK's leading literary figures and after a lifetime of writing and performing has established himself as a national treasure. His acute insights into people and their interactions have provided a lasting legacy and he remains a trenchant social commentator. His mistrust of the market and belief in the value of public services provide a clarion call for all those who continue to believe that there is still such a thing as society.

For Wendy, Jonathan, Sian, Katy, Ben, Rachel, Dom, Lucy, Alice and William.

To all probation staff past and present, who contributed to a public service often referred to as the jewel of the Criminal Justice System.

Introduction:
Probation — The Beginning or End?

Roger Statham

By the end of 2013 it was clear that, after decades of unpopularity, political forces were finally ensuring the end of the Probation Service in England and Wales. The notion of probation and the values it stood for seemed to resonate no longer with government and the public at large. Some of those, perhaps more appreciative of the wider significance that probation played in the dynamics of criminal justice, have fought a small rearguard action but to no avail. In 2014 as the new structure for probation emerges from the fettered imaginations of Ministry of Justice exercises, the political sop of retaining some kind of national probation service has a hollow ring given the parameters in which it is likely to operate. Sadly there does seem to be a lack of vision within Government and changes to probation do seem to be somewhat *ad hoc* and suggest problems lie ahead.

We should remember that the changes made by New Labour in 2001 when probation was effectively nationalised had already deprived it of an effective voice and shifted local accountability to national. It is axiomatic that both criminal and social justice essentially each have a local dimension; communities have different dynamics and in criminal justice terms sentencers do have to respond to local concerns. The ability of probation to be responsive in this way is slowly being lost, amid all the changes, and with it an important sphere of influence in the process of sentencing. It can only be hoped that the new Community Rehabilitation Companies (CRCs) can forge links with community organizations in order to provide the potential for local cohesion and long-term rehabilitation and reintegration that can help close the growing social divide in our modern world.

One bright note has been struck by the creation of a national Probation Institute which may yet help protect and sustain the values and skills nurtured in over a century of public service.

Amid the gathering gloom for those who believed in probation, there has been the sensing of the need to record something of its legacy. This aspiration has been reinforced by the realisation that much of the archive material in local services was being lost and indeed that there was little chance of much of it surviving; the Government apparently having little appetite for helping preserve probation's legacy. If the tree of probation is to be felled then here is a chance to create some of the tree rings. These chapters provide a cross-section of probation history and *in toto* they give a unique insight into the last half of the 20th-century, as probation grew, developed and modified in response to social and political pressures. I think it fair to say that probation had a self-conscious aspiration to broker a position in society for the disadvantaged and particularly those that might be termed the criminal classes. Probation as a service has never lost its belief in rehabilitation and at its heart has remained person-centred.

It was out of the talk about legacy that I began to reflect on my own personal probation journey which was from Stoke to Middlesbrough. It was to become the springboard for others to contribute their journeys, and for those amongst the ranks of the Association of Retired Chief Officers and Inspectors of Probation who could find the emotional energy — they have done so.

It is fair to say that this book has emerged from a political and social maelstrom, created by a Coalition Government that has produced a huge sense of sadness and maybe even an element of disbelief. The contributions, shall we call them essays, from some of the most senior and influential people in the service, are self-conscious in nature; personal recollections and reflections that, for the perceptive, say as much about the writers as they do about the subjects of their narratives. This is just as it should be because to get under the skin of an organization it is important to understand the people involved in it and the dynamic processes that shaped their efforts and achievements, individually and collectively. The Probation Service was never still, and here are insights into organizational culture locally and nationally; a political interface with the Home Office (and later the Ministry of Justice) and criminal justice system (CJS); and most importantly of some of those interactions with the disadvantaged and marginalised in society.

What has been so interesting about these emerging retrospectives has been the chosen focus for so many on early career experiences. A reflection no doubt of the values and aspirations of eager new probation officers, who could whiff injustice in every corner of the CJS, and that could still be stirred by memories. As a consequence in the modern world of the 21st-century there is a sense of wonderful naïvety in the compassion and altruism that is a common denominator in all the journeys. It is this that truly marks the prevailing social attitudes of their time. Inevitably the pieces are personal, but they create a mosaic and here is a lasting imagery of probation as it was. Aspiration, hope, despair, success, failure too, are all here for those who want to see it, and even courage, integrity and optimism. It is not too bold a claim to suggest that this book really does capture the golden age of probation.

Of the many patterns which emerge, it is the restless energy for innovation and initiative that is truly striking. Probation was an early advocate of equal opportunity and the recognition of need and social discord spurred continuous developments. Victim support, community service, day centres, drug and alcohol treatment, prison work and after-care, support groups of all kinds, risk-assessment, are but part of countless initiatives nurtured by probation officers. Many of these at a time when probation had responsibility for work with those going through divorce courts, adoption and juvenile courts, even neighbours' quarrels, permission to marry and any other problem the courts might pass on. If ever an organization was into multi-tasking then it was certainly true of probation, particularly through the expansionist years of the sixties, seventies and eighties.

Here too there are insights into the impact of unemployment and disadvantage, the social unrest and the civil riots of the eighties and nineties that have disappeared from consciousness. Most importantly there are insights into the struggle to understand racial discrimination and the challenges it posed in changing behaviours and attitudes both within probation and society as a whole.

There are no grandiose claims, but there are challenging questions that do emerge from these essays into the life of what was once considered an important public body. Probation has played a vital part in criminal justice and the lives of communities and for a considerable time significantly influenced sentencing in courts and the lives of offenders in the community. Its values and culture have shone like a beacon.

This beacon has shone further than these shores and there are examples of the UK Probation Service supporting developments throughout the world, and particularly in Europe. Ironically these influences seem destined to remain strong despite the fact that the service here is being dismantled.

One contribution to this book in particular facilitates a comprehension of the interface between the dynamics of government and an operational part of its machinery, in this case the Home Office and probation. The tensions around developing public policy and satisfying political aspiration are captured beautifully. Insights of this nature and the benefits of calmer reflection, provided by time, do illuminate the potential for some of the more base motives to be part of political aspiration. It also reinforces the difficulty we have now in modern politics of having a proper debate that can allow the influence of a broader consensus as we develop new approaches. Sadly without it, prejudice and narrowness win out. Perhaps we need to rediscover democracy.

For social historians the pages in this book provide a unique insight, and it is hoped that they will assist in future analysis of both public services and organizational culture. It is important that events and developments are recorded that may help those who wish to question, probe and to gain insight for themselves and these essays it is hoped will assist in this process. However this introduction would not be complete if it did not help to begin this process and provide some comment, even a modest analysis of the events leading to the demise of probation.

The Political Landscape Stifles Probation as a Local Service

Any analysis has to be put into a proper context because what is clear is that beyond the post-1979-to-1997-era there has been a prevailing view that there should be a reduction in the scale of the state, and also that there should be competition between the state services that remain. As the government struggles to cut expenditure, institutions that are deemed to be a waste of money or disappoint simply do not survive. However the Government has found difficulty in wholly distancing probation from the state, but instead has created a structure in which the service now has to perform in what is essentially a market-driven world.

On the face of it changes happening to probation are but part of a wider dogma, just another public service shunted into the private sector on the basis of little evidence, but simply on that of political ideological dema-goguery. What is being lost is an organization with a unique culture and value system, to be replaced with a small state-run Probation Service with a narrow risk-management brief and target-driven systems. The bulk of now old probation work will be farmed out to CRCs who will operate within an opaque financial and accountability structure that is being worked out in a piecemeal way and without a clear blueprint. The new structure will however give opportunities for profit to the Government's much loved solu-tions and logistics companies who are committed to shareholder value, but might be seen simply as public asset strippers. All of this will be covered with that wonderful old negligee beloved of Tory rhetoric, charitable and community work.

It is not intended to belittle voluntary organizations, now the independent sector, and the tremendous work that they do, but to simply point out that they are likely to receive scraps as the Government reduces its finan-cial commitment to working with offenders in the community. In reality, reducing spending is what the Government is about, and many deprived communities are beyond the reach of charities as there is neither the infra-structure nor resources to provide relief to, or sustain, the growing numbers of a social underclass. The marked increase in poverty is worrying.

In June 2014, it was announced that the new National Probation Service will be part of an agency within the Ministry of Justice accountable to Ministers. There will also be the creation of 21 CRCs which will be managed within the agency, but which will transfer to new private or social sector providers following to quote a "share sale" later in 2014. In order to justify the changes throughout the process the Government has relied on the mantra "Transforming Rehabilitation" as a positive sop and in an attempt to deflect from its real agenda. Whilst contemplating this agenda it should be remem-bered that many of the innovations in probation practice sprang directly from within the service and in performance terms the Probation Service has functioned in a way that has met expectations at all levels. It is as though probation is being treated as a failing organization when very clearly it is not.

What is being created now is an illusion, the sheer complexity of the unfolding structure beggars belief and the fragmentation of effort and aspi-ration that will inevitably follow will have a huge impact on performance.

Certainly the culture of the Probation Service with its steadfast rehabilitative beliefs will be lost as staff are shunted into the uncertainty of the new structures, which are hardly a boost to staff morale. Culture is important, it is in a sense the lifeblood of an organization. It is how positive aspiration, ambition and good performance are passed on to each generation of employees. Cultural norms become a positive affirmation of achieving and feeling good about being part of an organization and appropriate behaviours follow without the need to micro-manage. Fully understanding culture both organizationally and socially is so important, As Mary Midgley, that eminent and wise moral philosopher, reminds us,

> "In spite of the huge differences between cultures all that we know about human behaviour shows that it can be understood only through reference to peoples own thoughts, dreams, hopes, fears, and other feelings — This is not invented by a particular culture. It's universal" (Mary Midgely, *Are You an Illusion?*, Acumen, 2014).

There is something profound here. Behaviour is a response to people's own individual worlds, it is only through understanding this that we can gain insight and any chance for influence. For example, disadvantaged people feel disadvantaged, they fear disadvantage and behave in a way that often enhances the very disadvantage that is intrinsically part of their lives. Probation understood that and at its best could touch people and turn around their lives. This book gives insights into how probation worked and can still work and there are explorations of some of the moral and philosophical issues that impact on interaction with individuals. These very dilemmas exist as critically today as they ever did, it is just not fashionable to talk about them any more.

Understanding culture in the context of the lives of offenders is but part of the picture. I would argue that it is likely that it will be increasingly difficult for probation workers to practice in as sensitive and insightful a way as in the past because of the inevitable cultural changes they face. Their own experience of working within an organization will change as fragmentation through these enforced changes impacts. Organizational cultural identity is likely to be eroded or even lost. How will this impact on the hopes and fears and dreams of those employed in the new organizations? How will job satisfaction, the source of motivation be sustained? My own anxiety is that some of the intrinsic compassion that probation brought to criminal justice will disappear as members of staff begin to feel less valued and nurtured. There is growing evidence of this trend in health, education, childcare, the care of the elderly and elsewhere in both the public and private sectors. In over-regulated jobs people are reduced to parodying their rôles, avoiding taking responsibility and ultimately simply becoming automaton "jobsworths" desperate for the end of the working day. Zero-hours contracts are likely to produce zero-commitment, all a long way from the idealised model of John Lewis mutuality so beloved by government.

The changes now taking place in probation also give rise to fears that for staff there will be no time for reflection on the moral conundrums. In a world that is already more feral and arms-length, in terms of personal interaction, who is asking about such ephemeral things as hopes and fears and dreams. What is more as risk-assessment processes in the new probation structure become more mechanised the uniqueness of the individualism will be lost. It will also be increasingly difficult for hopes and dreams and fears of offenders to be explored, inevitably they too will be lost in a world of protocols and targets.

As all the changes unfold and probation begins to unravel it is telling that a raft of chiefs have chosen to go, the second significant exodus in 13-years. It is alleged that some others are only staying on as a result of being offered tangible incentives. This is hardly a vote of confidence for the changes and their exodus, after two years of consultation, is bound to have an impact. People at the top of organizations hold the ring in terms of culture because of their breadth of experience. The loss of this talent is surely a matter for regret.

For probation it will now be for others in future to assess the impact of the changes, not simply in terms of accountancy-led targets but in terms of culture and behaviours that reflect a proper set of values and aspirations in a civilised culture. To re-cap, I think that despite all the differences and tensions from time-to-time within the Probation Service itself there has remained a shared cultural understanding of social disadvantage that was often rooted in the criminal justice system for many and with it an aspiration for rehabilitation. It was the thread that held the service together and I do hope that it continues to do so.

These are enormous issues for all of us as individuals and as a society. Sadly, we cannot rely on politicians for answers and yet at the same time we seem unable to have the debate. Particularly as the media culture of doggedly pursuing yes and no answers from politicians has insidiously impacted on our capacity for nuanced discussion, and also the acknowledgment of difference and uncertainty in decision-making and policy-making. The politicians themselves however have to take major responsibility for their own spinning and dissembling to the point that they can no longer be believed. We live in a world of ego-junkies and this was never more clearly demonstrated than it is at that interface between politicians and the media.

Searching Questions Beyond the Present Political Hegemony

For me personally there will always be the question, "Was privatisation inevitable" or alternatively, "Might the Probation Service have survived if collectively we had been more politically astute?" So here is a brief section reflecting on some of the issues to ponder.

As part of unpicking these issues I might pose yet another question and a major one—"Why did probation become so politically unpopular? Was it because of perceived trade union antagonism to the government of the day?". This perception, it might be argued, made it difficult for chiefs to be seen as the real leaders of the service and to manage it effectively. Napo enjoyed considerable support in the service and had become an effective and much admired campaigning organization, but did not easily embrace the challenges of adapting to the new political forces. I had a real sense of unease about the dynamics of the time and in 1990 I wrote and circulated an unpublished paper that I called "Probation in the Market Driven World"[1] because I felt a deep concern that there was little or no awareness within the service of the threats that lay ahead. It highlighted the importance of leadership nationally and locally and suggested that senior probation officers were middle managers. It was in a *cri de coeur* as I felt that the service was under threat if the leadership was not perceived as receptive to the changes in the political landscape. However the political aspiration to include punishment in the probation lexicon which did not chime with probation culture was a significant problem.

1. "Probation in the Market Driven World", Cleveland Probation Service, 1990, Roger Statham.

Clearly the leadership concerns were real enough and I remember being part of a small group of chiefs at a private dinner with John Patten, when he was a junior Minister in the Home Office when it was discussed. A later personal discussion with Kenneth Baker when he was Home Secretary reinforced the importance of this as did an even later one with Lord Williams of Mostyn who was of a different political hue but had the same concerns about how probation was perceived. Certainly support for probation, both as a conceptual approach in the criminal justice system and an organization, which had begun to dwindle in the 1980s, a trend which might have been stemmed by the opportunities provided by the 1991 Criminal Justice Act, has continued to ebb in the 1990s and beyond. Certainly if there was an opportunity for probation to be centre stage with the 1991 Act the opportunity had been lost by 1995.

The change in government in 1997 did not change the perception of probation and nationalisation in 2001 saw probation lose its voice. Chiefs could no longer speak out as they had done effectively in the past either individually or through the Association of Chief Officers of Probation. Apart from stifling the voice of probation after 2001, Government has appeared to directly influence appointments in probation and even the tenure of chief officers. The cherished local accountability was now lost and government began to behave towards probation in a very different way to its approach to the police service for example.

This book is able to illuminate the culture of probation, and demonstrate a sense of common aspiration, and shared values. I have argued that these provided the cement that held the culture together despite the differences. At the same time it would appear that viewed from a political perspective it was being weakened by that human dimension of individualism and perhaps a perceived lack of a collective will to manage effectively. Was it a lack of collective cohesion and ultimately a failure of the Probation Service to be politically convincing, or that it is simply being punished for resisting succumbing to political hubris?

As for public attitudes, had they begun to shift too after the aspirational 1960s and when industrial unrest stifled the country during the 1970s? Or were public attitudes simply eroded by a sustained hardline political stance reflected ultimately in the prison works rhetoric? One thing that we can be certain of is that there was ultimately a change from a belief in rehabilitation to the desire for punishment.

Having briefly reflected on the dynamics of change in attitudes by Government we are faced with even more profound questions about the forming of public opinion and in the influences that are part of that. For now maybe it is sufficient to say that probation did become identified as being on the side of the offender, a position that did not sit easily with a wider shift to a belief in punishment and locking-up people for longer.

The parts of the academic world looking at policy shifts in criminal justice have become preoccupied with that difficult to define concept of neo-liberalism in its attempts to analyse the changes that have taken place. Neo-conservativism might provide a more accurate term for the forces that have created the shifts in public attitudes that have taken place over the last 20-years and more. The subtle use of propaganda promoted by the toxic chemistry of political spin and a self-interested media has worked. For example the welfare state has become the discredited nanny state, whilst proper pensions have somehow become elitist. How strange that there has been no debate about why Government is investing in stimulating the housing market, when the real reason is that ultimately those with no pensions will have a saleable asset to help fund their care in old-age. What the Government has lost sight of is that all disadvantaged people are destined to become wards of the state one way or another at some time in their lives.

There are many unanswered questions that for now must be left for others to ponder and maybe to answer. Sufficient to say that the contributions in this book reflect the preoccupations of those involved at the highest levels of probation over many years, their hopes and dreams of their time are here. We hope that we have described what was a golden age. However, the ultimate aspiration for this book is that it will foster debate.

An Unlikely Champion Emerges

Whilst this book was being written and developed the Government was implementing its changes to probation. It would be an understatement to suggest that these were ill-thought out and chaotic. Writing about a golden age in such dispiriting times was not easy.

What a delight it was to discover that Alan Bennett the author, playwright and actor was unimpressed about what was happening to probation and that he was prepared to comment. He agreed to write the Foreword to this book and also to allow me use his quotes from earlier writings. When I wrote back to Alan I thanked him and suggested that he had allowed us a few more days in the sun.

Here are some of the things he has said about probation and its predicament:

> "Walking along Wellington Street Leeds, towards the City Square I pass the offices of the Probation Service, now plastered with leaflets and posters from NAPO against the selling off of the service, protests that in my view are fully justified. The notion that probation, which is intended to help those who have fallen foul of the law, should make a profit seems beyond satire."[2]

> "I am uneasy when prisons are run for profit, or health services either. The rewards of probation and the alleviation of suffering are human profits and nothing to do with balance sheets. These days no institution is immune. In my last play the Church of England is planning to sell off Winchester Cathedral…Profit is now the sole yardstick against which our institutions must be measured and in pursuit of profit the state and all that goes with it is sold from under us who are its rightful owners and with a frenzy and dedication that calls up memories of an earlier iconoclasm."[3]

Roger Statham is Joint Secretary of the Association of Retired Chief Officers and Inspectors of Probation. For his personal contribution, see *Chapter 18.*

---

2. "Diary: What I Did in 2013", Alan Bennett, *London Review of Books*, 2013.
3. "Fair Play", Sermon Before the University, King's College Chapel, Cambridge, Alan Bennett, 1 June 2014: http://www.kings.cam.ac.uk/files/services/sermon-20140601-bennett.pdf

1. A Probation Officer in Coventry

Barrie Bridgeman

In the 1960s the probation office in Coventry was a series of interconnected wooden huts squashed between Drapers' Hall, an historic guildhall used as an additional magistrates' court, and the public lavatories. Each office within the timber complex was just big enough to accommodate a desk, two chairs, a filing cabinet and an electric radiator. However, all the probation officers had been trained; at a time when many neighbouring services had resorted to recruiting unqualified officers. I had been trained at Rainer House in London after the Home Office had paid for me to read for a diploma in social administration at Exeter University. The Home Office training course had also included two practical placements under the supervision of senior probation officers. My final placement had been at Winchester under Paddy Barratt.

My welcome to the office as a rookie probation officer by the late-Andrew Murray, principal probation officer, finished with my being told that my interviewing evening was on Thursdays and I had use of a dictating machine for recording case record entries on Wednesdays. He then escorted me to my office and left me to contact my caseload contained in the filing cabinet — all 69 case files.

The bizarreness of not having a facility for recording interviews until a week after the event was further enhanced by the necessity of not only finding a machine and a working microphone but also a micro-cassette. There was a typing backlog of two or three weeks, so most of the stock of cassettes were awaiting typing and it was necessary to be on good terms with the typists so that one could be set aside for me after it was freed. I soon realised that one evening a week was insufficient to see my "clients" (the terminology used then) so started to use Tuesdays for evening interviews as well. Even so it took a couple of months to make face-to-face contact with all my caseload.

At the time of my arrival in Coventry, the service had just appointed two senior probation officers (SPOs). This was an innovation and individual probation officers were somewhat bemused as to the purpose of these people. The SPOs did assume the responsibility of allocating social enquiry reports (also called probation reports and later pre-sentence reports) to officers in their "teams". In essence, however, each probation officer acted individually and there was little formal sharing of information except if different officers were preparing reports for courts on co-defendants. Later, I did have a case discussion with my SPO, which proved helpful and we promised ourselves that we would do it again but never did.

Our presence in court was considered by the service to be important. All officers with reports due for a particular day were expected to be in attendance in the magistrates' court when it started sitting at 10 am The practices in the adult courts and juvenile courts were different. In the adult court the probation officer handed in the report via the court clerk at the appropriate point in the proceedings and was afforded the opportunity after the magistrates had read the report to make any oral addition. I used this chance usually not so much to update the report but to stress particular aspects of it. My rationale was that this was an opportunity to "sell" what the service could offer. In the juvenile courts, the procedure was to hand in the report in as in the adult courts but then to read it aloud while the magistrates were reading their own copies. I started paraphrasing the report as I read it which immediately gained the bench's attention. No one objected to this development and it enabled me to address the sentencers directly.

By and large, the probation officers disliked the procedure of reading reports aloud in the juvenile courts. It was only at the retirement celebration of one officer, the late-Bob Buckingham, that the situation was clarified. He used his "thank you" speech to raise the question about the juvenile court reports. It transpired from those magistrates in attendance that they also disliked the system but thought that it was the probation officers who wanted it. After this clarification the juvenile courts assumed the same practice as the adult courts. It seemed that the original decision had been an agreement between the court clerk and the principal probation officer.

Mention of Bob Buckingham reminds me that he died within about 18 months of retirement and I discovered that that was a fairly typical pattern. Few officers in those days seemed to survive long to draw their pensions and indeed some died during their active service.

By the end of my first year as an officer, I had a caseload in the upper seventies and was preparing ten social inquiry reports a month. The day came for a visit by the probation inspector who was to decide whether or not I should be confirmed in my appointment. This was the late-Cliff Swann, whom I had met a couple of times previously. He had an unusual view about probation officer training. In his words all an officer really needed was training in logic and ethics; the rest would follow from that. I recall him also saying that one should not embark on a sentence without knowing how to finish it. I regarded him with awe. He spent the day reading a random selection of my cases plus one that I had chosen at his request for his guidance. At the end of the day, after also talking with the principal probation officer, he confirmed my appointment — to my great relief. He was also able to offer some helpful comment on my chosen case. It was only afterwards that I realised the chosen case record was lacking in the required quarterly summaries of progress and planning. I had done one 18 months summary. Interestingly, Mr Swann had made no comment about that.

In due course, as a result of negotiations between a voluntary local committee and the Langley House Trust a voluntary hostel for young male offenders was built and Mr Murray asked me to be the liaison officer. Some of the neighbours of the hostel were apprehensive about the development. The leading light of the objectors was identified and invited to become a member of the management committee. It was an adroit manoeuvre which resulted in the objector becoming an advocate to his neighbours on behalf of the hostel. It was a practical example of group and inter-group dynamics about which I learned on an excellent course I attended at Vaughan College in Leicester. This was probably the most useful course I went on throughout my career with the service and indeed I repeated it a couple of years later and enhanced my learning and appreciation of the dynamics that operate between people and within and between groups.

The hostel was staffed by employees of Langley House Trust. They comprised two married couples: one husband being designated as the warden and the other as the assistant warden and the wives respectively were the housekeeper and assistant housekeeper. I suspect such gender designation would be unacceptable these days but in that day and age it worked well. I was impressed by the commitment of these dedicated people and the good work they did in helping those young men in putting their lives back together.

Coventry was a good size in which to start a career as a probation officer. Officially a city it was sufficiently compact to feel like a small town. So there was a range of experiences to be found in the community and a number of initiatives taken by voluntary groups and individuals which made a difference rather than being swallowed up in a large conurbation. Indeed, there were about 30 people whom one met repeatedly on a variety of committees exerting great influence for the good.

Barrie Bridgeman, Probation officer, Coventry Probation Service, 1960s; Assistant Chief Probation Officer West Midlands, 1975-1997.

2.   Probation: A Journey in Caring

Basil Hylton

Introduction

It could be argued that authentic personal public *services*, such as the Probation Service, are institutions on a "journey in caring"; and that whilst they, as agents, might represent (and be paid for by) an otherwise necessary *controlling* state, they implicitly need to have a corresponding *caring* side also, seen and experienced by the actual or potential recipients of that "care".[1] So went the former "care and control" argument, now somewhat overshadowed by "tough-love" assertions which when said between gritted teeth simply implies "tough on you, mate". Reflecting then on my, albeit, small part in the 100-year journey of the Probation Service delivering care, I am somewhat forced to turn to a fading memory and largely to undocumented recollections. In doing so, I would neither want to exaggerate my own limited knowledge, nor my own modest contribution to that journey.

In sharing my bit of "journey in caring" within the longer, wider Probation Service's journey, I will restrict my focus mainly to my time as a main grade probation officer (1970-79),[2] and commence by mentioning a bit of my own background as a British-Jamaican. I am referring to my background since it is an important dimension to the context of the 1970s when I first joined the UK Service. In doing so, I hope to include peoples of the former British-owned colonies who contributed to that journey, and those who were on the receiving end of its statutory duties. However, as the essay's length will obviously allow only *snippets* of my own personal journey, I hope they will be seen as *pointers* to experiences valued, critical contestations fought, and

---

1.   Social work as a professional discipline seeks to improve the quality of life and subjective well-being of individuals, groups, and communities through a variety of methods (e.g. research, policy, direct practice, crisis intervention, etc.) and teaching for the benefit of those affected by social disadvantages such as poverty, mental and physical illness or disability, and social injustice (Wikipedia).

2.   I was an SPO for six years and for another eleven an ACPO within the West Midlands Probation Service.

instances of "tough love" and mutual appreciations shared.

I will therefore say something about that 1970s context itself, and a little about some significant happenings that impacted on me at about the time of my entry into the service. I will share some profound memories of my training, outline brief recollections of the first team of officers I worked with along with two or three outstanding memories of "clients". Finally, I will refer to some of my own disappointments regarding the current "death knell" of a much loved and socially significant *service*.

Context of the 1970s

As a young man in Jamaica, I once met a probation officer, a Robert Preston. I recall that he was involved in assisting two persons, an old tailor and a shoemaker, both owning small business workshops in Kingston. Because they were semi-illiterate, Mr Preston did their book-keeping for them but on the condition that they offered ongoing apprenticeships to two known "rude boys" (offenders) on probation to him. "Isn't Probation work sensible," was my then honest thought. Earlier I was schooled along with hundreds of poor, disaffected and socially-disadvantaged children, seemingly imperceptibly directed in a process of limited social outlets for the young — primarily sports, music/military, church or crime.

Meanwhile, within Britain, encouraged by the social reforms of the-1960s (e.g. abortion law, abolition of capital punishment and the decriminalisation of homosexuality), many fundamental social changes began to take place. "It was an extraordinary liberal period," commented Harry Fletcher, a criminal justice expert, in an *Observer* article (2 March 2014). He was the leading mouthpiece of probation staff facing what appears to be the final days of a service many of us knew and faithfully served. "People were pushing at every boundary — sexual, moral, legal…," he expanded, explaining that even paedophiles attempted to seek open support for their views. The door to immigration from the Caribbean was all but shut, and the meaning of the word "integration" was still masked by the maxim "when in Rome, do as the Romans do".

Within the context of this "liberal period" of the 1970s, we might also add the Civil Rights March on Washington DC in 1963 led by Dr Martin Luther King. Coincidentally, on that very day the well-publicised anti-racism demonstration in relation to the "Bus Boycott" in Bristol took place and along with other notable events (e.g. the Notting Hill Riots of the late-1950s onwards) gave rise to Britain's first two racial discrimination laws being enacted (1965 and 1968). Within this same context, the right wing Conservative MP, Enoch Powell, should not be forgotten. He "prophesied" rivers of blood in UK streets unless black people were positively encouraged or made to return to some place rather than remaining in the UK. "Race", poverty, discrimination and crime were interlinked, and any authentic "journey in caring" needed to have been cognisant of this. Prisons "bursting at the seams" were inescapably relevant to a caring rehabilitative service; and so should have been the increasingly disproportionate incarceration of members from the black community, as well as their being in receipt of hostile policing. Of equal significance was the noticeable absence of black CJS service delivery staff. Indeed, it was at the 1977 National Association of Probation Officers' AGM in Brighton that I moved its first ever motion against racism within the service, introducing myself as "Basil Hylton, a *token* black probation officer from Bristol" and getting an unexpected standing ovation. Of significance to me was the pressure placed on me to accept a composite motion linking my union branch motion to a condemnation of the National Front. That was a momentary distraction that signalled the need for an Association of Black Probation Officers (ABPO) aimed at holding the service to its responsibility for recruiting and supporting significantly more black staff.

However, it suffices to affirm that already a new Probation Service was envisaged and indeed being put into place. It was previously required to embrace some new legal responsibilities regarding "parole/after-care" amidst new forms of a slightly more punitive rôle for the service in ensuring the selected offenders did *"service within the community"*. The Home Office sponsored and controlled recruitment and training of predominantly ex-church and ex-military personnel to work as probation officers which began to give way to academic-based and hence professionally-based social work training. Area services were adjusted downwards to enable larger organized services; and in two or three areas some black achievers (e.g. a fellow Jamaican alumni and graduate of the Royal Military School of Music, Dr Leslie Thompson) were recruited mainly to engage with black offenders and their families.

Liberating and Motivating Opportunities

My entry into the UK Probation Service in 1970 was an interesting and challenging one. I had been in the UK for less than four years, having opted for a church-education vocation, and having decided that the perceived spheres of legal services (law), community involvement and church ministry were somewhat interchangeable. After all, I thought, "helping people" to survive and to achieve so as to enhance their personal and communal fulfilment seemed like what life's *real* vocation was about. How quaint, when so much of today's driving principle seems to be "me, me and me alone"!

So understandably, this came from a former young part-time musician and near "perpetual student" (it seemed) who 12 months earlier had terminated the final phase of his theological studies/training to be a Roman Catholic priest, and had secured a CQSW training place in Bristol. I had felt versed in relation to the turmoil and hopelessness in people's lives, articulated and emphasised at the time by the debates around "liberation theology",[3] in the iniquitous implications of the very notion of "race" and abuse of black people; and I had concluded that I needed a new direction to actually help me resolve my acute dilemmas. In other words, I felt a need to be *standing up* against social injustice, as well as to be more *selective* in my personal and social alignments, weary of those who would seek to *use* people—church and state included.

Thus, I walked into social work training in Bristol University Extra-Mural Department to commence studies/training after some six years of pastoral training, but feeling somewhat liberated and motivated to continue in a kind of quest or *journey in caring*. My hope was to return to my homeland post-qualification, but the Home Office had stipulated a training condition that I undertook to work as a probation officer in the UK for a minimum of three years. Later, however, I was wholly disabused on learning that in Jamaica the CPO post which was becoming available was directly accountable to the Minister of Justice—a possibility I could not contemplate.

---

3. It has been described as "an interpretation of Christian faith through the poor's suffering, their struggle and hope, and a critique of society and the Catholic faith and Christianity through the eyes of the poor" (Wikipedia). It now seems that Pope Frances himself came out of that same period of struggle.

Significant Learning Experiences

On the very first day of my dual certificate training course, we were to learn the first of many lessons: *that **significant** observations are best reflected on and shared when able. Subjective "certainties" are mere self-declared assumptions.*

On that first day in question we were sent out together in threes to choose and observe for no more than four minutes a single incident or event of our choice. We were then to write up separately and without discussion what we each *saw*; then return to the department the following morning with a brief written report on what was observed. To our surprise, members of each group reported on seemingly quite different scenarios. In my case, for example, three women of apparently different age groups were sitting at a table in a restaurant. Included in our separate reports and conclusions were that they were a grandmother, a mother, a daughter, or a younger female friend. One of the women was described by one of us as "hostile", and yet by another as "fairly friendly" to the others. One of our numbers reported them as having "tea" and another as "coffee". I confess I stated they were each "having a "drink" though in discussion I conceded that cups were being used by all — not glasses. I clearly recall a haunting thought at the time saying: "What chance have clients got without accurate assessments?"

Over recent years much has been made of the importance of determining and relying on "what works". Having had the opportunity of meeting up with many of my former colleagues (including one 30-year reunion), we occasionally reminisced about our training course, particularly about the famous (or infamous) "T-Group experience". Very few liked it; and too many seemed to have had no real appreciation of what it was meant to achieve. On the first of that two day event, we had sat in a large circle in a conference room, mainly in silence, in order to observe and analyse members' personal/group *behaviour*. However, the occasional and apparent inane comments by the facilitators were a constant source of irritation to most, even when conformity rather than rebellious outbursts were the actual behavioural norm of the group. I recall at one stage the group being told repeatedly that a specific bit of disruptive time-wasting behaviour by a renegade member of the group was being carried out *on behalf of its members*. Exasperated by this I decided to carry out my own related bit of *his* behaviour by repeating it for myself.[4]

However, unlike my renegade colleague, I received "shock horror" disapprovals from members of the group. I then defied them and repeated my walking-out and returning another couple of times with decreasing exasperation of my colleagues. I recall experiencing a great sense of personal psychological relief from doing so, and certainly felt less hostility towards the renegade colleague. I thereby concluded that the group was content in having its own known renegade colleague being defiant, but not me, a previously more "conforming" colleague. Indeed, I can still hear the shrill and stinging voice of my dear friend, Zina, disapprovingly exclaiming "*Basil!!*" I felt I had freed myself from the formerly imperceptible hold that both the group and some of my colleagues had on me.

There were many lessons to be learnt from this experience though we all might not have recognised them: for example, *that both social conformity and deviancy are imposed and maintained until or unless they are negotiated away; that social deviancy in some instances is invested in "pushing at boundaries" on behalf of others; and that group work processes can be used to enable social deviants to be free of **unwarranted** psychological constraints and thereby to enable greater freedom of choice.* The real challenge was how we would use this knowledge and skills to help protect the community from "mindless offending" and enable offenders to free themselves of unwarranted psychological constraints to live more responsible and successful lives. "Care *and* control" had to be acknowledged and actualised.

Team Friendships and Befriending

I commenced my professional career as a fully qualified probation officer in an office located in South Gloucestershire, three or four miles outside Bristol and some 35 miles from our Gloucester Head Office. My seven-officer team consisted of mainly experienced probation officers with a newly appointed senior probation officer, Bryan S, arriving a couple of weeks after my own arrival. Two older women, seemingly without cause, harboured some "unease" about me, but I guess the feelings soon became quite mutual. Once

---

4. "Disruptive" in the sense of "not normal" group behaviour. He was after all merely walking-out through one door and re-emerging through another without any apparent reason, drawing attention to himself.

when a client wrote on the wall of the waiting-room in big letters, "*Basil the Black Bastard*", it was nonchalantly left on the wall for some months without comment. Yes, there was some genuine caring interspersed by some "Nelsonian" glances.

The team served three petty sessional divisions (PSDs) which meant accounting to three separate case committees of magistrates. In those days the assumed and well-guarded "autonomous probation officer" status supported individualistic styles of working with SPOs being like "senior practitioners". A caseload of 40-45 was considered about normal, as well as the writing of five to six social inquiry reports (as they were then known) and one matrimonial court report per month. Written case records were subject to oversight by the SPO and occasionally submitted to case committee magistrates for discussion. I do not recall ever having a black client in my early days; but I remember being totally rejected by a black mother and daughter whose Caribbean husband had committed an offence of indecent assault on the 15-year-old daughter. Transference was indeed a reality.

I ran my first client/offenders group with Dorothy, a petite, attractive self-assured woman officer who drove a huge car that matched her great personality. The group was an all-white adult male offenders' group with a mixture of offences and backgrounds. We laboured over the risk of involving David, a 30-year-old on probation for an offence of indecent assault on a female. He had deliberately groped the breast of a young woman and then run away. He was assessed as shy and terrified of the opposite sex. Being an all-male client group but with the presence of Dorothy, we decided to include him though it could become an ordeal for him. In persuading him to voluntarily join the group, and having warned him that eventually members would pressure him to disclose the nature of his offence, we gave him the option of making reference to a much earlier shoplifting incident that he had never been charged with. The moral quandary caused by this suggestion was not lost on us. In the end, however, the group completed the eight sessions with David attending all of them. He had related well to both Dorothy and me, candidly admitted his "sex offence" to the group, and readily discussed the possible causes of his behaviour. He positively became a more open person following that group experience. I recall getting his probation order terminated early with full revelations of the circumstances to my case committee magistrates who supported my decision. Quite unusually for offenders, David even attended the brief court hearing in which I successfully presented the case for his order to be terminated for good progress. His prognosis seemed good; but alas there was never any feedback on him.

Most probation officers will from time-to-time admit to having had "favourite" clients/offenders, and they would not necessarily be the ones they got on well with. On the eve of my 65th birthday in 2008, I had a telephone call at home from one such ex-client, "Gary", whom I had not seen or spoken to for some 32-years. He had gone into my old Bristol cricket club, saw my name on its "Board of Honour", and in discussion with a club member, persuaded someone to give him my telephone contact. "Hello … this is Gary C….," said the voice in a recognisable West Country accent. He said he just wanted to say "Hello", and to see how I was doing; and would love to have a drink with me if I was ever in Bristol again.

I knew Gary as a 19-year-old, thrown out of home by his parents in the mid-1970s. Burglary and theft, and taking and driving away, I seem to recall, were his specialist offences. I had seen him through borstal, and at the time he had one love in his life — his Alsatian dog. His sole ambition was to be a "Hells' Angel" though he had no motorbike. The local groups had rejected him, and he was left to look more like a "greaser". I pursued him like "The Hound of Heaven"! Deep down he was a pleasant enough young man though somewhat detached from his family. Because of his dog and his own dishevelled appearance, for him accommodation was impossible to come by. Squatting was his best option. During one period of time, making a "home visit" (in my day, a casework necessity) involved going through a church cemetery, and then scaling a concrete wall before banging on the bolted door of a disused warehouse. At the time I dared not ponder the possibility of being arrested for trespassing! Showing that I cared enough was a lifeline to Gary; and a telephone call from him seemed a confirmation that he thought I did.

Mark, on the other hand, I had deemed my "failure". Unauthorised taking and driving away as well as damaging his father's property were the repeated pre-occupation of this 19-year-old. He was not prepared to leave home unless his mother also left; and although one helped them to talk bout the inter-family problems, Mark was not disposed to listen to any "elders". It was no surprise when he was sent away for a spell in a detention centre. So some 20-years after I had left Bristol but briefly returned to the area with my wife in tow, the driver of a bus stopped (blocking the road), chasing and calling out my name. *"Do you remember me…?"* he finally asked as he caught up. I momentarily hesitated, not wanting to respond too quickly as I remembered that a 20-year old in Bristol had threatened to "do me in" on his eventual release from prison. "It's *Mark S.……,*" he stressed. A furtive glance between me and my wife telepathically amplified her thoughts to me: "Oh yes, Mark! You were the one whose father was always on the verge of killing both you and your Mum — resulting in my husband spending weeks of late evenings trying to sort out the problems between you all!" *"Hi Ma-ark — nice to see you,"* I stammered.

Then as if in a single breath Mark *"reported"* that he was now married, had two children, and was employed. "Thanks for everything, Mr Hylton," he said looking at the traffic jam his bus had caused, shaking my hands — and in a jiffy he was driving out of sight. I would have liked an invitation to go with Mark for a drink. For there were many questions I could have asked him: Did he escape going to prison? Was his long suffering Mum now OK? Did his younger brother follow in his footsteps? Had he been on an anger management course? But, later I thought that somehow Mark's extraordinary efforts to say "thanks" seemed an immense reassurance to me that the casework friendships of hundreds of fellow probation officers over the years must have resulted in a generous measure of social stability we too often are *not* credited for.

Cricket was one of my passions, and annual games against penal institutions, such as HM Prison Leyhill, along with my former chief probation officer, John Burbidge, were usually delightful. Once or twice I had successfully recommended supervision orders *with intermediate treatment* to the juvenile courts for capable, promising but lazy youngsters who needed the kind of discipline, motivation and social interactions playing cricket offered. One youngster, Carlton D, was such a teenager. He was a Rastafarian who, if and when he bothered, could be a lethal fast bowler. Indeed, his occasional excitement about cricket was matched only by his loathing of the police. At 17, he achieved a club bowling record by taking nine wickets for 18 runs at Page Park, Staple Hill, in 1976 — against the Bristol Police Club!

He commanded their "respect" and they became human to him. Though he was to die young during a trip to Africa, an annual club trophy was established in his honour and memory.

Will that Pendulum Swing?

One of the many strategic changes introduced within the current Probation Service was to cease referring to offenders as "clients". In addition to this, the government changed the legal definition of the purpose of probation officers and of the service's rôle. Out went "advise, assist and befriend". In came ensuring punishment in the community and even closer ties with the prison regime. This signals the return of the "journey in caring" to civil society's partnerships where, ironically, professional-type dedication and outcomes are expected ("more for less"?).

The more recent changes within the service were largely made not just to re-emphasise whom it worked for, but to be in line with the "prison works" maxim of Michael Howard, former Conservative Home Secretary. This gave credence to the implied suggestion that as long as offenders were locked away in prisons — never mind rehabilitation — they were *limited* to commit criminal offences only against their fellow criminals if they were so inclined. How sad that the professional management-led leadership of the service was to add credence to yet another falsely projected maxim that "he who pays the piper calls the tune" — an affront, I guess, to jazz musicians!

Thus the death knell of the service's "journey in caring" had well and truly sounded. In line with its development, the management of the service had previously tackled the "autonomous probation culture" which tended to defy pursuing management-led objectives (via the Statement of National Objectives of Probation); SPOs' rôles were more clearly defined within management's responsibilities; and the setting of clear team goals and closer monitoring of officers work were put into place. I was proud to have supported these significant developments under more positive leaderships. My hope is that current probation staff will continue to believe that there is *intrinsic good in almost all offenders, and in knowing that an important feature of their rehabilitation* could be enhanced by not succumbing to the largely revengeful attitude underlying the stress being placed on "punishment".

Thus, the professionally-academically-based probation training once given in order to advise, assist and *befriend* offenders was curtailed; and the critical skills and professional freedom we had to involve and moti- vate a wide range of socially-damaged and disorganized individuals were relinquished. Otherwise, many positive elements of the 1970s were quickly brushed aside by the early-1990s. No more were we to be reminded by the likes of Goffman that we had the ever-present propensity to *stigmatise* and *scapegoat* the vulnerable; by the likes of Bion, Becker and McDermott that the largely imperceptible group-dynamic was a powerful enabling tool in influencing people's lives; and by the likes of Biestek that a "casework relationship" method of operation could effectively underpin and enable the professional engagement of trained workers with "clients/offenders". Disappointingly, it was the increased focusing on the experience and needs of victims of crime that was used politically to undermine training and reha- bilitative work with offenders.

Indeed, it was to the credit of the late Christopher Holtom, the former director of the Bristol University Social Work training course, that he also founded the first Victim Support scheme in the UK, highlighting the expe- rience and plight of victims who suffer at the hands of offenders. He believed that within the process of addressing the hurt and deprivations of victims of crime laid the potential rehabilitation of their respective perpetrators. Such a process, though challenging and not wholly guaranteed in all cases, is the antithesis of pandering to revengeful attitudes against on offenders.[5] Long may the "journey in caring" institutions complement the state's duty of upholding necessary legal and legitimate social control.

Conclusion

In concluding my bit of the "journey in caring", I should say it was an honour to have been invited back to Jamaica in the mid-1970s by the then CPO, Dudley Allen (British trained), who was in the process of his own succession planning. I would mention the invaluable experience of working under the leadership of a small number of CPOs and their deputies — and here I would name Bill Rutter and Lois Moores-Wheedon, John Burbidge,

---

5.　A process in which the crime victims (or relatives and friends of deceased crime victims) meet with the defendant after conviction to tell the offender about how the criminal activity affected them, in the hope of rehabilitation or deterrence.

Michael Day, John Harding and Susan Vidal/Hinds, whose contributions to the maintenance and development of the service during my particular time might too quickly and too easily be forgotten. Finally, I thank Adrian Whiting whose advice to me as my SPO student supervisor some 40-years ago seemed spot on. He said he thought I had a great deal to say and do, and some of it will be at some personal cost; but that I should not be afraid of doing both. Thank you, Adrian.

Basil Hylton, Probation officer, Gloucestershire, July 1972; Assistant Chief Probation Officer West Midlands, 1985-1996.

3.   A Road Well Travelled

Cedric Fullwood

Points of Departure

The question "Where did it all begin?" receives a reply, in my case at least, "It's complicated and somewhat uncertain".[1] At the Speech Day at Ecclesfield Grammar School in 1957 a young Richard Hoggart (who some years earlier had married a teacher from the school) gave a talk on his just published and seminal work *The Uses of Literacy*.[2] He was on his way to address the 51 Society in Manchester about his book. I bought it and found that it spoke, certainly in the opening section, to my own experiences. The bookshop in Sheffield where I purchased it also had a journal *The Universities and Left Review*[3] with articles by Hoggart and Raymond Williams on "Culture and Society".[4] A similar journal, which I subscribed to, was *The New Reasoner*[5] edited by E P and Dorothy Thompson. I avidly bought all the back copies. I was fascinated by the critique of cultural, social policy, sociological and political issues which flowed from their pens and from those of Richard Titmuss, John Rex, Peter Townsend, Brian Abel-Smith, Ralph Miliband, Peter Worsley and Stuart Hall. Titles of their books of collected essays set a tone and emphasis, e.g. *Out of Apathy*[6] and *Conviction*.[7]

A couple of years later, struggling with the need to find a job, I was interested in sociology and psychology and I was attracted to psychiatric social work, but that required a qualification and so I needed to gain experience in order to apply for a place on a course. I noticed that the Central After

1.   Rutherford, Andrew (1994), *Criminal Justice and the Pursuit of Decency*, Sherfield-on-Loddon: Waterside Press. A book that Andrew interviewed me, and others in the criminal justice system, for as to what motivated us to join, in my case, the Probation Service.
2.   Hoggart, Richard (1957), *The Uses of Literacy*, London: Chatto and Windus.
3.   Hall, Stuart (1957-59), *Universities and Left Review*, Vols 1-10, Various.
4.   Williams, Raymond (1958), *Culture and Society*, London: Chatto and Windus.
5.   Saville, John and E P Thompson (1957-59), *The New Reasoner*, Vols 1 and 2, Huddersfield: Norman Ellis, Vols. 3-10, Halifax: Fawcett and Greenwood.
6.   Thompson, E P (1960), *Out of Apathy*, London: Stevens and Sons.
7.   MacKenzie, Norman (1958), *Conviction*, London: MacGibbon and Kee.

Care Association[8] based in London wanted someone and I went down to be interviewed by the great Frank Foster. As I waited to be interviewed I heard, through the half-open door of his office, Mr Foster talking to a colleague about the handling of the horses at the Badminton Trials held over the previous weekend! He tore a strip off me when I said I wanted the experience solely to apply for a course, but, surprisingly, he offered me a post. On my return home, a letter was waiting for me with information that I had requested from the University of Sheffield, with details of the Social Studies Course, which I could apply for if I worked in a "real" job for at least a year.

I turned the Central After Care Association down and went to work in Samuel Osborne's Steelworks in the Wicker in Sheffield. This building later briefly became the headquarters for South Yorkshire Probation Service! The very old Mr Osborne still turned up for work and I was surprised many years later to find that as a magistrate he had been a member of the Home Office Review of Social Services in the Courts of Summary Jurisdiction[9] in the 1930s — a review that was not immediately implemented because of the outbreak of war, but later contributed to the 1948 Criminal Justice Act, which was so important for the development of the Probation Service.

My practical placements on the Sheffield course took me to the Family Welfare Association in London, a month at the original borstal named after the village of Borstal near Maidstone, and an attachment to the Sheffield Probation Service (pre-Hugh Sanders) led by a conscientious objector Mr Golding. Academically we covered human growth and development, also social policy and psychology but had the most amazing philosophy seminars engaging with moral and ethical bases for actions and interventions. We had anthropology as well as sociology, lecturers such as Dr Royden Harrison who was an authority on industrial relations and wider economic history. Park Hill flats had gained "fame" but Pearl Jephcott was working on her groundbreaking study of life in tower blocks, *Homes in High Flats*.[10] In our second year the staff group was increased by the appointment of a young probation officer from Brighton, Eric Sainsbury, who was inspirational, in

8.   Bochell, Dorothy (1976), *Probation and After-Care: Its Development in England and Wales* (pp. 184-186), Edinburgh: Scottish Academic Press.

9.   Home Office (1936), *Report of the Departmental Committee on the Social Services in Courts of Summary Jurisdiction*, Cmnd. 5122, London: HMSO.

10. Jephcott, Pearl and Robinson, Hilary (1971), *Homes in High Flats*, Edinburgh, Oliver and Boyd.

his quiet professional way, especially for those of us who were aspiring to join the Probation Service.

Sheffield was followed by a year on Priscilla Young's Applied Social Studies Course at Leicester University. Dr Howard Jones taught us criminology and we had a very young Fred Jarvis (then principal probation officer for Leicester) teaching us about probation, law and the criminal justice system. I knew of Mr Jarvis's books on criminology, social work and counselling but it was an unexpected joy, when I retired, to come across his later books on English poets, literature being a lifelong passion of his, especially English poetry of the early and late-Romantic periods.[11] The three probation sponsored students on the course were visited by a Home Office inspector to check on how we were doing. The inspector was Bob Speirs whose shoes were so polished you could use them as a mirror!

I knew that on leaving Leicester I wanted to return "up North" but not to my home town of Sheffield. Liverpool in 1963 had over 20 vacancies for probation officers and with some confidence I applied. The very large probation committee interviewed me in a grim, dark court building. The principal probation officer at the time (Nigel Grindrod) was, surprisingly, not present. Nine out of the ten questions focussed on why I had put a line through the question in the application form about religion. Did I not know that the first probation officers were police court missionaries, how could I work with Catholics and Protestants in the city without a religion, etc.? They did not offer me one of their many posts. I left somewhat chastened. In some anxiety I applied to Manchester. The deputy principal, Tom Holt, escorted me across Minshull Street to be interviewed in the splendid Victorian magistrates' court building. Seeing that I was nervous he turned to me and said: "Go in there and breathe and the job's yours". A lifelong indebtedness to Manchester was born. The principal probation officer at that time was Mr J J Macmillan, who had worked in the Gorbals in Glasgow, and who, after a period in Hull, came to sort Manchester out.

Early days in Gorton Town Hall

I was posted to Gorton Town Hall to cover Openshaw and Gorton. Our senior probation officer was Les Morrell, an ex-engineer who went to Ruskin

---

11. Jarvis, Frederick (1996), *The Rainbow Shell*, Lewes: The Book Guild.

College, Oxford, before joining the Probation Service. I was filling a vacancy left by a probation officer who had been sacked a few months earlier. I was shown into a small office and on the desk were about 57 case files. He suggested that I gave priority to the statutory cases, i.e. not the ones in "Kindred Social Work" files which listed domestic disputes, neighbours' quarrels, matrimonial referrals, unruly children, etc. I duly set about visiting all the probation and after care clients, and after about a month or so turned to one of the Kindred Social Work folders, and pulled out the papers, which to my growing horror, described a "lifer" who was on licence from Broadmoor Hospital. He had been sent there for murdering a prostitute, using a cricket pitch roller(!) and was certified as paranoid schizophrenic. Mr Morrell went mad, apparently oblivious to the fact that he should have highlighted the importance of this particular case. On a dark, wintry night I knocked on the door of a dingy terraced house and met my charge who lived with his mother in a type of Norman Bates ménage! I don't know who was the more nervous, a state that was heightened a few weeks later when he appeared on the court list charged with setting-fire to a local factory.

My first impressions of life in probation were of the camaraderie of a group of remarkable staff, both officers and clericals. As in other Probation Services many of the staff had been in the Second World War, had survived through heroic endeavours, and some literally bore the scars of their campaigns. These were people with "life experience", some having moved over from jobs in business, banking, retail, factories, acting and many from the church. They were characters. One officer called Gerda Marx was a descendant of Karl Marx and had been a juvenile judge in Germany having to flee as the Nazis came to power. A Miss Disney was a distant relation of Walt and another member of staff traced her family back to Beatrix Potter! One of my colleagues, who started about the time as I did, was Bill McWilliams whose annual memorial Cambridge lectures have become a beacon of sanity over the past 20-years. After a year new officers were inspected by a Home Office inspector. These were nervous occasions, not more so that when you had Miss Vandy, whose first act on sitting down in your office with your case files, was to pull a pipe out of her handbag and light up!

Young enthusiastic officers and more experienced ones were able to experiment with new approaches to our work with young, older and women offenders. Weeks camping at Brathay Hall in the Lake District before the concept of intermediate treatment was "discovered", meetings with head-teachers of local schools to share our respective expertise, partnerships with the voluntary sector such as the Rainer Foundation or emerging drug treat-ment units like Lifeline. We had to tolerate the, often, tedious examination of our case files by a trio of magistrates from the "case committee". Occasional visits from government Ministers to politely explain changes in policies such as voluntary after-care after Lady Reading's report, and later, parole, were stimulating and reflected a genuine investment in the Probation Service at the highest level. One particular highlight was the visit from the medical director of a new penal institution at Grendon Underwood in Buckinghamshire, based on therapeutic principles and respect for the prisoners, unheard of in our local Strangeways.

In the mid-sixties I chaired the Manchester Criminological Society and invited the great Dr Melitta Schmideberg to talk to us. She had gained some fame by her support for probation supervision through her *International Journal of Offender Therapy*. I looked after her all day, taking her round the sights of Manchester, completely oblivious to the fact that she was the daughter of Melanie Klein. Apparently mother and daughter had a very destructive relationship, and this was turned into a play, "Mrs Klein" by Nicholas Wright, in 1988. We heard a gaunt Richard Titmuss talk at Manchester Cathedral on "The Gift Relationship".

The service nationally was represented on Sir Kenneth Younger's Advisory Council on the Treatment of Offenders, and the sub-committee chaired by the outstanding academic and reformer Barbara Wootton worked during the 1960s to publish in the early-1970s her seminal report on "Non-custodial Alternatives to Prison". Her recommendations, which in the main were accepted by the Government, again saw the Probation Service as the bedrock for these developments. These were heady times for young members of what felt increasingly like an emerging profession.

Gorton was to be a name, along with Hattersley, which embodied one of the most heinous crimes of the 20th-century. I was supervising a young boy whose sister was to be a victim of Ian Brady's maniacal evil. My colleague, Geoff Pleasance, with whom I partnered our caseloads, was supervising David Smith, who the day after the last butchery of a young girl arrived at our office to confess what had happened. Geoff kept in touch with Smith until he died.

There was a great commitment to training and staff development. The head of the social work course at Manchester University, Jean Heywood, seemed to have a penchant for accepting on her post-graduate course able students with Oxbridge, often theology, degrees. She herself in the 1960s had a sabbatical in Chicago with the renowned social caseworker/teacher Charlotte Towle. Towle's approach and that of other American academics informed the Manchester course's approach to student training and likewise placed expectations on us as fieldwork supervisors of her students.

The American link continued when, in 1971, I obtained a place on the MA course in Applied Social Studies at the University of Bradford. My tutor was the inspirational Dr Sydney Wasserman, of Smith College fame. My practical placement was in the newly-established National Society for the Prevention of Cruelty to Children (NSPCC) "Special" Unit—special because of its concentration on child abuse. My caseload was drawn from the poorest deprived estates in Bradford. Dr Wasserman's supervision of me and my clients was one of the most rewarding periods of my professional career. He always had on his desk a copy of John Berger's *A Fortunate Man*—and I felt likewise. Even there in an ego-centred casework world change was in the air. As I accepted my degree from Harold Wilson a new professor had been appointed at the university, Noel Timms, who was to become famous for his work with the recipients of social work in a book entitled *The Client Speaks*. [12]

A theme in Home Office sponsored training was to pay for staff to go on week-long courses run by experienced trainers from the Tavistock Institute and later the Grubb Institute. A K Rice (who had written extensively on the behaviour of large groups and inter-group relations),[13] Pierre Turquet, Wilfred Bion and others worked with probation groups as well as interdisciplinary groups (from business, the church, health) to expand our understanding of organizations and organizational behaviour. It was an eye-opener to the likes of me from more restricted training backgrounds.

---

12. Mayer, J E and Timms, Noel (1970), *The Client Speaks*, London: Routledge and Kegan Paul.
13. Miller, E and Rice, A K (1967), *Systems of Organisation*, London: Tavistock.

First Experiences of a Centrally Driven Re-organization

In the early-1970s there were major changes to the organization of the National Health Service shortly followed by significant amalgamations and upheavals in the structure of local government. It was only a matter of time before this impacted on the Probation Service. Smaller services that had existed since the 1950s were brought together, especially in what became known as the metropolitan areas. Greater Manchester Probation Service was formed out of the Cities of Manchester and Salford, South East Lancashire, and parts of both Cheshire and South West Lancashire. Jack Marsh, previously of South East Lancashire, was appointed the first chief probation officer of Greater Manchester in 1974 and I was appointed as one of his three deputy chiefs, with responsibility for staffing and training. Expansion was part of the scene and about ten new assistant chief posts were created to cover this larger area. Magistrates from all the court areas had to be represented on the new probation committee, together with one councillor from each of the ten district councils. An unwieldy, inefficient and unnecessarily bureaucratic state of affairs resulted for the next nearly 30-years.

At one level it could be seen as a waste of resources, but at another there were benefits of scale, that allowed the creation of a central training unit with its own building and staffing. We were able to appoint specialist staff, such as a property manager, develop a range of probation hostels (recommended in the Wootton Report), and appoint specialist practitioners initiating new ways of working whether that was in divorce court welfare or intensive group work. Bringing groups of senior staff together, sparking ideas and stimulating new practices would today be called a "hub" or "co-conglomeration"!

Whilst managing a scale of organizational change few of us had experienced we were to a significant degree engaged with professional change of an equal order. Not only did community service orders need to be developed, probation hostels expanded, and the principles of intensive treatment and day training centres considered we were also being subject to the scrutiny of the new Home Office Research Unit, which had a base in Manchester with Martin Davies and Ken Pease making names for themselves. In addition, professional and policy change was being pursued including the introduction of parole with a national Parole Board, chaired by Lord Hunt, who received the call to take on the rôle whilst he was in the Himalayas. For me, one of the major aspects of the Parole Board was the bringing together of judges, criminologists, psychiatrists, lay members and, usually chief probation officers. The standing of the service was enhanced in such a distinguished inter-disciplinary group.

The Home Office sponsored the Cropwood Conferences at the Cambridge Institute of Criminology. In 1974 the theme of the conference was "Control without Custody" and I was invited to give a paper on "Probation and Control".[14] Papers had to be prepared and circulated in advance and each session was chaired by one of the attendees. The head of the Social Work Inspectorate at the Department of Health, Joan Cooper, chaired my session. Jenny West (later Roberts) gave a paper on the community service scheme she was running at the time in Nottinghamshire. There were papers on "Control in Hostels", and in communities. The eminent Professor Nils Christie was present as were officials from the Home Office including the chief inspector of probation, Mike Hogan. With all this excitement, little did we know that a storm was brewing in America in the shape of a meta-analysis by Professor Martinson entitled "Nothing Works" (later to be exposed as flawed and the author committing suicide!)

The 1970s saw the development in South East Lancashire/Greater Manchester of the voluntary partnership known as the Selcare (South East Lancashire Care) Trust. Its president was Lord Rhodes. The many, varied and exciting projects which Selcare initiated became models across the country and commended by Ministers in the House of Lords. Bearing in mind that I am writing this in 2014 it may be worth highlighting one project whereby a volunteer would befriend a prisoner whilst he/she was doing their sentence, meet them at the prison gate on their release, take them to their accommodation which we had found for them, ensure that furniture, food, and warmth were available, and then visit them regularly for months afterwards to ensure that the founding principles of the Probation of Offenders Act 1907, "to advise, assist and befriend", were fulfilled.

In 1978 I had been in Manchester for 15 years. One of my deputy colleagues had left to go to Scotland to become secretary of the Carnegie Trust UK.

---

14. Fullwood, Cedric, "Control by Probation Officers. Control Without Custody?", Paper presented to the Cropwood Round Table Conference, December 1975. Edited by Joan F S King and Warren Young. University of Cambridge, Cambridge: Institute of Criminology, 1976.

Scotland was implementing Lord Kilbrandon's seminal report on the future of social work in Scotland. It appeared an exciting place to be professionally and some chief probation officers (Nigel Grindrod from Liverpool) and a senior probation officer (Fred Edwards also from Liverpool) had already taken up some of the new posts of director of social work. Similarly (Sir) William Utting and (Lord) Herbert Laming moved from probation to become directors of social services in the post-Seebohm world in England and Wales. The stature of chief probation officers is exemplified by the appointment of Bill Pearce from London as the first chief inspector of prisons, and (Sir) Michael Day moving from West Midlands to chair the Commission for Racial Equality.

When I saw in *New Society* an advert for deputy chief social work adviser the temptation to apply was too much to resist. On the interview panel I was to meet Joan Cooper again (After she retired she wrote a history of the British Personal Social Services[15] and I loved her phrase "a public response to private sorrow").

A Scottish Fling

In the *Oxford English Dictionary* the fourth definition of "fling" is "a period of self-indulgence or pleasure, a good time, specifically a brief affair". Not that I thought this described my five years in the Scottish Office at the time, but looking back it was brief, it was a good, albeit challenging, time, and there were elements of pleasure.

I worked to the redoubtable Beti Jones, who before becoming chief social work adviser, had been children's officer for Cardiff and after World War Two had participated in the social reconstruction work in Germany. I had responsibility for the territorial advisers covering Scotland, the specialist staff working on services for offenders, including prisons and List D schools, and research. Looking back it was a move shot through with risk. I was moving to another country with quite different cultural and legal traditions from the one that I was used to. Its social policy framework had just undergone massive changes as a result of the Social Work Scotland Act 1968, none more significant than the abolition of the Probation Service(!). We were quite deliberately part of the Scottish Education Department, whilst criminal justice

---

15. Cooper, Joan (1983), *The Creation of the British Personal Social Services*, London: Heinemann.

policy, was handled by the Scottish Home and Health Department (SHHD).

I am left with many memories of my time in the Scottish Office. I was at assistant secretary level and as such had meetings with Ministers, and access to extremely confidential material (no more so than the Cabinet Office briefings about why there were riots in England in the early-1980s and not in Scottish urban centres like Glasgow). As in Manchester there were characters such as the under secretary at SHHD, David Cowperthwaite, who took snuff and listened to cricket matches on a tiny transistor during long and boring interdepartmental meetings on alcohol policies and the like.

Whilst in Manchester I had been used to national conferences but my time in the Scottish Office introduced me to international ones. An inspirational one on "Alternatives to Custody" in Toronto became the model for our "What Works" conferences in Manchester ten years later. One in Copenhagen on services for under-fives took me out of my comfort zone, as did being one of the two UK Government representatives at the Quinquennial Conference on Crime in the European Headquarters in Strasbourg. Lord Asa Briggs delivered a closing paper on "A Forecast of Problems Likely to be of Concern to Governments During the 1980s".[16]

In an attempt to summarise what the experience meant to me, I would highlight three things. Firstly, politics and policies in the kind of detail I had never experienced before. I took up my post in the dying days of Jim Callaghan's wounded Labour Government, and I was there for the first three years of Mrs Thatcher's Conservative Government. The scale of cuts expected and the type of radical approaches to the delivery of new policies intertwined with a monstrously detailed Financial Management System sent genuine shock waves through the upper echelons of the Scottish Office Civil Service. Some old hands retired to the New Club on Princes Street, shaking their heads saying it would all pass. They had seen this type of intent before. However this was political change on an unparalleled scale. The permanent secretary was sent for a "placement" at the local Marks & Spencer head office in Edinburgh for enlightenment! The experience served me well when I returned to be chief probation officer in Greater Manchester in 1982 — I knew where many of the Home Office approaches to management and direction

---

16. Briggs, Lord Asa (1980), *A Forecast of Problems Likely to be of Concern to Governments During the 1980s*, Strasbourg: Council of Europe.

were coming from and I had already responded to them whilst in Scotland.

Secondly, I began to have enormous respect for the civil servants who I worked alongside, those writing briefings for Ministers, drafting legislation, handling sensitive public crises. Their use of English, their ability to summarise with great clarity (usually on one side of A4) complex policy issues, and to understand both sides of an argument, were second to none. My experience in probation circles had often been the opposite: poor English, turgid prose styles, waffling reasoning, and a desperate attempt to pray in aid vague values and principles. Being part of the small team sitting in the box of the Scottish Grand Committee during criminal justice debates certainly sharpened ones wits. Opposition MPs would raise issues in their contribution, often attacks on the Government Minister, and a parliamentary aide would sidle over to the box expecting you to provide a note no bigger than the size of a playing card with an absolutely clear response for the Minister to use. Woe betide those who exposed the Minister in any way. Equally doing a review of a child death was not just doing a social work report, it was the basis for the Secretary of State, in my case Sir George Younger, to make a statement in the House of Commons, and your professional judgement could not be wrong.

Thirdly, I experienced for five years a different way of delivering social work services, including services to offenders, which were embedded in the new Social Work Departments. Lord Kilbrandon[17] had emphasised the centrality of education and a more integrated and preventative approach to social problems. Richard Titmuss's ideas had been influential with some advising the original review. One element of the changes that did not roll out as planned was the expectation that the new Social Work Departments would give equal emphasis to services for offenders as to children, the elderly, and the disabled, now that the Probation Service had been done away with. The sheriffs and procurator fiscals were frustrated by the poor quality of service they were receiving in the courts and in the supervision of offenders. By the time I left new arrangements had to be introduced to ring fence the money for services to offenders and eventually to fund it 100 per cent from the Scottish Office—not what Kilbrandon had in mind.

---

17. Kilbrandon, Lord (1964), *Children and Young Persons, Scotland*, Cmnd. 2306, Edinburgh: HMSO.

When I returned to Manchester we appointed community probation officers working from community centres based in troubled communities — seeing both officer and centre as a resource to the community and not just for criminal justice purposes. On leaving Scotland I was invited by the directors of social work to address their annual conference on my reflections on working in the Scottish Office and the differences, especially for services for offenders between England and Scotland. A year later I was invited by the Association of Chief Officers of Probation to address their Annual Conference in 1984 on the implications of my experiences in Scotland for the work of the Probation Service in England and Wales — a talk entitled "Bot, Wites and the Dooms of Alfred"[18] attracted a little interest! It was not until the 1998 Crime and Disorder Act that some of the ideas in the paper were taken up!

Return to Manchester

My 16-years as chief probation officer in Greater Manchester was a roller coaster of an experience in terms of practice developments set against a back-cloth of what felt like constant policy, administrative and legislative change. Some like the abolition of the Metropolitan Council, the Strangeways prison riots, and the build-up to and implementation of the Criminal Justice Act 1991, were on a seismic scale.

When Mrs Thatcher decided to abolish the Metropolitan County Council structure the Probation Unit at the Home Office had to work on the ramifications for the Probation Service. A phone call to me from the then head of the unit confirmed that civil servants, even with the probation inspectorate on tap, had little idea as to how the service was organized, and functioned administratively, at local level. They turned to us for help but persisted in some strange stances. In Greater Manchester, as in other areas, we decided to establish our own computer department now that we were no longer tied to the county council services. The Home Office wrote to me threatening that I and committee members would be held responsible for the misuse of public funds if we went ahead. Our legal advice was sound and we went ahead — not before one junior official in the Probation Unit had contacted me suggesting

---

18. Fullwood, Cedric (1984), "Bot, Wites and the Dooms of Alfred", London: Association of
      Chief Officers of Probation.

that we go down the road and buy some computers from Dixons! A more serious state of ignorance about the workings of the Probation Service on the part of senior civil servants at the Home Office was exposed with the publication of the Audit Commission Report of 1989 "Promoting Value for Money in the Probation Service".[19] The permanent secretary received a severe grilling in front of the Public Accounts Committee for the woeful state of financial understanding at the Home Office,

On a similar theme, I always assumed, rather naïvely on reflection, that Ministers would know what the policy and operational effects were of their legislation that they themselves had taken through Parliament in great detail. In the main there was little commitment to and ownership of their legislative and policy work apart from the odd soundbite. The wanton way in which subsequent Home Secretaries, even within the same party, could scythe through their predecessors' work was astonishing—not more so than in respect of the Criminal Justice Act 1991 that had been so carefully crafted by David Faulkner and John Patten (then Minister at the Home Office). The Criminal Justice Consultative Council that had recently been formed, and of which I was a founding member, specifically to coordinate developments and to be "consulted" with, was completely ignored by Kenneth Clarke in his haste to dismember those aspects of the Act he did not like.

I was blessed with superb staff at every level in our organization. Many senior staff went on to be chief officers themselves, or probation inspectors (one, Liz Calderbank, even becoming chief inspector). Others were seconded to local authorities or government departments. Still others did time-limited project work on such developments as the Financial Management Initiative (John Crawforth), work with the Audit Commission on their seminal report on Probation (Mary Fielder), and later on Youth Justice Policy.

On one occasion when I was speaking to judges at the Judicial Studies Board conference in Northamptonshire, a Conservative MP who was also a Crown Court judge somewhat aggressively said to me: "Well Mr Fullwood, now that probation has failed what are you going to tell us?" I made as good a reply as I could but on return to Manchester I asked Andrew Underdown, who was about to do the Cambridge Senior Course in Criminology, whilst

---

19. Audit Commission (1989), *Promoting Value for Money in the Probation Service*, London: HMSO.

there, to review the up-to-date evidence for effective practice. We were being more and more held to account by sentencers and politicians to demonstrate that our interventions were effective. Andrew's report[20] led to him being seconded to the inspectorate to develop effective practice programmes nationally. Unfortunately the Government only bought into elements of effective practice and left other key aspects to flounder. For nearly ten years from 1989 on the "What Works" conferences, which Jenny Roberts and I sponsored in Manchester, led the way, establishing a national and international basis for co-operation and sharing of research and practice. This was practically and symbolically important as they were held during a period which included the notorious one-sided "prison works" approach of Michael Howard.

Following my "Bot, Wites and the Dooms of Alfred" paper I was invited by David Faulkner, deputy secretary in charge of criminal justice policy at the Home Office, to join his "Discussion Group on Crime" held off the record at Nacro (as it now is) headquarters every few months. The group of no more than ten included Vivien Stern, senior academics (Rod Morgan, Andrew Ashworth, Roger Hood, David Downes, Andrew Rutherford), Navnit Dholakia who was at the Commission for Racial Equality at the time, and Mary Tuck, head of the Home Office Research Unit. We discussed topics of current policy importance: race and criminal justice, parole (Lord Carlisle was chairing the review), the notion of a Sentencing Council, and ideas that eventually became enshrined in the Criminal Justice Act 1991.

If there was one significant feature of the 1980s and early-1990s it was the increasing stature of the Probation Service within the wider criminal justice system. No longer "servants of the court" but true partners in that wider system. This was no more evident than in two respects. Firstly there was our working relationship with the senior judiciary. In the North West the CPOs met every few months with the senior presiding judge and the honorary recorders on the Northern Circuit. Secondly there was our attendance at the national Criminal Justice Conferences that David Faulkner hosted. For seven years in the 1990s I gave the talk on Probation to the Judicial Studies Board biannual seminars for experienced Crown Court judges, first with Mr Justice Auld and later Lord Justice Igor Judge. In my wider contact with

---

20. Underdown, Andrew (1995), *Effectiveness of Community Supervision: Performance and Potential*, Manchester: Greater Manchester Probation Service.

judges, I was always struck by the, barely disguised, contempt that they had for politicians in general, and Ministers in particular. At a very low point in these relations between the judiciary and Michael Howard, the permanent secretary at the Home Office (Richard Wilson) asked if there was anything I could do to smooth out relations!

Underpinning this enhancement of our professional status was the rôle of the Association of Chief Officers of Probation (ACOP), so ably led by Bill Weston (erstwhile CPO of West Yorkshire) and powered by the administrative skill of Jill Thomas.[21] It was a privilege to chair the association as I did in 1991, and the various sub-committees were veritable dynamos pushing through at national level a host of innovations. We were consulted on many policy initiatives, were confident enough to go to Ministers and officials to propose other ideas (I was particularly proud of the bail information schemes in collaboration with Chris Stone of the Vera Institute of Justice), and we developed a set of strong networks with the Local Authorities Association, Justices' Clerks' Society, Directors of Social Service, police, HM Prison Service Headquarters and the Director of Public Prosecutions.

I wrote many articles during these years and gave talks to numerous national conferences. They included the Manchester Statistical Society,[22] the annual McClintock Lecture[23] and the Department of Theology Conference on Penal Philosophy (both of the latter in Edinburgh). I was prepared to stand up for what the Probation Service represented. When the Association of Chief Police Officers began to use tabloid means to undermine the 1991 Act and ran a campaign about "bail bandits" and "rat boys" I addressed a Criminal Justice Conference condemning this approach which diminished their office. When the Prime Minister, John Major, spoke about the need for more condemning and less understanding of offenders I wrote an article as to why we needed more understanding.[24] I opposed the notion of

21. Association of Chief Officers of Probation (2001), *ACOP 1982-2001 A Brief Chronicle and Review.*, London: ACOP.
22. Fullwood, Cedric (1989), *The Young Adult Offender: Historical and Current Perspectives*, Manchester: Manchester Statistical Society.
23. Fullwood, Cedric (1998), 5th McClintock Lecture "Civil Liberties and Social Control in the Community", Birmingham: *Vista*.
24. Fullwood, Cedric (1996), "The Future of the Probation Service: The Case for the Compulsive Understander", pp. 118-126 (Article dedicated to the memory of Michael Willson), London: *Probation Journal*.

a Correctional Service and received a phone call from the senior civil servant in charge to say that they were only using "corrections" in an educational sense! Letters to the press,[25] interviews on radio (with the "Rottweiler" John Humphreys and the more gentle Martha Kearney) and television (alongside a postmaster who still had bullets in him from an armed robbery) were part of the staple diet of chief probation officers, especially when chairing their professional association.

In 1989 Lord Rhodes died and I was asked what would be a fitting memorial. I suggested setting up a scholarship fund to send probation staff around the world to examine new initiatives in dealing with offenders and bring back that experience to Manchester and the UK for implementation. It is the Rhodes Trust's 25th Anniversary in 2014 and we have sent over 50 scholars to five continents, their reports being given to an Annual Presentation Evening, currently held at Chetham's School of Music.

As the 1990s wore on, fatigue began to set in and as the New Labour Government was installed I could see another raft of criminal justice legislation on the stocks and more major organizational change for the Probation Service in the offing. I felt it was time to hand the baton onto others with more energy and fresh ideas. So in 1998 I bowed out. Apart from the many letters that I received, I was most appreciative of, and touched by, a plaque presented to me by the Association of Black Probation Officers for my support of them over the years; and a generous tribute from Lord Justice Rose for my work on the Criminal Justice Council.[26]

Retirement and Paths Less Travelled

One of my last national contributions in 1997 was being a member of the Labour Government's Task Force on Youth Justice, chaired by Norman (later Lord) Warner with, as tireless secretary, Mark Perfect, ex-Treasury, who had been seconded earlier to the Audit Commission to undertake their review of the subject.[27] I successfully applied for one of the board member posts and enjoyed a fascinating six years helping take through legislation, establishing

---

25. Fullwood, Cedric (1994), "Hope abandoned in these walls", Letter 5th March 1994, *Guardian*.

26. Rose, Lord Justice (1998), *Criminal Justice Consultative Council Summary of Activities 1997-98*, p.3, London: Home Office.

27. Audit Commission (1996), *Misspent Youth—Young People and Crime*, London: Audit Commission.

new youth offending teams, working within Government departments and acting as North West Youth Justice Board liaison.

I participated in the External Reference Group to John Halliday's Review of Sentencing Policy[28] and in 2000 I was invited by Paul Cavadino to take over his rôle as chair of the Penal Affairs Consortium. This brought me into contact with senior civil servants and Ministers again, and in 2003 I presented the consortium's views on the Criminal Justice Bill to the All-Party Penal Affairs Group in the House of Lords.[29]During this period I participated in the Lewis Review of Social Work in Special Hospitals that reported in 2000.[30] This involved visits to interview staff and patients in Broadmoor and Ashworth. This was set up by the Department of Health and Social Security (DHSS) after the Fallon Inquiry into how an eight-year old girl was allowed to visit, unsupervised, wards at Ashworth containing patients with records of sex offences against children. Our recommendations, which were accepted, led to a major overhaul of social work services in the three special hospitals.

Two-thousand-and-two saw me as poacher turned gamekeeper, as I became chair of the Cheshire Probation Board, a position I held for six years. It was a great joy to renew acquaintance with Steve Collett, the chief probation officer, who had worked with me in Greater Manchester. I have nothing but the highest praise for him, his senior management, and all the staff I came in contact with during those years. Although many of us had serious reservations about the introduction of the National Probation Service in 2001, especially with its quixotic and short-sighted ending of the Association of Chief Probation Officers, there was at least a national director sitting on the permanent secretary's Executive Board at the Home Office, and with access to the Prime Minister. We invited and tried to influence Lord Carter in his review of prisons and probation, but it was not an independent review, and the deals and template had been decided by the Secretary of State and the head of the Prison Service and the bringing together of prisons and probation in a National Offender Management Service was clearly a foregone

28. Home Office (2001), *Making Punishments Work*, London: Home Office.
29. Fullwood, Cedric (2003), Presentation to the All-Party Penal Affairs Group on the Criminal Justice Bill, London: Prison Reform Trust.
30. Department of Health and Social Security (2000), *Review of Social Work Services in the High Security Hospitals*, London: DHSS.

conclusion. It was one of the most negative and destructive developments in penal policy for many years. The big loser was probation.[31],[32] As we briefed members of the House of Lords and the Commons little did we know that a Conservative Government would arrive with even more destructive policies for the Probation Service. The irony was that this was happening when firstly there was a Centenary Celebration taking place for the founding of the service, with a splendid service in Westminster Abbey, and secondly, in 2013, an international conference on probation where the merits of the existing service in England and Wales was held up as an example to the rest of the world. The irony was lost on the current Minister of Justice (Chris Grayling). The moves to privatise 70 per cent of the service's work leave a raw feeling and a sense of helplessness in face of an intransigent and mean spirited Secretary of State.

From 2002 to 2004, I was a member of Lord Coulsfield's Independent Review of Alternatives to Prison, commissioned by the Esmée Fairbairn project on Rethinking Crime and Punishment. It was a very detailed review involving visits across England and to Scotland and Northern Ireland. We consulted with judges, police and the private sector. The newly created National Offender Management Service was reluctant to submit evidence — our messages were contrary to the received orthodoxy of NOMS. Ignored at the time I still believe that it will stay the test of time and maybe future generations will turn to it for inspiration.[33];[34] Wiser people than I have reflected on the state of criminal justice both here and in the USA. None more so than Professor Sir Leon Radzinowicz who, in 1992, with his kind regards, sent me a copy of his profound article, "Penal Regressions" which every Minister and senior civil servant should have on their desk to show them the potential pitfalls and errors of previous attempts at reform.[35]

31. Fullwood, Cedric (2005), "The Development of the National Offender Management Service: A 'Consumer' Perspective", Birmingham: *Vista*.

32. Fullwood, Cedric (2010), "Criminal Justice and New Labour: A Personal Valediction, pp.286-290", *Probation Journal* Vol. 57, No. 3 (A Special Issue on "Reflections on New Labour: Has Criminal Justice Changed?"), London: Sage.

33. Coulsfield, Lord (2004), *Crime, Courts and Confidence: An Independent Inquiry into Alternatives to cCustody*, London: Esmée Fairbairn Foundation.

34. Fullwood, Cedric (2005), "Crime, Courts and Confidence — The Challenge Ahead", pp. 11-20 *Judicial Studies Institute Journal*, Galway: National University of Ireland.

35. Radzinowicz, Leon (1991), "Penal Regressions", *The Cambridge Law Journal*, 50 (3) pp. 422-444, Cambridge: Cambridge University Press.

This was meant to be just one person's record of a life spent in the Probation Service and the wider criminal justice system. It has been indeed a "journey", and as the *Oxford English Dictionary* has as one of its definitions of that word, "the passage through life", I tried, in my talk to the newly founded Probation Chiefs Association in 2010, to convey a sense of "Hope, Voice and Passion" [36] but in 2014 I attended its last conference, symbolically for me, in Manchester (a hundred yards from where I had been told to "go in there and breathe and the job's yours"). Simon Armitage, surely the next Poet Laureate, whom we had appointed as a probation officer in the tradition of appointing Armitages (his father having been in Ashton in earlier years), was entertaining the assembled company with moving poems, and hilarious stories from his time with us in probation. [37]

Coda

How to end a road well travelled? In normal circumstances it might be a quote from Robert Frost [38] on "the one less travelled by" and "that has made all the difference" but that would be personal whereas although this had been personal it is essentially a professional probation journey. So let us turn to page 233 of Le Mesurier's *A Handbook of Probation and Social Work of the Courts* [39] published in 1935 where we read of probation:

> "It is a thing so large in its conception, and so immensely potent in its effect on the hopes and happiness of thousands of human lives every year, that perhaps it is better not even to try and find words of commendation, which might be unworthy of their subject, but to be content to make the way clear for its advance and let its deeds praise it."

Cedric Fullwood, Probation officer, City of Manchester Probation Service, September 1963; Chief Probation Officer, Greater Manchester, 1982-1998.

---

36. Fullwood, Cedric (2010), "Hope, Voice and Passion", Talk to the inaugural conference of the Probation Chiefs Association, London: PCA website (http://probationchiefs.org).
37. Armitage, Simon (1998), *All Points North*, London: Viking.
38. Frost, Robert (1951), *The Complete Poems*, p. 129, London: Jonathan Cape.
39. Le Mesurier, L (1935), *A Handbook of Probation and Social Work of the Courts*, London: Napo.

4. Probation Memories

Colin Archer

Before the Beginning

In 1963, I crossed The Strand from King's College, London. I was becoming disillusioned at the prospect of a well paid career in something scientific, to which my education and undergraduate course had been geared. I entered the Royal Courts of Justice. I have no memory of being searched, and walked into the public gallery in one of the courts. It was hearing a fascinating case which involved cheque fraud. The defendant was alleged to have altered the final initial on the payee line to make it into a surname. He then somehow diverted the money into one or more accounts to which he had access.

Sometime later, I spent a long weekend in Windsor Great Park at Cumberland Lodge. An impressive, inspiring contributor to the conference about Probation was Gordon Jones, then principal probation officer (PPO) in Hertfordshire, who died shortly afterwards. It was not long before I applied to courses for probation training and to the Home Office, where I was quizzed by a probation inspector whose name escapes me. A career in the Probation Service offered much less salary than a scientific career, but there was a good pension scheme and "prospects of promotion to senior appointments". It was on a snowy December day in 1964 that I was interviewed by Priscilla, daughter of J R R Tolkien, at Barnett House in Oxford and granted a place on the 17-month combined Probation and Child Care Course. This course was one of a number established to increase the number of graduates joining the service.

My main probation placement was with Ernst Lazarus in Beaconsfield. I was an extremely "green" 22-year-old, and recollect offering appointments to a man with "matrimonial" difficulties. The listen and nod technique may or may not have been helpful. I did of course prepare social enquiry reports (SERs), and supervised a varied group of people who were on probation.

First Probation Officer Job, January 1967

At the time I did not fully appreciate that the demand for officers exceeded supply, but following guidance from tutors, was successful in obtaining a post in Hertfordshire, after a rather perfunctory interview with Jimmy James, PPO. This was on the same afternoon that Lorna, to whom I was engaged, enjoyed similar success at an interview in the same building for a child care officer post.

My pleasure at this offer was held in check because I was to cover the whole of the south of the county, with work in Cheshunt in the south-east, and Borehamwood in the south-west. I mainly avoided work in Potters Bar, midway between the two. What is more, the administrative office covering Borehamwood was provided by the Middlesex Service in East Barnet, and the South Mimms (Herts) magistrates used the same court building as Barnet magistrates. These areas were covered by the Metropolitan Police, not the Hertfordshire Constabulary.

First Cases and SER Work

I could not have had a more helpful colleague in those early months than Malcolm Lacey, and it was quite a loss when he departed to an SPO post in the Midlands. It was a standard expectation that we would interview defendants at Barnet Court who had been arrested overnight, to establish plea, and provide a short oral report, usually aimed at asking for an adjournment for an SER to be prepared. I well remember Malcolm asking; "What's the history?" and thinking it was almost impossible to answer that on the basis of little time, no interviewing privacy, and inexperience!

One case allocated to me at the outset was a young man who had been placed on probation just before Christmas. I did not start until almost mid-January. Top of my in tray was a letter from his parents saying that they were about to write to the national press to complain that nothing had happened since the order had been made. This was the start of years of supervising him and eventually helping wean him off his drug addiction. Relationships at home resulted in him living in a shed at the bottom of the garden! I returned him to court for breach once, and was granted an extension of the two year order to three years.

One of the cases inherited from Malcolm was a young lad on a supervision order. One of the B-sheets read; "The past three months has been a period of masterly inactivity."! I am grateful to Malcolm for telling me that he followed John Haines (as he had at school where John was a prefect a year ahead of him) and he followed Fred Jarvis (Malcolm also followed John as RSDO but gave up when John became an inspector!).

Confirmation in post was then a responsibility of the Probation Inspectorate. My confirmation inspection was at the Cheshunt office, but shortly afterwards, I left Cheshunt to work solely in Borehamwood. Office interviews with clients took place in a room provided by the Health Service. Long "reporting" evenings from 4 pm to 9 pm or later on two nights a week seeing large numbers on of people on probation, after-care from detention centre or borstal, parole or voluntary after-care were the norm, as were home visits. Interviews for SERS took place in people's homes at least as often as the "office", even after we were provided with a new office building in Borehamwood some three years after I started there.

In the Courts

As a new PO, I was both young and 'green'. I remember the feeling of embarrassment when the chairman of the bench, referred to this "very experienced probation officer" when placing somebody on probation. He was not only the bench chair, he was also the chairman of the Probation Committee. There was none of the much heard about, in recent years, "lack of confidence in probation" on the part of sentencers. His comments were encouraging and confidence building. Those were the days when I felt great, if sometimes misplaced confidence in my professional skills and the ability and requirement to use discretion in all aspects of the job.

Another feature of my early years was attending applications hearings. I would often pick up work with individuals applying for a separation hearing, to see if there was any intervention that would remove the need for a court hearing in the matrimonial court. Preparation of divorce court welfare and *guardian ad litem* reports was also a responsibility at that time.

There were, of course, no computers. case notes—C sheets, Part Bs, and SERS were recorded on a dictation machine and decoded by ever-helpful secretaries. What a pain it was when the machines did not work or material was accidentally deleted!

I recollect only two instances of personal hazard. One was during a reporting evening when a young teenager, whose mother was schizophrenic, held me hostage for about an hour. Another was at Middlesex Crown Court (or perhaps Quarter Sessions in those days), when the father of a prolific young offender managed to land a punch on me, probably due to a wholly exceptional recommendation for borstal training.

"Political" Action

Loss of Malcolm Lacey led to the arrival of Arnold Barrow at the Borehamwood office. Arnold was another colleague, one of many, with whom I worked closely and for whom I had much respect. At that time we were not happy about the lack of success in negotiating decent salaries. We felt that the previous practice of appointing people who had, perhaps, made money in earlier careers, or were supported by better paid partners and were content with relatively low salaries, had led to less pressure for improvements than we thought necessary. As well as initiating something of a national campaign to try to "ginger up" colleagues around the country, we decided we would lobby the MP for the area in which we worked. After an initial refusal, based on his rôle in government, which we challenged strongly, we were invited to a meeting with Reggie Maudling, then Home Secretary, at the Home Office! He apologised for keeping us waiting, saying that he had had to deal with a "little issue" that had arisen in Northern Ireland. As the late-1960s and early-1970s were a particularly problematic time in Northern Ireland, we felt very satisfied that he gave us the opportunity to bend his ear for 20-30 minutes.

Becoming a Manager

With experience of supervising student placements, and nearly six years in post, I was encouraged to apply for SPO posts. It was customary to be away from home in St. Albans, from a day or two before Christmas until after the New Year, staying successively with parents and in-laws. We had packed, locked the flat, and strapped our two infants in the car. While driving out of the car park, the postman arrived and handed me a heap of letters. One of them invited me to interview in Worcester on December 28th, 1972. I attended, was offered the post, and remained in Worcester until retirement in 2001. Leaving home a minute or two earlier, or the postman arriving a bit later, and what might have been?

For the next few years, I was privileged to work with the two Gordons, Robb and Read. My main recollection of the interview was being met by a man in a bottle green corduroy suit! No prizes for guessing which Gordon that was! (For those who do not know — Gordon Read. Ed.) The SPO post, like my first "split" PO job, involved covering South Worcestershire from two offices 18 miles apart, and four petty sessional divisions. My diplomatic skills were rather underdeveloped at that time and the chair of one of the case committees refused to hold meetings! Eventually this was resolved by combinations of petty sessional areas.

Imprisoned!

It was not much more than a year later that I was required to cover the probation team in HM Prison Long Lartin, on an interim basis, and subsequently began a secondment lasting nearly two-and-a-half years. I felt incredibly anxious about this. I had not joined the Probation Service to work in a prison. I doubted that I could manage this assignment. It turned out however to be a highly significant developmental experience. First, I was privileged to work for just six months with one of the foremost Governors[1] of his generation, Bill Perrie. Second, it helped begin the process of assessing risk, in a way that had not been the practice before. And third, the two Gordons were excellent supervisors! Gordon Read has reminded me that we and Paddy Lowry co-wrote an article about working with prisoners, and the *International Journal of Offender Therapy and Comparative Criminology* published my article "Probation in Prison" in 1982 (Vol. 26, No. 1).

January 1977 — Now a Senior Manager

I was "released" to take up an assistant chief probation officer post in Hereford and Worcester in January 1977, working alongside Chris Brown. I remained as an ACPO for 20-years, with a further four years in an area manager post until my retirement.

When I was appointed ACPO, I wanted to know what the job was all

---

1.　Throughout this book an upper case G on "Governor" indicates the No 1 prison Governor; the one in overall charge at an establishment. In contrast to various lesser ranks of "governor".

about. Gordon Robb, CPO, told me that the job of the ACPO was to assist the CPO! There were many further humorous moments. Gordon told me about a social enquiry report he had prepared when working in Manchester. It read as follows: "The defendant is a man of few words, and when I saw him, he used two of them."

He also talked of his irritation at the requirement to complete Green Forms every three months for the Borstal After-Care Association. He recounted the occasion that his report said, "John has settled well at home, has found employment and has a new girlfriend". The reply from the BACA read, "I am pleased that John has settled well at home, has found employment, and has a new girlfriend." Gordon replied, "I am pleased that you are pleased that John has settled well at home......". A week or two later he was called to a rather uncomfortable meeting in the principal probation officer's office!

Gordon possessed a fantastic understanding of himself and other people. When Chris Brown took up post, Gordon was in great need of a holiday. Chris was understandably anxious about being left in charge of the service, and asked Gordon to leave him a list of priorities. Arriving at his desk on the first day of Gordon's leave, the list for Chris read as follows: "Where there is no vision, the people perish; but blessed is he that keepeth the law."

Provision to Meet Need

Those were the days when, in response to identified need, the service created an open access day centre, in Worcester, available five days each week. This was used by a mix of offenders, and potential offenders, who were often homeless, abusing drink and/or drugs. While this provision was welcomed by the local authority, it was frowned upon by the likes of Cliff Swann in the Home Office Inspectorate, and eventually had to be converted to provide programmes solely for offenders. Concurrently, in partnership with volunteers and local agencies and churches, a night shelter was set up, and a voluntary day centre created. It is encouraging that both of these are still operating, although local authority cuts may lead to a reduction in service or at worst, closure.

I arrived to work as SPO in the Worcester City and County Probation Area. It became the Hereford and Worcester Service in 1974, and West Mercia in 2001, six months before my retirement. In the late-1970s, the service budget was negotiated with the local authority, and the Home Office coughed up their 50 per cent or 80 per cent. There was a generally cordial relationship with the local authority with helpful secretaries and treasurers. The change to 100 per cent Home Office funding was major and severed or entirely changed the nature of the relationship with the local authority.

After Gordon Robb's retirement at the end of 1982, Jenny Roberts took up the CPO post. What were the main features and highlights of that enormous chunk of my service as ACPO? Achieving an understanding of my own racism and sexism and learning to adopt anti-racist and anti-sexist practice; helping others to achieve such learning; considerable involvement in probation hostel development; managing in-service training and providing an input for qualifying training on West Midlands courses and my original training centre, Barnett House in Oxford; assisting with the introduction and development of a computerised record system, which sadly was not, but should have been, chosen for a national roll-out (this was a great disappointment for Jenny Roberts who had devoted much time and effort to the development of the Integrated Operational Support System (IOSS)); involvement in the creation of the Perrie Lectures (I remain on the committee to this day)! I also benefited from some excellent training throughout those years; anti-racism; the Cambridge Criminology Course; a month on Management at Ashridge; and some Home Office seminars. I well remember John Haines introducing an event about what was rather unfortunately entitled "Internal Inspection" with the words "Where there is the will to condemn, there *will* be the evidence." That is a useful precept in many situations.

While I was not personally involved, the service was instrumental in initiating a Victim Support scheme during the 1970s, giving the lie to those who criticised probation for being unconcerned with victims. Jenny Roberts and other colleagues developed a ground-breaking theoretical and practical basis for separate and bespoke provision for women. Historically, the system tried to fit women into provision designed for men. Thus the Asha Centre was born in Worcester, and formed a model for provision for the particular needs of women, some of whom were offenders and others potential offenders if needs were not met.

Postscript

The current government, against all the evidence and informed opinion, appears to be hell bent on transforming, or wrecking, the Probation Service. This is a service with a proud history from its humble beginnings with the police court missionaries. It has an undoubted ability to create change, so that offenders become ex-offenders and citizens like the rest of us, albeit with a criminal record diminishing their citizenship in a variety of unhelpful ways.

Everyone is capable of change and personal development, given an appropriate environment and in particular, positive relationships. The system is also capable of change—anything created by human beings can be changed. Work to reverse and limit the damage to criminal justice about to be inflicted on us by an ideologically-blinkered Government, must continue. The safety and resilience of our communities must be strengthened by the restoration of an integrated Probation Service in the not too distant future.

Colin Archer, Probation officer Hertfordshire 1967; Assistant Chief Probation Officer and Area Manager Hereford and Worcester, 1977–2001.

5. A Home Office Perspective

David Faulkner

This contribution reflects on my experience of working with the Probation Service at various times while I was at the Home Office between 1959 and 1992. I have concentrated on those events in which I played some part, and on my own impressions as I remember them at the time, with some reflections influenced by later experiences or events.

My first memory of probation was as private secretary to the Home Office Minister Charles Fletcher-Cooke when he had been asked to speak at a probation conference near Preston. It was a cold, wet and windy afternoon in November 1961 and we were glad of the warmth of the conference room and of the welcome we received from the Lancashire Probation Service. I have no recollection of Fletcher-Cooke's speech but I remember thinking what nice people probation officers were.

Probation was at that time seen in the Home Office as an agreeable backwater, outside the mainstream of criminal justice and the department. Finlay Macrae (though we never used his first name) was principal inspector, and Winifred Goode—one of the few women in senior positions—was head of the probation division. Probation officers were more or less autonomous practitioners, whose work was loosely co-ordinated by (I think at that time 58) principal probation officers. Their accountability, if they ever thought about it, was to their clients, the courts and their employing probation committees (probably in that order)—certainly not to the Home Office and perhaps not even to the public as a whole.

But the waters were rising and probation was starting to be swept into the main channel. More clients were being supervised; the Morison Committee was sitting and reported soon afterwards, with recommendations about recruitment, training and inspection; and 18 months later, as a principal in the Prison Commission and then the Prison Department, I was given responsibility for the reorganization of prison welfare and after-care following a report by the Advisory Council on the Treatment of Offenders.

That early and much needed "rehabilitation revolution" was to be brought about by abolishing the voluntary Discharged Prisoners Aid Societies and the Central After-Care Association and transferring the work to the Probation Service, to be renamed the Probation and After-Care Service. The transfer demanded a large increase in staff and a degree of management which the service had not previously experienced. It also brought probation officers into prisons. Some welcomed the new experience, but others saw it as a betrayal of their professional values. It also offended the Prison Officers' Association who saw probation officers as taking over "their" work. More functions and responsibilities were added during the next few years, especially for parole and community service. The waters were becoming more turbulent, but the political climate was still relatively benign and debates in Parliament were still more often about the need to give more help to offenders than about increasing the severity of punishment.

I next had contact with the Probation Service as head of the women's and young offenders' division, again in the Prison Department, during the early-1970s. Most of the job was about bringing women's prisons and young offender institutions up-to-date with the social and cultural changes that were taking place in the world outside. Part of that, as I saw it, was to develop more contacts and if possible closer relationships between institutions and their local communities of which probation was obviously an important part. One venture was the "neighbourhood borstals" that we set up with the Merseyside and Greater Manchester services at Hindley and with the West Midlands at Hewell Grange. Probation officers were enthusiastic; prison staff less so, but the Advisory Council on the Penal System saw them as a possible model for the review of the arrangements for young offenders which was then in progress. The idea became part of a vision for the future which the Advisory Council set out in their report, but the pressures of overcrowding, the demands of "tactical management", and perhaps the Prison Service's lack of interest in anything outside its own walls, disappointingly brought the scheme to an end after a few years.

My main involvement with probation, and my first direct responsibility for the service, came as deputy secretary for the Home Office criminal and statistics and research departments from 1982 until 1990. Probation had in many ways been transformed from the service as I had known it 20 and even ten years earlier. There were fewer services following the amalgamations and local government reforms of the 1970s, but the service as a whole was much larger, covered many more functions and responsibilities, a wider range of activities (for example hostels and day centres), and it needed, and was beginning to receive, more active and systematic management. There were now large numbers of senior and assistant chief officers, and the Association of Chief Officers of Probation (ACOP) had just been formed. At the same time, many probation officers were still attached to their sense of professional independence, their traditional ways of working, their relationship with their "clients", and their social work values.

The 1980s and 1990s were a period of sometimes painful questioning and adjustment. The Home Office and the service were together faced with the challenges of the Conservative Government's Financial Management Initiative, with all that went with it; a hardening of public and political attitudes towards crime and the treatment of offenders; and an urgent need to find policies which made less use of imprisonment. To the familiar tensions between care and control, rehabilitation and punishment, and the interests of the offender and those of the public were now added those between the offender and the victim. They all became more salient, and more difficult to resolve, as the service's rôle became more prominent and exposed. New issues were emerging or were being recognised—racial injustice, the treatment of victims, and the need to do more to reduce crime than relying on the criminal justice process.

ACOP and most chief officers understood the situation and accepted the need for change, but I saw from my attendance at a National Association of Probation Officers (NAPO) conference that much of the service was ambivalent towards it and sometimes actively hostile. Most probation officers disliked any apparatus of management such as standards, guidelines and cash limits and saw them as an unnecessary intrusion. Many still thought of themselves as the "good guys" of the system and were inclined to look down on police and prison officers, and some still saw themselves as being "on the side" of the offender against a repressive social system. NAPO did little to conceal its dislike of Margaret Thatcher and all that her government stood for.

Those attitudes were all too visible to Ministers and other politicians. The service still had friends in Parliament, especially in the House of Lords and the Labour Party; Home Office Ministers like William Whitelaw, Douglas Hurd, David Mellor and John Patten respected the service and wanted to support it; but the government as a whole had no time for social work or what they and many others now thought of as its pretentious values. The service's main advantage was prisons were in a precarious situation, with unrest among prisoners and industrial action by staff as well as overcrowding, and the government needed its help to limit the pressure on the system. But to provide that help and retain its credibility with the Government, the service had to accept both the new management disciplines and "tougher" measures in the treatment of offenders to show that they were still being punished even if they were not sent to prison. In return, we hoped that the service would gain a more central rôle and a more influential position in the criminal justice system.

Throughout the 1980s the Home Office and the service, or perhaps more particularly chief officers and to some extent probation committees, worked together in what I felt was a mostly amicable and productive relationship. We had to reconcile the government's political demands with the service's professional standards and traditions, and to try to use the instruments of financial management and public accountability in pursuit of objectives and outcomes which we could all support. I hoped that joint aim might be expressed in a national statement agreed and owned jointly by the service's representative organizations and the Home Office.

That hope proved unrealistic, perhaps not surprisingly, and after consultation the Home Office issued its own more limited and more managerial Statement of National Objectives and Priorities (SNOP) instead. It had a mixed reception from the service, and there were some casualties, for example support for short-term prisoners after release and contact with families, but it served its purpose at the time.

The 1980s were a period of practical innovation and creative thought, inspired both by the service's own leaders and by the growing number of probation scholars in universities, many of whom had themselves served as probation officers. Practical innovations included day centres, bail information schemes and groupwork; there was increasing interest in evidence-based practice, often based on services' own research and management information; and the service began to form partnerships with voluntary organizations in providing support for offenders. Chris Stone, a visitor from the Vera Institute of Justice in New York, was a valuable interpreter and catalyst.

More theoretical debates took place at conferences and in articles in journals by writers such as Bill McWilliams, Mike Nellis, John Pendleton, Peter Raynor, Philip Whitehead and Maurice Vanstone. They brought new ideas to the management of the service and re-examined the underlying fundamental questions about the nature and purpose of criminal justice and of punishment and the service's rôle in relation to them. Examples include the sets of papers edited by Roger Statham and Philip Whitehead, and by David Ward and Malcolm Lacey.[1]

I set out my ideas for the future of the service at a Clarke Hall conference in Cambridge in July, 1989.[2] Although the talk had the title "The Future of the Probation Service: A View from Government" it was essentially my own vision. I discussed the service's identity as an "agency of the criminal justice system with a social work base" and what that implied; its rôle in punishment; the importance of its credibility and effectiveness in responding to crime, and especially in reducing reoffending; issues of performance measurement, management and leadership; and the distinction between functions which the service had to carry out itself and those which might be performed by others. On punishment, I stated the traditional but soon politically unacceptable view that it was imposed by the court and not by the Probation (or Prison) Service; it was the loss of liberty or opportunity required by the sentence, and not an activity or form of treatment that was somehow added on to it and intended to be degrading or humiliating for its own sake. The person should retain his or her own identity and place in society and the responsibilities that went with it should be restored as soon as possible.

In later years, as a non-executive director of a National Health Service community health trust, I sometimes accompanied health visitors on their visits to patients' homes. I was impressed by the extent to which they could, and often did, provide a social service to their communities which went well

---

1. Roger Statham and Philip Whitehead (eds.) (1992), *Managing The Probation Service: Issues for the 1990s*, London: Longman; and David Ward and Malcolm Lacey (eds.) (1995), *Probation Working For Justice*, London: Whiting and Birch.

2. The papers for the conference were edited by Roger Shaw and Kevin Haines and published in *The Criminal Justice System: A Central Role for the Probation Service* (1989), Cambridge: Cambridge Institute of Criminology.

beyond a strict definition of their rôle. I saw that service as having great value for troubled families and households where several members were having problems of different kinds, although it was becoming hard to reconcile that kind of service with the culture of targets and performance indicators which had become prevalent. I made a comparison with the potential work of the Probation Service, and wished it could have been possible for probation to develop in that direction instead of becoming an increasingly office-bound agency of punishment and law enforcement.

Idealism and charismatic leadership had come to be viewed with suspicion by the 1980s, and appeals to values were often regarded as precious or self-interested. We rarely mentioned them in the Home Office. The Thatcher Government's reforms, with their insistence on measurement and quantified results, reinforced those attitudes and debates about criminal justice were conducted almost entirely in terms of cost or quantified evidence, or later "what works". Arguments for moderation in sentencing and the use of imprisonment could be presented convincingly in those terms and they prevailed, more or less, until the early-1990s. They did not however prevail against the populist, dogmatic and "common sense" arguments which have been set against them for the last 20-years and which can now be seen to reflect a different set of social, political and perhaps moral values. Faced with arguments and values of that kind, appeals to cost and effectiveness can no longer succeed unless they are supported by a more compassionate and well-articulated vision of the kind of country we want Britain to be. No political party seems able to offer that at present; how that can be done in a market society is part of what Eric Hobsbawm has described as the dilemma of the 21st-century.

David Faulkner, Home Office 1959–1992; Deputy Secretary with responsibility for Criminal Justice, 1982–1990. The author has written a more extended account of events during his time at the Home Office in *Servant of the Crown: A Civil Servant's Story of Criminal Justice and Public Service Reform* (2014), Sherfield-on-Loddon: Waterside Press.

6. Remembering Probation in the Sixties

David Millard

When I became a probation officer in 1963 the discipline within which probation officers practised was almost exclusively Freudian and had been so for many years. There was a huge emphasis upon one-to-one casework and family contact; criminal behaviour was "explained" entirely in terms of the childhood experiences and anxieties—often allegedly "oedipal"—that stemmed from upbringing.

It was all great fun of course, but I soon realised that it was all a sort of elaborate intellectual game. In fact nothing was really being explained at all. How could it be? The probation officer entered the life of a person (nearly always male, especially in those days) who was already anxious about a court appearance and its possible outcome. He or she ferreted around for a bit, trying to put together some kind of social and personal history but, apart from the record of convictions, usually had no way of checking the accuracy of the facts he or she was given. Then he or she brought all this together with some very personal impressions of the person in front of him or her, and cobbled together a version of events which somehow put them into a coherent explanation. But really it was only coherent because this type of psychologising had managed to achieve a supremacy within the criminal justice system. This indeed had been the story of criminal justice in the 20th-century—the growing acceptance of the psycho-social determinist, and therefore therapeutic position. But all that was happening in the individual case, as I soon realised, was that *a story was being made up*. By this I don't mean that our work was an elaborate confidence trick. Far from it. What I mean is that the kinds of explanations that probation officers offered within this (often pseudo-)Freudian framework could in no way be *validated*. By definition they were endlessly subjective and impressionistic. This does not mean that they were dishonest; it means that probation officers were making use of the only professional language that they had available to them at that time.

What I quickly came to realise was that I had joined not so much a profession that was exercising a verifiable empirical discipline, but one whose task was to inhabit and make use of *a system of professional discourse.* In this the crucial thing to be learnt was the language—the *jargon,* in other words—and the permissible limits within which it could be deployed.

The public arena in which all this was most visibly played out was of course the court. Here the task of the probation officer was to help the court determine the appropriate penalty in specific cases. The assumption was that it was possible to provide explanations of criminal behaviour that could justify therapeutic—i.e. counselling—programmes of intervention that would reduce the risk of re-offending. And although their work was endlessly subjective and uncertain, the probation officers continually deployed their professional language in such a way as to underplay this fact. The implication was always that the "trained" probation officer had access to some source of special esoteric knowledge, inaccessible to lesser mortals, which entitled him or her to pontificate about "diagnosis", "therapeutic interventions", "likely prognosis" etc, etc. But in truth it was always a tentative proposition at best. Probation officers soon learned to protect themselves from the realisation that their particular emperor didn't have too many clothes by routinising their work. They learnt how to deploy the language, tailoring it to a real situation in which the emptiness of their rhetoric would not be subject to too much scrutiny. Thus, once the new probation officer had realised that the actual factors most relevant to sentence were frequently such things as the perceived seriousness of the offence and the number of previous convictions, he or she could play his esoteric language game to his heart's content, safe in the knowledge that he wasn't going to be called to account.

For myself though, it wasn't long before I found myself struggling with the issue of how it could be possible to justify my work—not least to myself!—if the overt language game in which it was being played could not really be substantiated. Here I was, standing up in court and arguing for particular outcomes, and in effect *pretending* that I was making use of some kind of sophisticated knowledge base; whereas in fact what I was doing was little more than making guesses. Sometimes they may have been well-informed and educated guesses, but they were guesses nevertheless.

In my own mind it was very important to try and resolve this, and I think that things began to fall into place for me when I realised that what I was actually doing in court was not so much claiming some kind of esoteric know-how that could turn crooks into honest men; rather, what I was doing was playing out a specifically defined rôle in a *moral debate*.

This requires explanation. It became apparent to me that every sentencing decision marks the resolution of a particular kind of discussion—a discussion that entails a consideration of questions like:

Who is really blameworthy here?
Where does the weight of guilt lie?
Who deserves punishment and who merits mercy?

In other words, sentencing is always an exercise in individualised social philosophy. This is what I was doing! Practical social philosophy. It wasn't a technical empirical exercise at all. It was an exercise, necessarily uncertain, in working out the relationship between punishment and mercy in any particular case. And the language that I was using—the *given* language of the probation officer—was the language of explanation that *for the time being* was culturally acceptable.

For my own practice, some things seemed to follow inevitably from this realisation. The first was to understand that the use of the language was acceptable as long as it didn't make unreasonable claims for itself, that it didn't aspire to *knowledge* that wasn't in fact available. The language should always be couched in terms of hypothesis and possibility rather than dogma. *This might be the case*, not *This is the case.* It could never be the probation officer's job to seek to *decide* on the balance between punishment and mercy, but only to contribute to the in-court debate. The decision rightly belongs to the court itself as the final arbiter of the will of the community.

Perhaps a more important thing to follow from this understanding of the moral dimension to a probation officer's work was the realisation that I needed some working principles to guide my own practice. Without such principles there was a constant danger of the *routinisation* of practice, of not entering into genuine debate. And I think that there were some probation officers who fell in love with the language of psycho-babble but totally failed to appreciate the moral dimension that I have described. Trapped within this language, and not fully apprehending its limitations, they would eventually fall into the trap of using the language to play to the prejudices of the court. Their primary working tool became their realisation that sentencing was often weighted in terms of the two categories of *perceived seriousness of offence* and *number of previous convictions*; they then constructed social and personal identities for their clients which re-enforced the tendency of the court to put these categories at the top of the list of sentencing criteria. Effectively this meant that they gave up on the opportunity to involve themselves in the in-court debate. It seemed to me that the only way to avoid this pitfall was to develop a set of working principles of my own and try to keep them permanently in mind. And for better or worse, this is what they were (more or less!):

- An acknowledgement that human beings are endlessly complex, and this has nothing to with their level of intelligence or ability to articulate their thoughts.
- An acknowledgement that the causes of crime are also complex and probably unknowable in any absolute sense in the individual case.
- That culpability is always, and necessarily problematic.
- That punishment—i.e. retributive pain—ought *therefore* to be used only as a last resort.
- That reparation and reconciliation are frequently the better moral option.

It seemed to me, and it still does, that these are essential assumptions for a Probation Service that does not conceive of itself in some kind of mindlessly punitive way, but rather as a force for reconciliation and mediation. Moreover they are assumptions that also need to be invoked once the work in the court has been completed and the offender has been placed under supervision. I am of course describing a time long gone! But the essence of probation work became for me the creation of a certain kind of *climate* and a certain kind of *space*. Having negotiated a particular outcome from the court, the probation officer needed to hold on to these principles and seek to create the space and the climate in which the client could think about and reflect on his or her life in a certain kind of way. Most importantly this was to be done in the context of a *relationship* with the client, one built on knowledge and acceptance.

What I mean by knowledge here is the probation officer's awareness of some of the worst things that are to be known about the client, including the behaviour for which he or she has been judged, but with regard to which, the probation officer *does not condemn*. Rather, by his manner and tone of conversation, indeed by his *courtesy*, the probation officer makes it clear that this behaviour can be variously understood, forgiven, controlled and moved beyond. It is not the probation officer who does this; the work is always done by the client. Not that it necessarily follows that the client is able, willing, or interested in following this path. But it is the opportunity that the probation officer offers, and my argument here is that essentially it is *all* that the probation officer offers. In order to achieve it the probation officer may follow a variety of short-term interim paths to gain trust and confidence. For example, he may elect to be his client's friend and advocate in a variety of impinging social realities — with his family perhaps, the employment services, social services or benefits.

There may be further work to be done within the criminal justice system itself, and from time-to-time the probation officer may be called upon to be interventionist in a more or less authoritarian way. Whatever form these kinds of interventions take, the essential task is to create the trusting conversational environment in which the offender does his or her own reflecting and decision-making, his or her own thinking about the possibility of living his or her life differently.

After five years of work as a probation officer, thinking about these issues of theory and working out a basic philosophy for myself, I became a senior probation officer in 1968 and immediately was given paid leave of absence for a year to study for an MA in criminology at Keele University. This was a great year for me — really a sabbatical — and I enjoyed it immensely. There was plenty of time for library work, both the set course and other reading, but it was also quite a relaxed year with time to spend at home. So I had a thoroughly good time and this made up quite a lot for the dreariness of my undergraduate years.

Be that as it may, by the time it was over — the summer of 1969 — I was ready to return to work as a senior probation officer running a team, which I was going to do for the next seven years. I felt now that I had acquired a new level of intellectual confidence in the whole area of "understanding" crime. Mostly this was to do with the sociological dimension to the course, an area which until then was completely unfamiliar to me. The psychological dimensions I was already familiar with; but the sociological stuff—class theories, labelling theory, organizational issues with regard to prisons and the police, etc,—all this had been new to me. And it did give me a new breadth of outlook and a new confidence. When I was confronted with a particular offender I now felt the confidence to review a number of explanatory *versions* of what had happened and choose, *eclectically,* the one that seemed most appropriate.

Although there was still a lot of room for "traditional" practice—and I had no desire to throw the baby out with the bathwater—I now found that I was frequently coming into contact with cases in which traditional practice no longer seemed to be relevant. Working with so many lives that were caught up in an escalating spiral of conviction upon conviction, with little possibility of breaking out of it, the use of labelling theory, for example, could provide one with both a different kind of story and a different kind of relationship to be worked at. One began to realise that it was really true that offenders had sometimes taken upon themselves the identity which had been given to them by the very nature of their involvement with the system. *I must be a crook because they **say** I'm a crook* (David Matza's 1969 *Becoming Deviant* became a key text here). Starting from such a realisation one found oneself working at a different kind of relationship—not so much an attempt to help the client unravel the past, as one to engage with the way that *current* behaviour had been brought about by a variety of causes some of which were as much social as they were personal.

So—a great broadening out in the way I came to conceptualise my work. A broadening out which led me to think of explanations not as absolute expressions of reality, but as *versions* of reality which could be employed for their usefulness in contributing to the punishment or mercy debate. This then is how I began to make sense of my work, and for some of us, another key text became the unpublished paper of 1969 by the Home Office civil servant D H Morrell, "Does Social Work Hinder Social Reform?".

"If it is part of the social worker's function to help people adjust to the expectations of the society in which they live, it is equally part of their function to criticise these expectations, describing some as unrealistic or irrational, and others as unethical. Society has no business to expect social workers to further a one-sided process of adaptation, all change being demanded of the clients and none at all in social expectations. On the contrary, society must expect the social work profession to derive from its experience of working with the client's understandings about society's responsibility for the attitudes and behaviour which it finds damaging or inconvenient. And it must expect to be told by social workers that their role is to mediate an active reciprocity of relationships involving social as well as individual change; it is not that of engineering passive conformity to unchanging social norms."

(Quoted by Zofia T Butrym in *The Nature of Social Work*, Macmillan, 1976)

The probation officer's job — as I had now come to understand it — was to argue that the individual offence and offender could be made intelligible, that causes were at work for which the offender was only partly responsible, and that something could possibly be done about this without the need to resort to punitive repression. All of this relied upon a sentencing philosophy which adopted the notion of complex culpability as a first principle. In effect the court was able to say, on behalf of the community:

"We cannot be sure who is to blame here. It may be this offender before us; but it may also be society itself, the pressures and disadvantages to which the defendant has been subjected. If this is the case, therapy may at least be as relevant as punishment."

Such a philosophy of criminal justice was an extraordinary achievement of the 20th-century, a truly civilised, humane, and liberal approach to the problem of crime. Sadly however, it is very different to today's pragmatism which has a distinct lack of interest in any acceptance of the kind of moral complexity that I have been describing here. It often seems to me that today's practice is not at all interested in the development of a system that accepts that the very notion of blameworthiness may often be problematic.

The time I am writing about is the late-1960s and into the 1970s. And when I returned to work after the course I found not just a new kind of professional confidence, but also that I thoroughly enjoyed being a team leader. And that I was good at it. In 1971 I moved with my team to an area office in Shelton in Stoke-on-Trent and here we began to develop a new kind of teamwork. We began to realise, partly because of our particular clientele, that it wasn't going to be enough to just go on practising in the same old one-to-one way. The office as a whole, the building and all its facilities, could help us in creating the climate of space and time through which the work could be done.

A significant proportion of our clients came from the very poorest and most disadvantaged sections of the community. For example, some of them were residents of the Salvation Army hostel in the town, or the nearby hotel that catered for unemployed Department of Health and Social Security (DHSS) clients. Some were single mothers in the very poorest accommodation that was available. These were disaffected people, often lacking in motivation or hope, frequently at a loose-end during the day, drifting aimlessly around the town and the pubs.

Somehow it became the most natural thing in the world for part of our office to become an informal drop-in centre—for chat, coffee, listening to the radio, etc. But all done within the same ethos—that of creating the time, the space and the support for the client to do his or her own work. Perhaps it doesn't sound much now. Indeed it sounds impossibly dated. But this was before the time of any *structured* day centre work at all. Virtually all probation work was one-to-one or family counselling. For us this was a time of questioning and optimistic innovation. Old habits and practices were being queried, and people were keen to experiment with new ways of working. In our office at Shelton, something which began spontaneously and informally—a group of demoralised and unemployed petty offenders meeting for tea, chat and problem sharing—grew and grew. And soon the old *boundaries* between probation officers and clients, previously quite formal, became eroded. Sharing on a much more human level began to take place. First names began to be used, and this itself became the symbol of a new kind of climate.

Out of all this, as the probation officers began to reflect on what was happening, there grew a whole new sense of possible opportunities that could be developed under the same roof. At different times, and sometimes all at the same time, we made use of informal discussion groups, structured discussion groups, women's groups, a play group, an art group, a group producing an office newsletter, visiting speakers. And also at the same time the officers continued to have their individual cases allocated to them in traditional ways, but found that when it was appropriate they could feed them into one or other of the groups which might help to meet their needs.

This is a period of my working life which I look back upon as immensely rewarding. I felt that I was doing something innovative and important for the Probation Service, thinking about working in new ways and doing this successfully. And I was working with a team of people whose morale and commitment were extremely high. Moreover, because we were writing about our work, and being invited to address conferences about it, I am sure that we were able to enthuse other people as well.

In retrospect, I don't think that it was surprising that my commitment to probation at this time was a commitment to the idea that, given the opportunity to do reflective work on their own inner worlds, people might discover in themselves the possibility of change. *For this is what I had discovered about myself.* The past determines us but it doesn't have to imprison us. Freedom is not absolutely attainable. But the *struggle* for freedom, the long slow process of working for some kind of personal moral progress *is* possible, and it is a commitment worth making. A proportion of the clients that we saw at this time did make some such progress. Such a statement is not of course amenable to empirical or statistical proof, but it is justified by the response that we sometimes saw, and the things we heard said. It has nothing to do with the task of the Probation Service today—social control and policing for the duration of a statutory supervision period. This seems to me to be an infinitely depressing scenario, but perhaps that is no more than a symptom of my age.

David Millard, Probation officer, Stoke-on-Trent Probation Service, 1963; Assistant Chief Probation West Midlands, 1976-1989.

7.   Probation: An Earlier Life

Gordon Read

Tho' much is taken, much abides; and tho'
We are not now that strength which in old days
Moved earth and heaven; that which we are, we are;
One equal temper of heroic hearts,
Made weak by time and fate, but strong in will
To strive, to seek, to find, and not to yield.

Alfred Tennyson (from Ulysses, 1842)

Probation Encounters

When thinking about "A Life in Probation", as Cedric Fullwood has described his brief memoir in *Probation: A Celebration of Achievement* (2014), it tends to be contacts that come to mind; with colleagues, court and prison staff, social work teachers and — in pre-privatisation days — local authorities and voluntary organizations as well as those to whom we all had responsibilities. I knew nothing about probation until a few months before I left the army. However, from its first mention to my becoming actively involved I think, on reflection, I began edging towards it though I should probably have known more about it given the amount of alcohol-fuelled offending behaviour that accompanied the necessary camaraderie of military life.

That first mention was by a young woman sociology undergraduate thinking of a probation career I'd met while on leave. While that may have accounted for my joining the Sociology Society when I eventually arrived at a university myself, I gave it little further thought until attending a week's introduction to social work in its widest sense at a settlement in Bermondsey where I met Ron Howell, an Inner London senior probation officer (SPO) about to head up the Rainer Foundation. His commitment captured my interest and just prior to a long trip to the Indian sub-continent I applied to and was accepted for the London School of Economics' (LSE's) Social Studies Course.

I really enjoyed the LSE with such luminaries as Richard Titmuss, Brian Abel Smith and David Donnison as well as the placements provided, including research into letters dealing with housing problems in the *Daily Mirror's* offices (where there was never a dull moment). What LSE provided was not only grounding in social work and psychological and psychoanalytic theory, but an historical introduction to the origins of the welfare reforms introduced between 1944 and 1948. That familiarised me with earlier Poor Law studies and the identification of the roots of poverty in the UK's successive low wage economies at times of huge wealth.

It is painfully ironic to see that reappearing again with zero-hours contracts and the reversion by the Department for Work and Pensions (DWP) to the "less eligibility" mantras of the 1834 Poor Law Amendment Act which overhauled 200-years of workhouse provision and established the baleful system prevalent in Dickens' time, parts of which were only discarded with the coming of the Health Act of 1948. It is easy to forget — though necessary to remember — that the legislation between 1944 and 1948 liberated my generation and those that followed, up until now, from the inequalities and ever-present poverty of our earlier childhoods.

On the Job

My first experience of a probation office was at Old Street courthouse with the thoughtful John Ferguson where Stan Ratcliffe, then an SPO, managed duties standing against a filing cabinet in a cramped back office. Many folk heroes of the Inner London Probation Service (ILPS) dwelt there and others passed through; Geoffrey Parkinson was one, he of "I give them money" fame and other eye-catching insights including, if my memory serves, the notion that one of the strengths of probation was the creativity that its workforce "smuggled in".

I next joined the irrepressible Fred Hambrook in Kingston-upon-Thames. He had an energetic commitment to the novel concept of psychoanalytic "probation casework". I then took up post with Harry Hilton — the "Mr Young" of John St John's 1961 book, *Probation: The Second Chance* — at Wallington where I joined Michael Day, Ray Robinson and others including Chris Brown (then a local curate). I shared the Mitcham patch and the totter community and, standing in for Michael at court one Saturday morning, had to field a loudly confrontational aside from one of his supervisees nodding towards the somewhat pompous clerk to the justices with a "Who's that little old fat xxxx then?"

Harry's was a lively office committed to experimental groupwork and group supervision as well as undertaking liaison with a number of London's large psychiatric hospitals (still asylums in those days) with Ray Robinson bringing back insights from his liaison with the renowned Henderson Hospital. It is in work in such settings that the clientele teaches probation staff their job.

Not having heard from someone I'd been bequeathed for some weeks, I decided to undertake the time-consuming three buses journey to "outer" Tooting only to find him with three children under three, a partner who'd pushed off and the National Assistance Board (NAB) not getting money to him. On another occasion I was met with surprise by a West Indian mother who'd never dreamt that a white official would accept a cup of tea from her. Elsewhere I also worked out that it was important to remove your overcoat if you wished to indicate you were staying put and meant business. Our court's thoughtful gaoler also taught his probation staff a thing or two and once requested me to accompany a seriously disturbed young man into the defendant's box to explain to the magistrates that he didn't feel he could remove his cap or his damaging thoughts would fly round the courtroom.

An important lesson for a literature graduate was the discovery that many of those we met didn't understand quite commonplace words, "conflict" for example or that a "bench" was an *ad hoc* coterie of magistrates. A harder lesson, following the Howell example, was the need to be prepared to run the extra mile—occasionally marathon—for people one served. I still reflect shamefully on those occasions when I failed to do that, whether for those under supervision or for members of staff; bearing in mind also that not everything any of us have endeavoured will have had positive outcomes.

After four years in post, I undertook the one year Advanced Social Work Course at the Tavistock Clinic. Apart from the working experiences and insights gained there, there was the ongoing benefit of a widespread and talented former student network—including many within probation—which helped keep ideas and practice up-to-date. I then relocated to Kingston to find, early the first morning, a rough looking youngster in a sleeping bag in the doorway who asked if I was the new bloke—a practical example, we may all recollect, that colleagues can, hopefully unwittingly, "leave out their dead". A few weeks later he turned up at the UK consulate in Geneva wanting the fare home. I asked how he'd got there, was told he'd hitch hiked, so said, "Give him a few bob and tell him to hitch back". He soon returned. I also recollect a particularly complex and violent family drama from the juvenile court with three of us, including Geoff Childs, submitting separate reports outlining how we proposed working with the family dynamics.

A year or so later I made an application to Inner London for an SPO (Student Training Unit) post but, on being offered a different job, caused a mild tremor by turning it down. However, when a similar post became vacant I was offered it and accepted. The unit was relocated within the complex of probation teams in a West Kensington office building and linked to both the Notting Hill and Marylebone offices. Not only did students have an office mentor as well as unit supervisor, but the supervisor was also able to provide relief cover for a range of other SPOs as well as run groupwork sessions, as did Michael Day and others, at Rainer House. Rosemary Deane, the assistant chief (ACPO), also had additional training tasks up her sleeve like linking-up with the emerging social work courses and there was even time, occasionally, for an article in the *Justice of the Peace* or a letter to the *Guardian*.

It was when Bill Pearce, ILPS's then chief probation officer (CPO), was on an office visit that I made my next move. There was an SPO vacancy at Pentonville Prison. I told him I wouldn't have minded that job in another six months, whereupon he told me it would be mine! While I'd worked as a relief SPO at both Wandsworth and Brixton Prisons, I think I had a more enlightened Governor there than I'd hitherto encountered who told me to settle in and then he'd let me know what he wanted. I made it clear that when I'd looked round, I'd let him know what I thought was needed. Thereafter, he gave me a free hand. With something like 23,000 arrivals and departures a year at that time and six probation staff—one of the former the elderly ex-jazz trumpeter Leslie Thompson—we needed more help and, having determined between us that about 15 minutes was the minimum required to realistically connect with each arriving prisoner, recruited additional one-day-a-week part-timers along with one-day-a-week students from the training network to increase our capacity (mentoring them on the prison wings). With the initiative of a very dynamic team of London NW3 mothers (one now in the Lords) a visitors' centre was set up—symbolically in retrospect—opposite the prison in a former off-licence. Prison staff raised safety concerns about that until I prayed my young drama teacher of a wife in aid by explaining that if she could take their unruly adolescent sons from one end of the Holloway Road to the swimming pool at the other, there shouldn't be too much difficulty getting visitors over a pedestrian crossing. For me, lessons to be imparted about working with prisoners include never promising what can't be fulfilled; saying "No" and meaning it; using volunteers to mentor prisoners on release; and ensuring that as far a possible someone is waiting at the gate early in the morning, even if it's you, to assist resettlement on discharge and get things sorted before the off-licences open (fortunately there were no wall-to-wall booze shops and supermarkets back then).

Management

After Pentonville I moved to Worcestershire (later Hereford and Worcester) as Gordon Robb's first assistant principal (APPO). That meant more supervision for SPOs in the area as well as a refocus of attention on matrimonial and family court work. It also brought me Parole Board Local Review and Probation Hostel Committee work and, as a sideline, running a Social Studies class at the dispersal prison at Long Lartin. One particular aim was to bring people from all walks of life inside to engage such prisoners in the realities of their eventual release. Those imprisoned in the dispersal sector are often difficult for staff to manage without sanitising the offences that their charges have committed—but very likely to be repeated if not engaged with.

Staff Training and Development

Quite early on I was recruited by Malcolm Lacey, then Midlands region staff development officer (RSDO) to help organize and teach on national courses for those recruited by way of direct entry and later for the burgeoning number of SPOs. Those were intellectually stimulating engagements and led to partnerships with some very talented in-house probation contributors like Los Coates, John Jones, Deidre Flegg and David Millard (he of *Why People Offend* and *Social Work and the Literary Imagination*) as well as an occasional inspector and staff of the Grubb Institute and the National Marriage Guidance Council (now Relate) whose premises we used.

It wasn't too great a transition, therefore, to move fully into the RSDO rôle when Malcom crossed into higher education (HE). It also led contact with the energetic creativity of the three other RSD units, headed respectively by Bill Bayley, Laurie Foster and John Harper, their assistant RSDOs and staff they attracted from universities plus freelancers like the unpredictable and always challenging .

It was in this time of rapid service development that RSDOs worked with the encouragement and support of Roy Taylor, then deputy chief inspector of probation responsible for training. Along with David Millard at RSD and various local HE teachers, we commenced a programme to develop—*in situ*—"Teamwork in Probation" and, together with our RSD peers provided programmes which, increasingly, became useful mechanisms for coordinating and expanding developmental approaches to new responsibilities like community service, day centres, hostel management, sexual offending and—in probation's then the family court welfare rôle —mediation and conciliation. Often provided on a workshop basis, or at monthly forums, these enabled staff of all grades to develop a real authority when exchanging ideas and skills. For me the South East RSD ventures in international exchanges and research—as with a Poland on the brink of better Western European relations—sat happily with work arising from my contact with the Grubb Institute which had linked me into the University of East Anglia's (UEA's) Development of University English Teaching (DUET) project—really about creative writing and not just criticism—in Norwich, Katowice and Amherst, Massachusetts.

Move to the Chief Probation Officer (CPO) Rôle

In early 1981 I succeeded Royston (Roy) Bailey as CPO in Devon and inherited his impressive head office staff. They had been involved in the establishment of a highly innovative community development outreach team (the Devon Consultative Group—DCG) chaired by a former director of prisons, David Hewlings, and led by John Harding prior to his move to the West Midlands and successively thereafter by John Anthony and Michael Vizard. Aside from having to cope with my share of our family's grief at the death of our elder daughter in a mountaineering accident, I had my work cut out getting to know all members of staff and meeting magistrates and judges, whom I always looked upon as my key "constituents". One of the first challenges I had was introducing the recommendations of a ground-breaking report from the DCG on the supervision of those who are potentially dangerous which had been commissioned following a serious incident in Devon involving a released prisoner the year before.

This forerunner of multi-agency public protection arrangements (MAPPAs), with guidelines drawn up by John Anthony, recommended a partnership with the police and other public agencies, based on the key worker principle of the then area child protection teams. It set out a protocol for supervising the most dangerous people, including those who had committed all manner of sexual offences however minor the presenting factors might be—something we (unlike the current Ministry of Justice) understand better now with respect to people like the amiable, apparently innocuous and plausible Fred West. The decision to categorise for such supervision was made on referral by members of the head office management team, which might also include the chief officer if there were particular concerns, and then passed to a serious offender rehabilitation team (SORT). Such teams comprised the proposed supervising probation officer, his or her office manager, and the appropriate head office member who set up the police links. As with child protection, police and workers from other agencies were integral to such teams.

Each of those on the team had a clear rôle in the supervisory plan and the process cut across time-honoured principles of confidentiality because it required supervisors to be aware of, and if necessary in contact with, all significant people the supervisee was involved with: partners, step-children, friends, employers, social workers, etc. A team meeting could be requested by any of the participants, with monthly reports, signed by the team manager going to the head office member who had assigned the case. Because of that, there was—to quote from Barry Palmer of the Grubb Institute—a real sense that the people who ran probation would carry within themselves the emotional realities of doing the supervisor's job, and helping them hold the tension of befriending and helping; working to obtain the co-operation and motivation of someone who is potentially dangerous and—the difficult part — remaining sceptical in order to avoid becoming captured by their rationalisations or insufficiently aware of the very real dangers they posed.

Rôles in the Association of Chief Officers of Probation (ACOP)

From the time I became an APPO I was involved in ACOP (formerly the Conference of Principal (later Chief) Probation Officers) activities at a local level and, as an RSDO, at national level, especially with training, development and skills issues. That involvement increased as a CPO when I joined the Management Services Committee, taking over the chair when Ieuan Miles went as director to the Central Council of Probation Committees (CCPC). In that context I advised the employers' side as well as proposed the establishment of a separate Financial Services Committee, initially chaired by Jim Cannings. In 1989 I became vice-chair of ACOP during an 18-month transition period when Graham Smith was chair. One of my duties then, leaving aside addressing the National Association of Probation Officers (NAPO) conferences, was chairing ACOP's group preparing the input to the White Paper that later became the Criminal Justice Act 1991. When Graham's time in office ended, it seemed appropriate to bid for the ACOP chair. However, looking back, I realise that would have been a bridge much too far without the excellent support of Bill Weston and Jill Thomas, and with the dazzling Mike Ward undertaking ACOP's public relations.

Probation and Criminal Justice Politics

Picking up on the Criminal Justice Act 1991, it is possible to say that this was a great gift to probation as well as being David Faulkner's crowning glory. It was — the 1967 Act abolishing capital punishment apart — the next most rational and creative step on the road to civilising the criminal law since the great Criminal Justice Act of 1948 which not only abolished penal servitude, hard labour and corporal punishment (though clearly not capital punishment) but, with its Schedule V, established probation as a key public service. However, the 1991 Act contained one major flaw. It changed the probation order from a sanction which was "instead of a punishment" and requiring the consent of the defendant to its imposition, to yet another punishment. That returned courts to objectifying all defendants instead of treating at least some of them as citizens to be fully engaged in their own responsibility for their breaches of the law. Gordon Robb, a mentor of mine as of many others in probation, always insisted that the issue of consent was a highly symbolic aspect of the probation order in so far as the humblest magistrate and the greatest judge in the land both had to seek the agreement of a defendant to impose it.

Sadly, the attempt in the 1991 Act to strengthen the fine as a sensible and realistic sanction based upon the means of the defendant was sabotaged by the popular press, missing the point that the proportion of income the "day fine" brought about was the level that was imposed on "ordinary" defendants every day. The fine had to be based on income as well as capacity to pay; otherwise where was the realism of the sanction. However, much of the Act stands, for example the "so serious" clause through which the imposition of imprisonment has to be weighed. Since the Act, the strangely punitive nature of so-called New Labour Home Secretaries and their determination to restrict the quite proper discretion of the judiciary with mandatory sentencing at the same time introducing a similarly previously discredited mechanism, the indeterminate sentence, ramped-up sentencing powers and the prison population; ills that continue.

Legacy?

If those of us who worked in probation in the past have any legacy at all, it is what we were able to give when we were in our working rôles. In that respect we have to trust that those continuing in such work or benefiting from our interventions will pass our messages along or act them out in their behaviour. It appears something of an irony that probation colleagues are being supported to work in countries like Turkey and Jordan to introduce the concept of probation developed in England, Wales and Northern Ireland over the past 100-years at a time when it appears to be being abandoned here.

But I still preserve some hope. When I visit New Zealand, as family commitments require me to, I encounter the song thrush that used to be common across the UK and is rarely seen now and joke about re-introducing it here. However, the analogy has a downside in the way the ubiquitous European blackbird flourishes there as well as here. They are the mellifluous privatisers that blast their alarm calls in every New Zealand forest, drowning the even more mellifluous calls of the native bell birds and tui.

What we might hope for in the future, therefore, is a legacy mediated in the forums of the newly established Probation Institute where the remnants of the Probation Service will meet with the yet to be appointed commercial and voluntary organization providers—some of whom will be our own former colleagues. In that context and setting, probation values could still be carried forward and my hope is that it will happen in a manner that those for whom they have responsibilities will be engaged with and treated with respect as people and not as targets associated with some binomially driven financial formula.

Gordon Read, Probation officer, Inner London, June 1962; Chief Probation Officer, Devon, 1981–1996.

8. A Personal Probation Journey

Howard Lockwood

I grew up in Lincoln, a farming town in the East Midlands with some heavy engineering industries. My background was steeped in Methodism, father being the Sunday School superintendent and mother in the choir. In my teens I joined the Methodist Youth Club and gradually became chair of the members committee (16-years), assistant leader (18-years), leader (20-years). Too much responsibility too young or an early indication of the work I wanted to do?

In my early-20s I worked as an engineering buyer for a larger excavation manufacturer, Ruston Bucyrus, in Lincoln. During this period (1966-1970) I ran a "skinhead" youth club with a friend on a new large council estate (Birchwood). I seemed to have some affinity with these rebellious young people and started to search for more meaningful employment. I considered full-time youth work but in the end I chose probation. I remember reading the booklet from the Home Office describing the rôle of the probation officer as: (1) an officer of the court; and (2) helping offenders through "advise, assist, befriend".

At the age of 27 I went on the Home Office one year mature students course with placements in London, Scunthorpe, Whatton Detention Centre and Birmingham. It was a great course which provided me with so many positive experiences as well as rocking me to my foundations. I remember Mollie Samuels tutoring us on probation practice saying:

> "The vast majority of you are here because you are Christians and want to improve the lives of others, by the end of this course I will have knocked those views out of you as there is no such thing as altruism! Now let's hear why you are really on this course".

I chose Nottingham as the place I wanted to work and on June 1, 1973 I started my career in the old Shire Hall. Health and Safety were not a top priority in those days. I remember my senior, Brian, giving me a thick file and asking, "Do you want to monitor this case or have a go?" Being young, enthusiastic and naïve I said I would have a go. "Well," said Brian, "don't read too much of this then, but be careful. Martin has a long criminal history of violence, drugs and alcohol."

I saw Martin for his first interview in the office at about 7 pm one Monday evening. He sat down and said, "I am an unstable psychopath with a personality disorder and I am sitting between you and the door." I have no idea what happened next. I recall that I had not checked to see whether or not there were any colleagues left in the building. There was no panic button in those days. In hindsight I must have stayed sufficiently calm to keep listening and talking to him because in the event it all passed off peacefully. But to say I didn't feel too great at the time would be an understatement (Lesson No. 1—Do not let the offender sit between you and the door!).

I remember being Martin's probation officer for two years. I went to see him in Ranby Prison to say, "Well Martin (we always had considerable disagreements), you will be glad to hear that I am moving on and that you will no longer have me as your PO." As a complete surprise to me he became rather tearful and said that whilst we had had our arguments I was the only one who had stuck with him (Lesson No. 2—Things aren't always what they seem).

During his periods of absence in prison I worked with his petite wife (Martin was a strapping young man). She had made it clear that she wanted a divorce as she was fed up with Martin smashing the house up and getting into trouble. I helped her get the court forms and a solicitor, then, as so often happens, she backed out. I asked her why and she said that Martin was not very well at the moment and she rather liked that. He had stomach ulcers and she enjoyed making them worse by squeezing washing up liquid into his shepherd's pie (Lesson No. 3—Be sceptical about who the perpetrator is and who the victim is).

"Office duty" in my first year comprised an afternoon a week meeting people who came without an appointment. I was not on duty but I remember a drunken offender getting very angry and throwing a chair out of the probation office window onto the street. He and the duty PO had the shock of their lives when the chair came flying back into the room having been returned by a passer-by.

In those days (1973), the duty officer could give an offender 50 pence for something to eat, but this was poor casework and it didn't really work. Rather we were proud not to give them money, used for booze of course, and as a result we didn't spend much of the petty cash. The finding of bed and breakfast accommodation for the homeless was much more important, but not easy especially on a Friday afternoon.

As anecdotes go, the least successful home visit I made (yes we did those regularly) in my opinion at the time was meeting a woman who was in a terrible mess. Husband left, loads of debt, electricity cut off and three children under five. She had been arrested for shoplifting and was placed on probation. Not knowing what to do I said, "You are in a mess"—she burst into tears and said that I was the first person to have acknowledged her position. After that we took one bill at a time and very slowly got her back on track financially (Lesson No. 4—Sometimes when you have no idea what to do just to acknowledging a person's situation can be good work).

From a "field" probation team in Nottingham I became the "welfare" probation officer on the senior wing, for those aged 14 to 17, of Whatton Detention Centre. We worked closely with the prison staff, education officer and the trade supervisors to encourage these young offenders to learn and have more order in their lives so that they might "go straight" in the future.

After this, in 1977, I joined the community service team organizing and supervising unpaid work for offenders. This scheme was still in its comparative infancy, having been rolled-out nationally only a couple of years before. Nottinghamshire was one of the pilot areas for this in 1973. In my opinion the Probation Service contributed greatly to the rehabilitation of offenders through community service. It was popular with the courts and probation staff as an alternative to custody and it made sense to offenders who understood that they were repaying the community for their crimes.

The best placements were when there was a direct link with a beneficiary, e.g. doing painting and decorating or gardening for an elderly or disabled person living on their own—even better if they were able to make the offenders and their supervisors a cup of tea. I saw some offenders visibly change when they realised they could do some good in this world by helping someone. A number of those offenders stopped re-offending and eventually we could employ them as supervisors themselves. That was a joy and made the work really worthwhile.

In the period of the copycat riots of 1981, I was a senior probation officer based in the Hyson Green area of Nottingham. In those days probation knew what was happening on the street because of our community-based approach to the work. During the riot the only windows not to be damaged were those of the fish and chip shop and the probation office. I suppose you need fish and chips while you are rioting!

My association with the Methodist Church ended soon after that. I went to my local church on the Sunday morning for some fellowship and comfort only to be met, almost to a person, with, "Why don't they go back to where they come from?" Later it was discovered through analysis that 70 per cent of the offenders were white and came from nearby council estates and were not local residents of the area.

In the late-1970s and 1980s field probation teams were very much community-based. In the Western team, for which I was responsible, we created a "drop-in centre" at Balloon Woods and on the Broxtowe council estate. In our social enquiry reports to the courts we were able to provide a community context, describe home circumstances as well as an analysis of the offending behaviour. This seemed really important at the time, so that we could provide the best possible information to the courts who would then have a thorough understanding of an offender's circumstances as well as the details of the offence. The social information was then be passed on to those who were working with the offender after their court appearance, and became the basis for the casework.

In 1983, I was seconded to the Training Information and Development Section (TIDS) in Headquarters. There I worked with others on organizational development based on the three cornerstones of our work—courts, custody and community. I remember assisting with wording on a "Client Access to Records" policy. Before that offenders were not allowed to see their records. Training was a priority and I was lucky enough to be sent on courses which addressed how to behave in court, how to develop a community-based approach and managing offenders in and out of custody. Underpinning this was a belief that training should address underlying issues. I was able to attend courses on Stress Management, Transactional Analysis and Group

Dynamics all of which I later went on to become a tutor in myself. The use of information was always central to the ethos of Nottinghamshire Probation Service and an evidence-based approach was attempted there long before it became the fashion nationally.

When I joined the Probation Service I wanted to be an officer of the court and "advise, assist and befriend". It was through the Nottinghamshire Probation Service that I was able to achieve that ambition and for that I will be forever grateful.

In 1984, I left Nottinghamshire to become an assistant chief probation officer in Leicestershire. The culture there was very different. Attention to courts and prisons took precedence. Officers were keen to do the bidding of the dominating resident judge and saw their rôle first and foremost as an officer of the court. Prison-based work was also a priority with Leicestershire having five prisons to staff.

During the time I was there I was pleased to encourage a more community-based approach through groupwork, the day centre and a local partnership scheme which were really important to help reduce re-offending. However a Leicestershire Employment and Education Programme (LEEP) went a bit pear shaped! We discovered after an audit that money was going missing and that this had to be the responsibility of the organizer and his administrative assistant. One morning I was required to be in a police car at 8 am with sirens blazing heading for the LEEP premises. I was the only one who could identify the staff prior to them being arrested. They were taken away via the back door and I had arranged for a senior probation officer to come in the front door to take over responsibility for running the scheme. The local paper got wind of this and the *Leicester Mercury* reported that assistant chief probation officer "Harold Lockhart" had carried out a dawn raid! From then on it was banter in the service that this had been "one LEEP forward but two steps back for mankind!"

One of the most rewarding aspects of my career was in 1989 when I was seconded to be regional staff development officer for the Midland region. This comprised ten probation areas who had a big say in the type of training/staff development to be provided. Through the regional staff development we had some great successes and watched staff change and blossom on courses such as, Do You Want to be a Manager?, Women in Management and Stress Management.

Staff training had become a theme in my life and I appreciated the transformative characteristics of staff development — I went on to run training courses funded by the Home Office for middle and senior managers.

In 1993 I became chief probation officer of the North-East London Probation Service (NELPS). One colleague suggested that this was one of the toughest jobs in probation, not just because of the deprived nature of this area of Greater London (comprising the boroughs of Newham, Waltham Forest, Barking, Redridge and Havering) but because of the militancy of the local trade union — the National Association of Probation Officers (now Napo). When I arrived the Napo chair said that morale was at rock bottom. When I left he said it was worse!

The big contrast with other places where I had worked was that the level of violence, especially knife crime, was so much greater. Important work was done with offenders in East London in very difficult circumstances and because of the target driven culture the staff never really received the credit they deserved from the Home Office and Government Ministers.

In those days we were translating information into 43 different languages. Working in such a multi-racial community it was very important that diversity issues came to the fore. I was delighted that, over the time I was there, that I, with others, was able to change the profile of the service. When I arrived there were 33 middle-managers, one of whom were women and one was black. Nine years later a quarter of the number were from ethnic minorities and half were female. The administrative staff profile also changed completely and in the end it reflected the ethnic mix of those North East London boroughs.

Some years earlier, under the courageous leadership of chief officers of probation, the Probation Service nationally had accepted that it was an institutionally racist organization. This was in the light of the MacPherson Report on the murder of Stephen Lawrence. Race awareness was a high priority for my leadership in North East London Probation Service (NELPS) and anti-racism training, although the struggle was cutting-edge. Once race awareness was embedded, the "problem" of race changed completely to a "joy". Being able to walk down the Barking Road and pop in and say hello to the different stall holders and cafe owners, from many different backgrounds, and who knew many of the offenders we were working with, was just a delight.

I was pleased, as vice-chair of ACOP in 1998 to be part of a movement to introduce evidence-based practice. This "What Works" concept came out of years of being told that, in relation to re-offending, nothing works. Since then many programmes have been run based on international research findings in order to help to reduce re-offending.

When I became chair of ACOP in 1998/9 we negotiated with a first-class Home Office Minister, Lord Williams of Mostyn that probation would not be amalgamated with the Prison Service and that the word "probation" would remain in our title. There would be a National Probation Service of England and Wales managing 42 areas. I was very proud that the word probation was retained as it is a meaningful concept throughout the world. Chief officers presented a united front to Government to fight for a better resourced Probation Service. These same chiefs ensured that, locally, a first-class service was being delivered to courts, prisons and the community. I am immensely proud and feel privileged to have been their chair at such a difficult time.

Over the last three decades, probation has been heavily politicised and used as a "toy" to kick around by all Governments. In the 1980s we were told the word "client" could not be used and was to be replaced by "offender". In the 1990s "punishment in the community" was the order of the day and "advise, assist and befriend" was discontinued by legislation.

Now, in 2014, privatisation of 70 per cent of the service is in full swing. For those in the "probation family" for that is what it is, and who have worked in the service for many years, firmly believe that "advise, assist and befriend" is still the key to reducing re-offending. Community-based work to help with rehabilitation will always be needed. Work with offenders has to continue whatever the government in power says. If the Probation Service did not exist it would have to be re-invented!

In 2001, I and a number of other chief probation officers were subject to compulsory redundancy. Not a happy position to be in! I had little idea of what I would do because I had been so busy closing down NELPS and ensuring it continued in a healthy state when it amalgamated with the other London services to make one huge Greater London Probation Service.

I suppose I re-invented myself at this time by going "solo" and becoming a consultant, trainer, mentor and investigator. I worked in the private and public sectors but mostly with Probation Services.

I became a keen advocate of the European Excellence Model for top quality management and worked with services to self-assess their performance before inspectors came in to do the same. I mentored chief officers and counselled members of staff who were in need.

I am still in awe of how probation staff are able to gain the skills to listen to and engage with colleagues across all the criminal justice disciplines and with offenders too in a way that other organizations cannot. Probation staff can talk to judges, civil servants, prison officers, police and offenders alike. Often very alike!!

So, despite my pessimism about the political climate within which probation has to work in England and Wales, there will always be enthusiastic people wanting to make a difference in the lives of those less fortunate than themselves. Working in communities continues to be vital for rehabilitation. I am so glad to have been part of it. The proudest moment of my life was to become a probation officer and on reflection that is still the case.

Howard Lockwood, Probation officer, Nottinghamshire Probation Service, June 1973; Chief Probation Officer, North East London, 1993–2001.

9. A View of Probation in the 1960s: From the Bottom

Jim Cannings

In 1963 it was very different. There were roughly 2,000 probation officers in over 100 separate areas in England and Wales, some with only a handful of officers. London with a couple of hundred officers was by far the largest. There was no community service or parole. Offices were staffed by probation officers and secretarial staff—no ancillaries of any kind. The service was expanding and its one training centre, Rainer House in Chelsea, run by members of the inspectorate, could not cope with the demand. A particular shortage in training graduate applicants had been delegated to a small number of universities. After an interview and tests at the Home Office, I had spent a happy 18-months at the University of Nottingham.

Seeking a suitable post, I went to meet the chief probation officer of London, Selden Farmer. I wanted a job and he was short of probation officers. Having been briefed by insiders, and with the naïvety of someone applying for a first job, I also had my conditions—I was only prepared to work in one of four offices. Wearily he told me that I had been well-advised. He offered me a post at Lambeth Magistrates' Court and then drove me to the Home Office in Whitehall. After a short wait in a small room, overheated by a coal fire, I was interviewed by him and a couple of bored civil servants (London had no probation committee and was directly accountable to the Home Office).

The outcome was that on 30th December I reported again to the London head office. After being issued with a plastic briefcase stuffed full of Statutes and Probation Rules I took myself off to the Lambeth Probation Office set in a condemned house in Renfrew Road in Kennington. I was shown my office: a basement room with a window overlooking the outside lavatory. This was the introduction to five of the most enjoyable years of my career.

The office was in a dreadful state of repair and decoration. Every couple of minutes the building shook as a Northern Line train passed underneath and some time after I arrived "goalposts" were put up in one of the basement rooms to reassure the staff that the bowing of the joists holding up the ground floor, caused by the weight of filing cabinets, was not the prelude to collapse. On the ground floor there was a general office and a waiting room. Security, as a modern office would demand, was non-existent. Callers would come into the general office, which also acted as a reception area, but they could get access to any office in the building without calling there first. Yet nobody thought twice about this and it was quite normal for a probation officer to hold a reporting evening and be alone in the office until 8.30 pm or 9 pm.

Geoffrey Orton, the senior probation officer was a delightful man, competent and conscientious and I owe him a great deal for the way he nursed a young and immature officer through his first post among a group of older staff who could have been ready to dismiss such inexperience. While I was apprehensive about them, the male officers could well have felt threatened by me as a trained graduate. The oldest of them, Bill Cotton, was secure enough to feel no threat, but the others had been trained either on the Home Office's own one year course at Rainer House or were direct entrants with no recognised qualifications.

The gender differences were very obvious in the London service. There was a distinct group of upper middle-class single ladies of at least partially independent means. Some had graduated on the early social science courses and they were a significant intellectual force. While some were at this time approaching the end of their careers, Lambeth had two younger women of a far higher calibre than the men. In my time in London the character of male recruitment began to change as more younger people with no previous careers and better qualification arrived and it was more obvious that newly-appointed women were much more varied in background. The Probation Service was not seen as an undesirable occupation as, perhaps, it later became when the public sector as a whole was seen as unfashionable.

The service was also appallingly badly paid. I might have felt pleased with my first monthly cheque of £50, but it would not have kept a family and it was less than some of the young men on probation working earned as scaffolders or digging tunnels on extensions to the Underground. Nearly five years later when I left London I was still only earning £1,100 per year.

The Lambeth team was responsible for a slice of London running from the river at Waterloo south to the Elephant and Castle and on through Camberwell and Peckham to Dulwich, Sydenham and Gipsy Hill. It contained, therefore, the old Lambeth Walk and Walworth communities gradually to be eroded by the onslaught of "slum" clearance and the arrival of tower blocks. Walworth had a marvellous and thoroughly crooked street market at East Lane. While some of the community feeling was strong, some of the housing needed to go; I knew at least one house with gas lighting and without an electricity supply and there were a number of rat-infested tenement blocks with shared lavatories. Camberwell was different as the boundary of the black immigrant centre in Brixton spread eastwards along Coldharbour Lane. Much of it was still streets of Victorian terraces, and included the base for Charlie Richardson and his gang. Richardson, in his autobiography said that he had gained some of his criminal education in the probation office waiting room (not Renfrew Road but we had contact with some of the peripheral members of the gang and one of the women officers even received a wedding present from him). Further south, prosperous Dulwich provided little work, but the estates of Sydenham and Gipsy Hill produced their share and were my particular beat in my first year.

Compared to other areas, London was unusual not just in its administration. For instance it tended to separate adult and juvenile work. Juvenile courts did not sit in court buildings but in rented premises. For the Lambeth area this was a hired church hall in Brixton. It suited the service to run this separately from the adult court work and the juvenile court probation officers had their own office in Camberwell. Although this began to change during my time, there was historically little contact between the two offices.

Working with a purely adult caseload became much more normal as juvenile work was transferred to local authorities, but was then confined to London. And the adult caseload was itself hardly typical. The Lambeth area contained the Union Jack Club, at that time a magnet for homeless ex-servicemen down on their luck. This attraction was increased by the existence of two large hostels for homeless men, one, Rowton House, just round the corner from the office. In Camberwell there was the "Spike", the reception centre run by the National Assistance Board often still referred to as the UAB by the customers. Drunkenness, including a great deal of meths drinking, and begging was rife and affected both the work of the court and the probation office. For us, casual callers wanting money were daily visitors and removing drunks from the office was routine. Vouchers for David Greig's the grocers, Salvation Army clothing and a local store's shoes were part of the local currency. But it was money they really wanted.

Lambeth Magistrates' Court actually covered more of Southwark than of Lambeth. The building still exists but is now a Buddhist Centre. There was only one courtroom with a lead-lined floor intended, it was said, to dull the noise of dockworkers' boots.

Whenever the court was sitting there was a police inspector present and next to the seat reserved for him sat the duty probation officer together with any other officer with an interest in a case. Sitting here brought me my greatest public accolade. One particularly cocky south Londoner started to bargain with the magistrate.

"I am fining you £20."

"Oh come off it your worship that's far too much."

"Silence. I repeat I am fining you £20. Do you need time to pay?"

"Yes please. Three months."

"Nonsense. I'll give you seven days."

"Well, how about a month?"

"Seven days."

"Two weeks then."

"Cheeky little bastard!" — the court inspector, *sotto voce*.

"I quite agree with the probation officer. Next case."

The court sat every morning and afternoon, six days a week (no lay justices of the peace (JPs) just two stipendiary magistrates (now district judges), each sitting on three of the days). Apart from a couple of motoring courts and including on Saturday afternoons there was always a probation officer on duty to present reports prepared on defendants, to interview any offender on-the-spot where immediate information and assessment was required and to take referrals for reports to be prepared on remand. It was never acknowledged, but quite frequently such reports were prepared on defendants in custody, not because there was any great risk if they were on bail, but to give them a taste of prison — the clang of the gates. This was technically a misuse of a custodial remand, but often happened nevertheless.

The regulars made up a significant minority of any morning court list.

These were the drunks from the hostels. The proximity of Waterloo and Victoria Stations also acted as a magnet. They were fertile ground for begging. The technique was to approach people in a fairly aggressive way when they were anxious to be elsewhere. I once watched one of our regulars doing this amongst the audience leaving the Old Vic. In court or in the office he was polite and mild even when he had been drinking. As a beggar he was intimidating and not easily put off. We knew most of these men well and spent a great deal of time on them, even though they were very rarely put on probation.

When the hostels were full they slept rough and often sheltered in the railway stations at night. Their activities, whether when offensively drunk, or begging or "trespassing" on railway premises often led to arrest and they appeared in court to be given a fine (which they couldn't pay) with the alternative of seven days imprisonment. Every so often one irritated the police to such an extent that he was charged under archaic legislation with "being an incorrigible rogue". This carried a much longer penalty of imprisonment and removed him from the area for a few months. Serious offenders they were not.

I remember one man in particular who had been a brewer's representative before he succumbed to alcohol and meths. He had a pension, but lived rough, usually on Waterloo Station. His technique with unsuspecting young policemen was to loosen his belt so that, when they tried to arrest him, his trousers fell down and embarrassed them more than him. He often came to the office for temporary assistance until his pension became due and a couple of times even arrived by taxi, asking the Probation Service to lend him the fare. I always paid and he always repaid, which was quite unique. He became so fed up with being arrested at the station that he got himself a season ticket from Waterloo to Vauxhall, the next station down the line so that he always had a valid reason for being there and could not be arrested. An intelligent man, he finally and tearfully allowed himself to be taken to a mental hospital and I never saw him again. To me he was an amiable nuisance in comparison with some of his fellow drinkers who were much more frightening and prone to violence.

Most gradually deteriorated and succumbed to the rigours of sleeping rough, but just occasionally one stopped drinking and rebuilt his life, frequently with the help of the voluntary projects for down-and-outs or of a handful of charismatic and devoted probation officers in central London courts. One, Manchester Fred, was a big man who used his size to intimidate people. He was an ex-soldier who could not adapt to civilian life and took to the bottle. He seemed fairly typical and one feared for his future. Some time after I had left the area I saw him on a television programme—as an assistant warden in a hostel for recovering drunks.

It must be fairly clear by now that the work of a London probation office took its tone from any special problems in the surrounding area. For us it was the alcoholics and beggars. At Marlborough St, for instance, it was the prostitutes. Nevertheless it would be a mistake to give the impression that we only worked with minor offenders. The Elephant and Castle was a rough and potentially violent area. Just before I arrived it had seen the arrest of the train robbers (and it has always been a regret that I was too late to prepare one of the social enquiry reports). One of the first people I dealt with was a young man aged 18 who had been assessed as "too mature for borstal": for reasons best known to the court and certainly not to me, he was placed on probation and nobody was particularly surprised when he was found in the back seat of a stolen Jaguar armed with a pickaxe handle.

Although the death penalty was abolished in 1965, it was still in force when I started work. In my first year I was asked to provide a routine put-back (later stand-down) report on a man who clearly had a violent temper and had been in a fight. It may have been my inexperience, but while I realised that his level of self-control was tenuous, there was little to single him out from many others. As a result of my report he was fined. A week later I was on court duty when he appeared charged with capital murder. I did not sit through the trial, but was in court for the committal and heard the full recital of the prosecution case. The atmosphere was like nothing I had experienced before or since. He was a man who would hang if found guilty and the tension in the court was extreme. The consequences were so clear in the minds of the magistrate, the police, lawyers and everybody in the building that it was a relief to get out into the daylight of the street. When people call for the return of the death penalty, my mind is still taken back to that time. Concern for the victim and those who had lost a loved one, is surrounded by the burden of the weighing of evidence, what the process of the trial does to those involved and the ever-present danger of making a mistake. In the event the trial at the Old Bailey resulted in an acquittal because some of the evidence pointed to a domestic dispute running out-of-control, rather than an offence involving theft. For me there was and always has been the question of whether I made a mistake in my original interview. If I had come to a different and perhaps wiser conclusion in my report, might a life have been saved?

At the other end of the scale was the absurdity of having on probation a young man who had been convicted of a consensual homosexual offence. He was gay, though that was not the way it was described at the time, and his mistake was to be caught. What on earth was the point of having him on probation? He could not change and I was certainly not going to try to make him.

Indeed what were we trying to achieve anyway? The legislation laid on us a duty to "advise, assist and befriend" and those words were used for 50-years even as the issue of criminal justice came to be a matter of greater political significance in the late-1970s. Within this we were certainly expected to take public safety into account and to breach those who failed to keep to the terms of their supervision. Although it did not assume major importance until debates about the purpose of the service in those later years, the question about whether the probation officer was a social worker or an agent of social control was a feature of my training. It always seemed to me that control was a vital part of post-war welfare state thinking.

Experience quickly taught me that I was most comfortable dealing with younger adults including those with a tendency to aggression. I felt that there was something to work with if the aggression could be turned to something constructive. I felt far less able to deal with older inadequate offenders who had given up all thought of making any kind of effort. I wanted to tell them to pull themselves together and found patience very difficult to maintain. Some of the young thugs were just that and far too well-adjusted to a way of life that could not be easily broken. For those who were not yet in that category there was the chance of change. I don't know whether you like dealing with those that you are best-equipped to help or you come to like working with those who have shown some improvement. The chicken or the egg, it doesn't matter!

Certainly in London, a probation officer was an all-purpose court officer.

Before the court sat we would interview all those applying for summonses, usually for domestic disputes but also for neighbours' quarrels and even consent to marry. We would refer some to solicitors, others we would take into court and apply for the summons on their behalf. We would be present in all the courts and prepare reports as required, on custody and access to children; we could be asked to mediate; in adoptions we acted as *guardians ad litem*. Within the office we spent much time on matrimonial concilia- tion or reconciliation work to the extent that on a Monday morning we had three rather than the usual two officers on duty to pick up the pieces of weekend domestic mayhem. This was such a major part of the job that it would be quite wrong to think of ourselves at that time as simply workers with offenders.

While a breadth of skills was necessary, the range of posts was limited. Unless one wanted to work entirely in the higher courts, the choice was between working with adults or juveniles (I did later ask for experience of working in a juvenile court and was allowed to do so).

There was no community service. There were no residential workers because all the probation hostels were run by voluntary bodies. The Prison Welfare Service was not incorporated into the Probation Service until the mid-1960s. At first there were no ancillary workers of any kind. The first four money payment supervision officers were introduced in about 1966 and this was the start of a major change which altered the nature of the service. Gradually other staff appeared.

The consequence was that the route to wider experience or promotion was twofold: through work for the National Association of Probation Officers (now Napo) or through training. Napo at this time was far from a union in the accepted sense. It had a rôle in salary negotiations, but was much more a staff association The national chairman was usually a principal or assistant principal probation officer and local branch meetings were often attended by the service's senior managers. Radical activism was unknown and the holding of office in the branch was seen as a positive indication of interest and potential rather than a sign of latent anarchism. In due course I became branch secretary and a member of the London's joint consultative committee.

Although later I became far more interested in policy and management issues, this was not my major concern at this time. It felt it was far more important to become involved in the training of new staff. As a young graduate I was used by the Home Office as a university liaison officer which meant very little except that if a London University student made enquiries about applying for training, he or she could be sent to see me to get more information about the job and perhaps spend some time observing officers at work. I had found this helpful when deciding to apply for training and had spent time with a very experienced officer at Marlborough Street Magistrates' Court seeing the subtle differences in technique he employed in dealing with each offender.

In terms of establishing one's professional credentials the direct supervision of students was the signal of acceptance. If you were lucky, the offer of a first placement student, i.e. somebody at the beginning of his or her training course, might come after about two years. In retrospect, I was extremely lucky. Not only was a student allocated to me, but he created waves. Ivan was a few years older than me and was an active member of the Labour Party. He had been adopted as a prospective parliamentary candidate for an unwinnable constituency and an election was called during his placement. He asked for three weeks leave to campaign and I rang the Probation Inspectorate for advice. The inspector, Mollie Samuels, was adamant that it was an impossible request and she arrived in the office within the hour to lay down the law. A short interview later she emerged to say, "You know, I think he can do it". Ivan duly took his three weeks leave, lost the election and returned to complete his placement. He was a good student and the last I heard he was an assistant director in a social services department.

The incident helped me as well. Other students followed and I came to be seen (not necessarily by myself) as a skilled trainer. Within a year I had been added to the group that supervised students from the London School of Economics, at that time the most highly-rated of the London courses and the most demanding. It also influenced the way in which I saw my career developing. Student supervisors were in short supply and the Home Office established and financed a small number of student units in which a senior probation officer would provide fieldwork training for six or more students at a time. There was a vacancy in Bristol (where the holder of the post had jumped a grade and been appointed as a principal probation officer). I applied and got the job. I left London with some regrets to work in a completely different service, small and covering no more than a single city court area.

The London Probation Service had become the Inner London Probation Service. It had grown and changed as I had. The Lambeth office had provided excellent supervision and a wide range of experience, but even that had been demolished. Three of us who worked there went on to be chief probation officers, two became assistant chiefs. Geoffrey Orton went to the Inspectorate and he, together with our assistant principal probation officer, the incomparable Doris Sullivan (who regularly came to work the Saturday morning shift) had provided a model of how an office should be run. It is difficult to imagine a better start.

Jim Cannings, Probation officer, London Probation Service, December 1963; Chief Probation Officer, Derbyshire, 1977-1997.

10.   A Probation Memoir 1965 to 2001

John Harding

I remember asking Christopher Holtom, my Bristol University tutor, in 1965, which Probation Service would he recommend for the start of my career in probation. He replied, quite unequivocally, Nottinghamshire under Peter Paskell. He was right. Nottinghamshire was a lively county within a great city in the mid-1960s, rich in cultural and industrial background plus sporting heroes. Brian Clough was at Nottingham Forest, Gary Sobers was at Trent Bridge and John Neville ran the best provincial theatre in the country at Nottingham Playhouse. Besides which, the market place had mushy peas on Saturdays and the bitter tang of Mansfield Ales became an acquired taste.

Peter Paskell was an inspiring chief officer — blunt, committed, highly intelligent and deeply loyal to his staff, giving younger members a sense of belonging to a service which applied high standards of professionalism. He and the service were well esteemed by the courts and the judiciary as well as the county council. My colleagues included Howard Lockwood, Jenny Roberts, Eric Morell, Chris Brown, Roger Ford, Colin Fishwick, Frank Cooper, Alan Morrison, and Cath Hollway, many of whom became chief officers. My first senior probation officer was Herbert Laming, now Lord Laming, a former chief inspector of social services. Herbert was painstaking, thorough, challenging and analytical. He paid you the compliment in supervision of reading your files before a session, making acute observations about your strengths and weaknesses as a worker. The other senior probation officer was Bob Norman, latterly chief of Buckinghamshire, a solid, totally reliable man, not academic, but immensely wise and engaging.

Support was not just within the service but outside. Interdisciplinary links were prized by probation. We had the benefit of monthly sessions with a forensic psychiatrist at a local hospital to discuss how we could manage dangerous offenders and dual diagnosis cases. Mordecai Woddis was part of the Jewish diaspora who came to Nottingham as a young man to escape Nazi persecution in Austria. He was a gentle Jungian, full of common sense, inspiring us to think carefully about the way we worked with difficult cases. Nottingham also had a pioneering regional addiction unit with inpatient beds run by Dr Bruce Ritson, who had trained in community psychiatry in Boston, Massachusetts. Ritson was an open and inclusive psychiatrist, who taught us the value of therapeutic communities and educated us about amphetamine abuse and heroin misuse.

I spent seven years as a probation officer in Beeston, a suburb of Nottingham, a mainly working-class area, which boasted important employers like Boots, Eriksson's, Beeston Boiler Company, John Players and the university. The caseload consisted of juvenile offenders and adults. Within a year, I had a caseload of 50 and an average 12 to 15 pre-sentence reports to write a month. I had a report centre in Beeston one evening a week and usually worked till 8.30 that night. There were also two home visiting evenings focusing on juveniles and their families. It was demanding but manageable.

Too many juveniles were placed under supervision for minor offences which would in later decades have attracted a caution. At the other extreme I had a life licensee, who had murdered his wife and children in a psychotic episode in the war years. He served 25-years in Broadmoor. I made an annual trip with him to see the celebrated superintendent of Broadmoor, Dr McGrath. My licensee was for some years, McGrath's hairdresser. "The best clipper I ever had," he often remarked. The other psychiatrist I recalled with affection was Mary Ellis, who worked from her base at Feltham Young Offender Institution with some deeply troubled trainees, a few of whom were on my caseload. Back in Nottingham, when some of the Feltham licensees came to see me for reporting, some asked if they could speak to Mary on the phone in Feltham. She never refused those requests, always making herself available to listen to those who were troubled.

Peter Paskell was willing to take risks. He asked me as a probation officer to organize some afternoon training sessions for local magistrates at our office. I recruited two ex-prisoners, a gambler, two drug addicts and alcoholics to tell them about their life experiences. Consumer stories were not commonplace in the early-1970s. One of the ex-prisoners was Dick Pooley, the founder of the organization Preservation of the Rights of Prisoners — PROP. One pompous young court clerk said it was quite inappropriate that I should be exposing magistrates to offenders in this workshop. The chairman of the magistrates, Diana Barley, a much loved person, told him that she had learned more from these face-to-face encounters than reading a dozen books on criminology and attending magistrates training.

My interests were particularly focused in those years on releasing community resources for offenders and opening up entry to neighbourhood networks and voluntary organizations. Peter Paskell allowed me to attend, as a secondee, the National Institute of Social Work in London for ten months focussing on their community development programme. I worked two days a week on a Greater London Council estate with homeless children and families. The sessions on community organization and anti-poverty programmes in the institute were of a high standard.

The National Institute of Social Work experience gave me the background to apply for the senior probation officer/community service position in Nottinghamshire in 1972. Community service was launched by the Home Office on a pilot basis in six probation areas, including Inner London, Shropshire, South West Lancashire, Durham, Kent and Nottinghamshire. I have already written about this pioneering episode trying to recapture what happened 40–years ago down the line.[1] Community service was a worldwide innovation in criminal justice. The first community service order in the world was made in Nottingham Crown Court on 2nd January, 1973. Peter G was a student and cannabis supplier, and was given 120-hours community service. He was feted with publicity from media outlets globally. After I published an article in the *Guardian* in 2013,[2] to celebrate 40-years of community service, I had an e-mail from Peter completely out of the blue. He reminded me that he was grateful not be sent to prison and had spent the rest of his occupational life working in residential homes with troubled adolescents.

In 1974, I moved to Devon as an assistant chief. Roy Bailey, a philosopher king, was the chief. He was the author of the seminal work called *Authority and Social Casework* (Pergamon Press, 1968). Apart from the responsibility of managing a division in Devon he gave me an open brief to make

---

1. Harding, J (2013), "Forty Years On: A Celebration of Community Service by Offenders", *Probation Journal*, Vol. 60, No. 3, September 2013, London: Sage.
2. "Forty Years of Community Service", Harding J, *Guardian*, 9 January 2014 (Society Section). http://www.theguardian.com/society/2013/jan/08/forty-years-community-service

communities more relevant to offenders. It was possibly one of the most challenging assignments of my career. We used Manpower Services Commission
job creation programmes to appoint employment specialists in the cities
and towns of Devon to advise and place offenders within private industry
and public services. Three hundred offenders were placed in the first two
years. We also set about developing bedsits, half-way houses and bail hostels,
utilising resources made available by housing associations and the Home
Office grant aid scheme. The accommodation consortium was chaired by
David Hewlings, a retired director of the Prison Service, who himself was
recruited before the war years, by the charismatic, Alexander Patterson, the
best-known prison rehabilitationist of the 20th-century. Our efforts were
augmented by the quicksilver fixer from the National Association for the
Care and Rehabilitation of Offenders (later Nacro), Nigel Whiskin, who
later went on to pioneer and direct Crime Concern.

Such was the nature of interdisciplinary work that in liaison with the
police and social services we were able to set up an experimental youth justice
team in Exeter in 1979, some 18-years before youth offending teams came
into legislation under Home Secretary, Jack Straw. The Chief Constable of
Devon, John Alderson, was the national pioneer of community policing and
became a natural ally for intelligence-led crime prevention and diversion of
juveniles from court proceedings.

We also explored victim/offender mediation within the Exeter team. I
had visited the United States in 1980 on a fact-finding mission, funded by
the US Embassy, looking at restorative justice, with a particular focus on the
work of Mennonite communities in Indiana and experiments in Boston and
Maine. The Mennonite experiments were led by Howard Zehr, now univer-
sally acknowledged as the godfather of restorative justice in the criminal
justice process. In the early-1980s, I played a rôle in inviting Zehr, together
with Burt Galloway, another American restorative justice pioneer, to conduct
seminars for probation practitioners and social workers in England and Wales,
inspiring many to set up more demonstration programmes in this arena.

I had moved to West Midlands by the end of 1980 and was a deputy chief
under Sir Michael Day, the third of my inspirational chief officers (I once
asked Michael, shortly after arriving in Birmingham, what he expected of his
new deputy chief. His reply set to one side fanciful job descriptions. He just

said, "'Make sure you guard my back" by which he meant we needed to know what was happening in the service, the good and the not so good, so that we could take preventive action should we be going off the rails or not taking the appropriate turning). In truth, there was plenty of scope for things going wrong. The West Midlands in the 1980s, like other metropolitan services, suffered from a full-scale economic depression, loss of jobs in the industrial sector and race riots. The service responded by setting up largescale urban aid programmes, employing hundreds of workers, including offenders, creating the Birmingham Wheels Project in the city, the largest of its kind in the UK, and establishing an innovative day centre that provided cultural opportunities for disenfranchised black offenders and others. Accommodation services, bail hostels and housing association development were expanded, led by our youngest ACPO, the very able, David Walton, later the chief of Staffordshire.

In 1983, I remember attending an Association of Chief Probation Officers conference at Durham University and leading a workshop on the reparative approach. David Mellor, the Minister of State at the Home Office, slipped into the room at the back. We had a few words afterwards. On his return to London he made it known that officials were impressed by the potential of restorative justice saying that funding applications from the service would be treated sympathetically by the Home Office.

By January 1985, the Home Office sponsored four demonstration projects in restorative justice in Cumbria — designed to divert offenders from the courts; in Coventry, which allowed reparation to become an order of the court after conviction; in Leeds as an alternative to imprisonment in serious cases and, finally, in Wolverhampton as part of the neighbourhood centres run by the local Wolverhampton Crypt Association. All the schemes were evaluated at length by Home Office researchers.

In 1985, I took up the post of chief officer for Hampshire and the Isle of Wight. The two counties consisted of large cities and towns, countryside and six prisons. The Home Office, in those days, encouraged us to expand and develop facilities for young offenders and adults in the shape of creating day centres, as a condition of a probation order, bail hostels and engage with voluntary organizations. This action led the way for the partnership approach initiatives of the early-1990s. We were empowered for the first time to grant aid non-government organizations (NGOs). During this period of Home Office largesse, committed staff established day centre provision in Portsmouth and Basingstoke alongside older centres like Southampton. Programmes focused on deep-end offenders addressing their offending behaviour in groupwork sessions. Ironically, one of the probation officer group workers, Richard Marshall, was a graduate of a community service order in Nottingham in 1973. Richard, subsequently, had degrees from Bristol and Leicester universities. When he applied to Hampshire for a probation officer post, the committee were told of his full story. Richard died in 2012. The programmes were the precursors of "what works" evidence-based practice of the 1990s.

The Hampshire Probation Service had already started two major initiatives before I joined: a drink-driving programme designed by a senior probation officer called John Cook, which was later nationalised throughout the country and sports counselling, whereby locally recruited staff with an activity background, placed offenders referred by their probation officers to a range of sporting activities including football, gymnastics, canoeing, judo, tennis, archery, cycling and so on. The venture was funded by the National Sports Council in conjunction with Manpower Services Commission.

Once again, young offenders became another priority for me. By chance the Director of Social Services for Hampshire, Arthur Hunt, had been a probation officer in Nottinghamshire, years before me. I put it to him that instead of splitting our services quite wastefully with young offenders we should set up a joint juvenile justice initiative. Both our committees supported the idea which did not need primary legislation.

By 1987, four juvenile justice units consisting of probation and social services staff were in place. The aims were very simple — through dedicated screening and assessment and enhanced supervision for at-risk young offenders; we hoped to lower the rate of remands in custody and use of custody in young offender institutions. The police were an essential part of this process particularly in relation to higher levels of cautioning. We were assisted at the professional level by the wholehearted support of enlightened clerks to the justices like Bryan Gibson (later founder of his own criminal justice publishing company — Waterside Press) and the criminologist from Southampton University, Andrew Rutherford, who had a decade earlier, worked as a researcher for Jerry Miller, the director of youth services for Massachusetts, who led the decarceration movement in the USA. Incarceration rates in Hampshire over the next five years, in all forms of custody, were reduced by 70 per cent.

We were further helped by a Home Office grant to the National Children's Homes, who joined with us to set up a young adult fostering scheme for offenders between the ages of 16 to 21. Two seconded probation officers recruited over 30 paid foster parents to provide both short-term and long-term accommodation to offenders without family support, most of whom had multiple convictions and previous custodial backgrounds.

I joined the Inner London Probation Service as its last chief at the beginning of 1993. The eight years were memorable, challenging and difficult, coinciding with the increased politicisation of probation, first under Home Secretary Michael Howard and, second, under his successor Jack Straw. Every aspect of probation was under scrutiny including the demands of National Standards, breach regulations and the need for better evidenced practice. Much has been written about the changes that have taken place within probation after nationalisation in 2001. Committees were replaced by boards, boards by trusts on the grounds that probation proceedings needed a more businesslike approach. The political rhetoric from Ministers suggested that committees made up of magistrates, district judges, judges and leading members of voluntary organizations could not possibly oversee the changes that were necessary in probation areas. I can only recall that the Inner London committee was made up of dedicated, experienced, clever and resourceful people who knew what worked in the world of criminal justice and who valued probation. The price of the semi-privatised probation estate, as we see today, is that probation has lost its umbilical cord with the courts, the police, the prosecution service and our partners in local authorities. It will be difficult for the courts, in particular, to understand the transforming rehabilitation agenda when services for low and medium-risk offenders will be carried out by an origami of commissioned enterprises, whose experience, for the most part, is in the private sector of running prisons, mostly in the USA, and whose staff may not necessarily have the qualifications to properly assess and supervise known offenders.

Finally, I would like to finish up on a positive note in describing one of my cherished memories of working in London. The experience could not be repeated in current times. I refer to a joint initiative by the Inner London service and the Metropolitan Police to provide goods, services and volunteer staff to orphanages in Romania, particularly in Constanza and Bucharest. One of our deputies, Roy Gray, spent all his vacation time working in Romanian orphanages in his latter years. Sir John Stevens, as the then newly appointed Commissioner of Police for London, wanted an initiative to raise the morale of his staff and achieve something useful. I put to him the idea of providing goods and services to certain Romanian orphanages. He agreed with alacrity.

The first convoy took place in May 2000 to be followed by further convoys in 2001 and 2002. It consisted of 15 fully-loaded, articulated lorries driven by police officers. Our contribution to the first convoy involved a larges-cale logistical exercise. Our workshop manager from Hackney, Don Gibbs, made a preliminary visit to Romania, carrying out a careful assessment of what needed to be done. He set in motion an ambitious work schedule of goods and materials to be installed in the orphanages. Over a period of nine months before the convoy set off in 2000, the workshop-based community service offenders, under supervision, built 75 bunk beds and made adventure playground equipment including swings, climbing frames and wooden toys. Police and probation staff also persuaded London-based wholesale outlets to donate duvets, pillows, soft furnishings and building supplies for the construction of play areas in the orphanages. The convoy's work was covered by the *Sun* newspaper and they donated £25,000 towards the cost of the mission. The publicity for probation from this red top was unusual to say the least! We sent ten volunteers, all of whom gave up their leave. Three ex-community service workers also went along with clearance from the Home Office and the Metropolitan Police Commissioner.

Looking back, the value of the mission was shown in the expression of children clambering over bunk beds and testing playground equipment with delight and pleasure. There were several lessons for us, too. The police officer volunteers were stunned by the quality of our goods. They, like the public, did not sufficiently understand the demands of a community penalty and the discipline of a workshop setting, whereby offenders, often with little practical skills, can be taught how to use equipment safely and to a high standard of quality and finish. In addition, offenders not only gained the satisfaction of producing equipment for a social purpose, but acquired foundation skills in the world of work.

I have attempted to cover 37-years in five services, each of which provided me with much satisfaction. The foundation stones of my experience were created by some exceptionally talented people from within probation and outside. Many of them are gone, but I learned so much from them as I did from service users and their families over the years.

John Harding, Probation officer, Nottinghamshire 1965; Chief Probation Officer, Inner London, 1993–2001.

11.   My Life in Probation

Michael Vizard

Nineteen-sixty-seven. I had seen an advertisement in the newspaper: the Home Office were recruiting probation officers. Some months later, I found myself at the Home Office, together with a group of other hopefuls. At that time, there were two selection processes: first, the Home Office approved you; if successful, you could apply for admission to a training centre. I successfully negotiated phase one. What training was now open to me? As a non-graduate, I had limited choice. However, I was strongly attracted to a new combined graduate/non-graduate two-year social work/probation course at Leicester University School of Social Work. I applied, and some weeks later I was interviewed by Mark Monger, previously an assistant chief probation officer in Leicestershire and author of a standard probation text-book. I was about to embark on a life-changing journey.

Life was very different, and I felt very different, from the very first day of my training. The School of Social Work staff had wisely decided to begin this experimental course with a weekend residential event. The programme included a showing of *Cathy Come Home* (Ken Loach, 1966), a docudrama that was to have a powerful impact on central and local government housing policies. It had an equally profound effect on me. It was the beginning of my swift political radicalisation, from vaguely Tory to socialist.

The course recognised the wide spectrum of knowledge required in social work, its curriculum covering: psychology, psychiatry, law, philosophy, physiology, social policy, sociology and social casework. The director of the school was Professor Derek Jehu, a psychologist in the behaviourist mould. The training included a number of practice placements; mine were: the Family Service Unit, Leicester; Northampton Probation Office; Bedford Prison; Mapperley Hospital Drug and Alcohol Dependency Unit, Nottingham; Mile Oak Approved School, Portslade, Sussex; and Lichfield Probation Office. The practice placements brought me into contact with all kinds of people, and conditions that were sometimes at the extremes of poverty and deprivation.

I remember many of those "clients" to this day. As I write this, decades on, I experience again the sense of anger, indignation and frustration at the injustice, deprivation, and at the hopelessness, which marked many of these lives.

Those two years at Leicester constituted one of the most important formative experiences of my life. It was a wonderfully rich experience, a comprehensive education, and a revelation. It has, in some senses, formed a foundation for the rest of my life.

So to Oxfordshire, my first post and a very happy berth. How do I now capture the following 24-years of my probation career: an incredibly enriching, demanding, transforming, illuminating, and entirely central part of my life? How can I possibly do justice to the numerous clients and colleagues, to the places, the institutions, the conditions, settings, the camaraderie, the training and tutoring, the students, the volunteers I encountered? I will never lose the sense of privilege and surprise that it could happen to me.

When I joined the Probation Service in 1970, it was expanding, and still had its feet on the solid ground of social work, its focus and sense of duty located more in the wellbeing of its clients than in its station within the criminal justice structure. With hindsight, it is clear that some readjustment was necessary. The principal aim of the service was that of crime prevention. That needed greater emphasis and clarity of purpose, even though the achievement of that purpose would still be, in the main, of "advising, assisting and befriending" offenders. In time the focus shifted appropriately, especially in the light of increasing expectations by the governments of the time that the service should move up-tariff and supervise more serious offenders. We began to recognise that we were in partnership with the courts, the custodial services, the police and — much later — the new Crown Prosecution Service. As an assistant chief probation officer in Devon, years later, I was responsible, with the rest of the chief officer's management team, for developing strategies for dealing with serious offenders in the community. With such offenders, our remit was very much that of securing the protection of the public.

However, back to the beginning. As a probation officer, I was responsible for a range of duties, principally: the management of a caseload of offenders, both in custody and in the community; the preparation of social inquiry reports (later pre-sentence reports); and, occasional specialist reports for the civil courts in my other rôles as divorce court welfare officer and *guardian ad litem*. I was always impressed with the diversity that characterised the Probation Service. Over the years, I met hundreds of colleagues from across the country, many of them bright, talented people, and from extraordinarily diverse backgrounds.

My first team covered the toughest areas, including the council estates at Rose Hill, Cowley, and Blackbird Leys. I also had a rural patch which included Berinsfield, a former military living quarters, which the council took over, building-up the place as an overspill estate. It became the subject of sociological research. As the solo officer for the estate, and a neophyte worker, I can now see how far the task was beyond me. I did make good connections with other workers on the estate but the work was more appropriate to a full-time community worker, part of a multi-disciplinary team. At a later stage, I acquired "reporting centre". However, I was only able to be there for a day a week, seeing people in their homes or at the reporting centre up to nine o'clock at night.

Back at base, one of the worst jobs was the weekly "duty officer" rôle, when one was expected to deal with anyone who came in without an appointment. These mostly transient characters were frequently looking for a handout. If they were drunk, they could be aggressive, threatening. Self-preservation became the first consideration. Occasionally, the police had to be summonsed when a caller became violent. But there were very few clients I did not come to like and want to work with. A tiny minority—in all my years in the job—alarmed me with their pathological potential and their absence of ordinary human emotions. A small percentage of any caseload was made up of very serious offenders: rapists, murderers, paedophiles. I undertook, perhaps once or twice a year, a social inquiry report on a killer or other seriously criminal defendant. This required me to read the Crown Court depositions in the case—the witness statements, police evidence, and forensic data. Some of this information was toxic, searing, and indelible. These experiences were invaluable to me when I helped to formulate and manage the SORT policy in Devon.

After six years, I began to apply for senior posts within the Oxfordshire area. At this point, the chief asked me to join the Crown Court liaison team. I agreed to move, with the proviso that I would be free to apply for any senior posts arising during the period of my secondment. I enjoyed my time in the Crown Court team, but, three months or so into the job, a vacancy arose for the leadership of an Oxford City team. It was now 1976, and the start of my managerial career. I had a strong team of very able, mostly young, officers. I was not entirely confident of my abilities. I needed time and experience to secure the confidence and competence needed. Looking back, life was very different then. The senior probation officer was not a manager but a team leader. These were still the days of social casework, with the team leader as the casework supervisor, advisor, and allocator of work. As time went on, I did move more into managerial mode, with a greater sense of the need to manage the boundaries between the team and the other agencies: the courts, the police, judges and lawyers, social services, housing, and hospitals. My senior post opened up other avenues of welcome experience in a represent-ative capacity. I joined the management boards of some associated bodies: the Housing Aid Centre, Relate and Phoenix House residential drugs reha-bilitation unit.

A particularly welcome opening was that of probation and social work student selection for the training course in High Wycombe. I had always enjoyed my periods as a student supervisor; now I was more deeply involved in the selection of students and provision of their practice placements within the team.

Prior to my promotion, I had been part of a team creating and running a training course for probation officers, under the South-East Region Staff Development unit. So began a long involvement in an aspect of my proba-tion career that was deeply formative. I joined John Harper, regional staff development officer (RSDO), and the senior probation officer from the Inner London Creative Therapy Unit, Peggy Thornborough, leading a week-long residential course called "Freeing Yourself for the Job". It was designed to help officers get to grips with their hang-ups, those aspects of the job which caused them personal angst, the dimensions of the work which evoked personal insecurity, distress or defensiveness. The work is highly stressful; staff need help to untangle themselves, to sort out the rôle from the personal, to help them to manage their vulnerabilities. I was a tutor and group leader on the course for five years. John Harper later pulled out, replacing himself with Brenda Palmer, a bright young officer from the Camberwell Intensive

Treatment Unit. Later, another new member joined the team, Michael Willson, a consultant group worker, a charismatic man of formidable and creative intelligence.

I remained within the Oxfordshire service for ten years before securing an ACPO post in Devon. The CPO, Roy Bailey, was a "name" in the service, the author of a standard text on probation practice. I quickly realised that the jump from SPO to ACPO was far greater than that between PO and SPO. As a divisional ACPO with specialist responsibility for training and staff development, I had a total staff complement, including support staff, of something like 80 personnel, and a geographical remit covering Exeter, north and east Devon, plus a Home Office student unit in Plymouth. As it happened, Roy was soon to move on to become the secretary of the National Council of Probation Committees. When he retired from that job, he gained a PhD through qualitative research into the views of probation clients on the service they had received. He was replaced as CPO by Gordon Read, regional staff development officer for the Midlands, previously ACPO, Hereford and Worcester, a man with an admirable concern for human rights and social justice: another much respected mentor.

Throughout my whole time in Devon, I retained specialist responsibility for staff training and development. My final senior management rôle, as quality assurance officer, encompassed: public relations, inspection services, the chief officer's inspector for disciplinary matters, library and information services, community development, equal opportunities, and computerisation and statistical services.

My principal interest and fulfilment continued to be found in working with people, both clients and colleagues. The management rôles were enriched by opportunities that enabled me to engage with others to help develop their skills and confidence. I greatly enjoyed developing our public relations, working closely with a specialist public relations officer. My satisfaction was always in innovation and creativity. Projects included redesigning the annual report, introducing a quarterly newsletter for sentencers and others (called *On Probation*), publishing a range of leaflets on the range of probation service functions, and setting up a complaints procedure.

But, as I have indicated, my greatest satisfactions were always to be in the area of training and staff development. The rôle included significant work with the Certificate of Qualification in Social Work (CQSW) training courses at Plymouth Polytechnic and Exeter University. With the arrival of the new social work and probation "licence", the Diploma in Social Work (DSW), the university staff, with agency representatives, set about constructing the new DSW qualifying course. It was a formidable undertaking leading eventually to approval from the Central Council for Education and Training in Social Work (CCETSW). A Home Office Probation Inspectorate inspection of the course a year on resulted in an "Excellent" rating.

I so enjoyed all this developmental work, including the establishment of a new Home Office Student Training Unit in Exeter. Devon Probation Service became one of the first services in the country to achieve formal CCETSW approval as a practice teaching agency.

In the latter three or four years of my work in Devon I was also chair of the south-west peninsular post-qualifying training consortium. Its remit was to establish a unified post-qualifying training structure for staff in the statutory and voluntary agencies in Devon, Cornwall and Somerset. The qualifying processes were to be accredited, leading ultimately to grade five of the newly-introduced General National Vocational Qualification (GNVQ), and, possibly, award of a Post-Qualifing Studies (PQS) degree. The consortium PQS training programme was ratified by CCETSW, a great day for the peninsular agencies. With a CCETSW grant, we appointed our first PQS coordinator to administer the scheme, opening-up to all qualified staff the opportunity of obtaining further qualifications in a wide range of professional studies.

I had also been working with academics and agency representatives to construct a post-qualifying masters degree at Plymouth Polytechnic (University from 1992), open to qualified social workers and probation officers in the peninsular. The degree — MA in Policy and Organization Studies — eventually received the approval of the academic awards bodies and started in September 1989. This was a two-year part-time course, with a taught element in the first year and a research dissertation in the second. Some four or five Devon Probation Service managers, including myself, enrolled and achieved masters degrees over the ensuing years. I enjoyed this privileged departure into academic work, especially as a non-graduate, a boy who had left school with two scraped-by GCE O-Levels! I chose to research the influences (and influencers) operative in and on the magistracy. It was necessary to begin with the question, "Did magistrates always live by their oath, '… to do right to all manner of people after the laws and usages of the Realm without fear or favour, affection or ill-will?'" Although some magistrates were supportive of the research, and interested in its conclusions, the response from the county magistrates committee was adverse, censuring me for my "intrusive" survey. I had certainly not set out with any ill-will towards the magistracy. My interest was in the nature of the institution and its decision-making influences.

The regional and national scenes also featured importantly in my Devon years. At various times, I was south-west representative on the Association of Chief Officers of Probation (ACOP) policy committee; a trainer on the new senior probation officers induction programme; a trainer on the new assistant chief probation officers induction programme; and a member of the ACOP training group. One very enjoyable job was that of organizing the annual ACOP conference in the year when it took place at Exeter University. I was the local coordinator on the organizing committee headed by the then CPO for Kent, Dick Whitfield. One of my rôles was to coordinate security arrangements with the police, because the Home Secretary was to be the principal speaker at the conference.

Two other highlights are worth mentioning in this account. Not long after I started in Devon, I received a call from the Home Office offering me a grant to undertake a study tour of Swedish prison and probation facilities. It was a memorable trip, and an experience that confirmed for me the importance of cross-cultural studies. What I saw in Sweden inevitably made me ask questions of the systems and attitudes prevailing in my own country.

My second foreign foray was to be part of a Regional Staff Development Unit (RSDU) UK-The Netherlands probation exchange in 1985-6. I was paired with a senior colleague from Amsterdam. Like my earlier Scandinavian tour, I was very impressed by my Dutch colleagues and with the criminal justice system in Holland. In both Sweden and Holland, probation officers had a very healthy attitude towards the necessary balances in life. I envied the Dutch officers their status in the justice system, giving them direct, mutually-respected access to prosecutors and judges.

I have barely touched the surface of the myriad experiences, successes and

failures, highs and lows, the breadths and depths of my 25-years as a probation officer. It was, truly, a privilege. I cannot claim that I loved every day
of it, but, given the opportunity, I would not rescind the decision I made
way back in 1967 to try for a career in probation. Who would have thought
that, back in the early–1950s when I accompanied my friend, Jimmy, to see
his probation officer in a room in the back corridors of Acton Town Hall,
that one day I would be a probation officer, too?

Michael Vizard, Probation officer, Oxfordshire, 1970; Assistant Chief Probation Officer,
Devon,1980–1995.

12.   The Hat on the Office Door

Malcolm Lacey

I joined the probation service in the early-1960s, when:

- Case committees, composed of local justices, supervised the work
  of probation officers. They met quarterly when each probation
  officer presented a written report on each person under supervision, recommending some for early discharge and asking for
  guidance on problematic cases (As the service grew, this became
  increasingly to be seen as professionally *infra dig* and they were
  transformed into liaison committees. What goes around comes
  around and we now have magistrates meeting with those whom
  the service supervises in a much more direct and at times interventionist way).
- Napo (as it now is) meetings still began with prayer (I know of
  two probation officers, known then as prison welfare officers,
  who were disciplined for getting on their knees with clients in
  their cells and praying for help in their reformation. Perhaps this
  becomes a little more understandable when one of them had
  come into the service from being a prison officer who had sat with
  a condemned man in the weeks before his execution by hanging).
- Probation officers, not frequently but not completely unusually,
  might take distressed or homeless clients (to use a now seen to
  be inappropriate word) home with them (One such was Mark
  Monger, the author of the first two textbooks on probation
  practice).
- Probation offices did not have notice boards outside the building
  as this was felt to add an element of shaming if people could be
  identified as offenders. It went so far as probation offices being
  prohibited from being situated in the same buildings as courts
  or police stations (This was based on the view that such shaming

would make it harder for offenders to re-integrate into society
rather than the current practice of "community payback").

- Probation officers acted as mediators in the magistrates' domestic
courts (now family proceedings courts) and as divorce court
welfare officers to the senior courts. A substantial proportion
of cases—around 10-15 per cent—were children under supervision following a domestic breakdown (It's worth mentioning
that this came about because the domestic courts were presented
with—mainly on Monday mornings when women came to the
court because their husbands had either drunk the housekeeping
or beaten them up over the weekend—situations they felt powerless to deal with So they turned to the probation officer not just
for information but also to suggest ways in which the situation
might be made manageable.

- The monthly statistical form contained a box to enter—and you
hoped it would be empty—the number of neighbours' quarrels
you had dealt with. Untrained though we were to "mediate" as
we would now call such work, it does perhaps suggest a potential
future for the service of community social work rather than the
route which was actually taken.

- I remember a woman colleague telling me that she used to have a
hat hanging on the door of her office in case she were called into
court. She was, of course, known as a *lady* probation officer.

- Girls and women could only be supervised by a woman; and a
girl could be placed under supervision as being "in moral danger"
if she had allowed a boy to unbutton her blouse.

- Probation officers also supervised money payment supervision
orders which courts made when they were unsure of the willing-
ness or the competence of offenders to pay off their fines.

- Home visits were regarded as essential before writing a report for
the court and for effective continuing intervention. Probation
officers set aside one or two evenings to do home visits—necessary because there was full employment and you didn't want to
jeopardise their job or you wanted to make sure you caught the
father.

- Probation officers were formally appointed as *guardians ad litem* in adoption proceeding.
- A child ordered to attend an approved school would be taken there by a probation officer in his or her own car, quite often some days after the hearing (Occasionally members of the probation officer's family would go too — It was a nice day out).
- At the end of their first year, probation officers were confirmed (or not) in post following an inspection by a Home Office inspector (not yet promoted to being one of *Her Majesty's* inspectors) rather than by their employing authority.

This is, of course, a personal recollection, nostalgic, neither claiming to be comprehensive nor completely accurate. To a modern generation it may seem quaint, a rag bag of disparate activities.

Yet it was to this service that Government turned in responding to the increase in the crime rate which began towards the end of the 1950s and climbed inexorably for the rest of the century. It did so because it had great strengths. These stretch back to the beginnings of the statutory service when the original probation officers were appointed by local courts and were personally responsible to those courts by name. This had two effects. They themselves felt, and others recognised, that they carried the authority of the court; and they were directly accountable to the court for their actions. This autonomy got into the bloodstream of the service and carried on long after the introduction of professional supervision and managerial systems. In fact, the 1960s and 1970s were marked by arguments over how much "autonomy" maingrade officers had and how much entitlement did seniors and other managers have in directing the work of staff. Even the phrase "maingrade probation officer" was contested as indicating his or her rôle in the hierarchy rather than a personally responsible professional.

It is worth remembering that, in the post-war period, probation officers were widely regarded as the leading social work professionals and this stemmed from the way in which they were able to make their own decisions. In contrast, child care officers and welfare officers always had to refer upwards to their managers and in most cases were not allowed even to sign their own letters.

Probation officers were also better trained. Some two-thirds of them were qualified in contrast to a quarter of child care officers and negligible numbers of welfare officers. Most probation officers were trained at Rainer House and, later, at Cromwell Road which combined two practical placements in probation offices with three months of attending lectures and teaching. There was also a substantial number of "direct entrants" recruited mainly in the Midlands and the North of England who were trained on the job.

My own training was on the "generic" course at the London School of Economics, newly set up with inspectorate help and advice in which almost all of the course was taught alongside social workers, except for a probation "setting" seminar and a one month placement at the beginning and a second concurrent main placement at the end. The first concurrent placement was in an agency other than probation; concurrent meant two days in college and three days in placement. It was an attempt to get an interplay between theory and practice, an arrangement which became quite widespread as further training courses were set up in universities. But the more important point was the stipulation that the student's first placement should be in an agency other than the one in which they would be employed. So child care workers and medical social workers would have a placement with the Probation Service and trainee probation officers in other statutory and voluntary agencies. This is in sharp distinction from the Rainer House model in which both placements were probation-based. My own placement was with the Family Welfare Association where I learnt that clients would only continue their contact, which was completely voluntary, if they felt it was rewarding in getting a better grasp on how they could handle their problems. Translating that into dealing with people who had to attend but who did not necessarily believe they had a problem was quite challenging. But it did teach me that effective work with offenders required some kind of "deal" if they were to benefit from the opportunity they had been offered.

The more important point about this system was that it was an assertion of a new profession—social work—whose members shared common values, knowledge and skills which could be applied in a variety of settings. Those settings might well require specialist knowledge but this would be built onto a shared foundation.

I suggest that these simple differences—agency-based or profession based — were at the root of the divergent ways that social work and probation were to develop over the following half century.

Let me digress for a moment. One of the characteristics of the service as it developed was the extraordinary ambivalence with which the service regarded the Home Office. My own view is that the inspectorate and those senior civil servants within whose remit probation came, represented the service with skill and determination, yet the service rarely acknowledged this. There was a deep-seated suspicion of Home Office motives while at the same time a recognition that the service was dependent on inspectors and others to fight its corner, to ensure the maintenance of standards and to guarantee adequate funding. For example, when the Home Office set up the regional training office (later the staff development office) it was seen by some CPOs as a Trojan horse to infiltrate Home Office ideas into the service by stealth. This despite the fact that the regional staff development officers (RSDOs) reported to committees comprised of three probation committee members and three CPOs independently appointed from within the region. Of course, the Home Office had identified the need for more consistent and professional staff development if the service were to be able to cope with the increasing demands upon it. I think this ambivalence stemmed from the fact that probation officers had been trained by inspectors to whom they would eventually become accountable. To be dependent on and grateful to those who trained you and then to go on being dependent on that same institution for resources and advancement, is quite a tricky balance to hold.

To return to the main point of this part of this essay, which is to try and understand how the service moved from that post-war practice intimated at the beginning to where it is now situated, and the kind of arguments and legislation that brought this about.

Two innovations in the late-1960s mark the start of a new and different practice. The first was community service. The emphasis here was not on the needs of the offender but on his (usually) obligations to make some recompense for the wrong done. I don't think anyone would deny that the service managed this development really well with a variety of placements and considerable benefits to local communities. But it would also be true to say that the service struggled with the disciplinary aspect allowing erratic attendance and poor performance to escape breach action. The same was also true of too much probation supervision.

The second was the introduction of parole. The expectation of close supervision was emphasised by the new power placed on probation officers to effect, following consultation with local senior staff and the Home Office, a recall to prison without recourse to the courts (though that action had to be justified later in a court hearing). These recalls did not depend on a crime having been committed but on behaviour likely to bring the scheme into disrepute or the likelihood of further offences. This responsibility to take administrative action affecting a person's liberty without recourse to the courts was a major expansion of the probation officer's powers. As an SPO at the time, I well remember feeling obligated to take the first parolee simply because it was felt to be such an important extension of powers and responsibilities. It was also significant in that, written into the Home Office circular, was the requirement for the probation officer to obtain the consent of the local management before recommending recall. It was a direct challenge to "autonomy".

At the same time, there was a vigorous debate about the future of social work, underpinning and contributing to the work of the Seebohm Committee. They were concerned about the best way to work with what were then called "problem families" who were the ancestors of our current dysfunctional "feral" ones (Incidentally, I don't recall this type of derogatory language being used by policy-makers and commentators at that time). They heard of cases in which a family could be visited by various social and welfare workers, sometimes reaching double figures. The solution was the creation of social services departments within the local authority and the advent of the "generic" social worker who would take the place of this myriad of specialists. The need for co-ordination would be met by combining welfare, child care, mental health and related functions into one large department. There was also a wish to raise the importance of social welfare by creating a large department which would have a considerable budget. Probation was very much on the sidelines. I can only speculate why. At an immediate practice level, it was as though these problem families did not have any men with offending backgrounds around. They would be dealt with separately by the probation officer although in fact they were the root of much of the mayhem. All the more strange in that the rôle of the earlier probation officers, as outlined at the beginning of this part was as a kind of prototype generic social worker. I think that community service and parole strengthened the perception of probation as a specialist service which had enforcement at its core. To include probation within social services entailed the risk of stigmatising all the other clients.

Not that many probation officers wanted to be included. They saw the new departments as administrative nightmares and felt they would lose their distinctive identity and curtail their ability to make independent judgements. Most were glad to escape the administrative turmoil involved in setting-up the new departments and even more glad that they preserved their own specialism when observing the unrealistic demands placed on the "generic" social workers. It is also true that many probation officers did not, and do not, see themselves as social workers but rather as having their own distinctive rôle within the criminal justice system.

A significant minority did advocate being included within social services departments and there were also those who felt that Napo should be merged with the British Association of Social Workers as it began to articulate the case for social work being recognised as a profession in its own right. That argument fell on deaf ears for much the same reasons, bolstered by the hardheaded argument that we needed a trade union not a professional association.

Concurrently, the Central Council for Education and Training in Social Work (CCETSW) was set up. The Home Office gave up responsibility for training and all entrants were trained in university social work courses with a probation option. The exception was those recruited as direct entrants. That route into the service also came to an end when the RSDOs, who had been asked to organize in-service training for them, realised that, while the training they were given was in fact very good, the trainees themselves were being short-changed in that they did not have a recognised qualification. Stopping the recruitment and training of direct entrants was an unpleasant and conflictful process and, again, was felt to be yet another loss by the service of its control over its own focus and standards.

CCETSW were very keen to keep probation training as they wanted to keep it within the social work fold. The service never really wholeheartedly accepted this position and there was a constant undercurrent of criticism that new recruits were not sufficiently prepared for the setting in which they were to work. The demise of CCETSW, never loved by social services, universities and probation alike, gave the opportunity to re-cast probation training. The current arrangements are service-based and criminal justice focused. It is completely separate from social work training.

The present position is that to become a social worker you do not have to be employed as a social work assistant (though you may be) and you apply to one of many university courses. Such courses are regulated by the General Social Care Council which is independent of central government. Further, it independently requires social workers to register as fit to practice. In contrast, to become a probation officer, you have to be employed by a probation trust, then take a course, which is work-based with the academic input provided by one university—Plymouth—delivered via distance learning. There is no independent register. Practice development is "in-house".

Even before the new social services departments were in being, the 1969 Children and Young Persons Act took away from probation the supervision of young offenders under the age of 18. It was a recognition that the educational, social and residential resources that might be needed were more easily accessed and co-ordinated by local authority social workers. Probation officers might be seconded to young offender teams but, in essence, young offenders were deemed to be in need of help and guidance which would be more appropriately provided within the non-stigmatising ambit of social work. Many probation officers were saddened and shocked by this and felt they were being cut-off from their social work roots. But it seems to me that the feelings and perceptions that led to this legislation must have been heavily influenced by the fact that probation had just taken on community service and parole which were primarily disciplinary and aimed at adult offenders.

In short, all these developments pointed down one path which was that probation was becoming a correctional rather than a social work service. Despite this, the service hung on to being the divorce court welfare service until 2001. In this, it was supported by the judiciary. In its initial phases, the transfer to the Children and Family Court Advisory and Support Service (CAFCASS) suffered from both managerial and professional incompetence despite the transfer of many skilled probation officers into the new agency. Nevertheless, it was impossible to argue that the Probation Service, with its predominant focus on criminality should retain responsibility for working with children and parents who had done nothing wrong.

I have a recollection of an article in the *Probation Journal* during the 1970s (or 1980s) (which I am unable to trace) by (Michael or Malcolm) Murch who was then a lecturer at Bristol University. He put forward the idea that the service should be designated the Court Social Work Service and so could continue to serve both the civil and the criminal courts. In this way the service could remain true to its social work roots and concentrate on skills in assessment, referral to appropriate community resources, supervision and mediation. I doubt whether such a solution would have been possible but it is a shame that the argument he put forward was never given a proper airing.

In 1983, the first national plan was published by the Home Office and much time was spent in getting the service to think managerially, that is to say, to set objectives and match resources and skills to achieve them. Later, there was also the recruitment of people to probation committees who were not magistrates in order to strengthen its local, community-based characteristics and to access business skills. The purpose of this was to ensure that the service was resilient enough and efficient enough to bear the weight of the demands that were being made on it. It was hoped that these demands would materialise from the Criminal Justice Act 1991 with its philosophy of assuming that offenders would be punished in the community unless the offence were so serious that only gaol would meet the expectations of retribution and public safety. The Act never met the high hopes of those who drafted it within the Home Office. In fact, for political reasons, it was the high point of what might be called the rehabilitative movement. What followed was a doubling of the prison population.

It was but a short step from there to incorporating the Probation Service into the National Offender Management Service.

Earlier, I used the word "correctional", an American coinage, indicating the social control of offenders through a system of imprisonment, probation and parole. It has a narrow focus on offending behaviour. It is centrally directed. In practice it concentrates on compliance with the conditions of the community order or parole. Its rehabilitative concerns would be with enabling offenders to gain social skills through cognitive behavioural methods rather than any psycho-dynamic or community-based approaches.

The NOMS website is quite clear that probation *is* one of the *correctional* services; and the page devoted to a description of "The National Probation Service" is illustrated by pictures of a pair of handcuffs and of bladed barbed-wire on top of a prison wall—all the more ironic, one may think, of a note which begins with a nod to its origins in the police court missionaries.

The modern riots have stimulated a great deal of ministerial and public discussion on the best way to confront serious criminality. The Prime Minister has declared that, "Criminality and a lack of personal responsibility were at the roots of the disorder" while his then Justice Secretary wrote, "The general recipe for a productive member of society is no secret..... It's about having a job, a strong family, a decent education and beneath it all, an attitude that shares in the values of mainstream society." In truth, I suspect that there is little difference between David Cameron and Kenneth Clarke but the two statements do rather neatly capture the two opposing approaches of correction and rehabilitation, the first placing total responsibility on the individual and the second acknowledging the importance of social issues in shaping behaviour.

This divergence of views can also be seen in papers by David Faulkner and Andrew Bridges, Chief Inspector of Probation.

Faulkner first:

- Emphasis and use of evidence on influences and motivation, with a preference for social rather than criminal measures as the primary means of preventing and reducing crime;

- A cautious but determined movement towards greater localisation and involvement of communities, working towards "justice reinvestment" in the longer term;

- Greater attention to the social and economic contexts in which crime is experienced and committed, and the means of reducing its volume and seriousness and mitigating its direct and indirect effects on communities and families;

- Higher expectations of what offenders and ex-offenders can do, both for their own and other offenders' rehabilitation and for their communities and their families.

Bridges:

"What is the practitioner being required to achieve? I've previously suggested, and I still do suggest, that there are three measurable core purposes to be achieved in all cases. There are some additional purposes in some cases, but the core three are:

First, Compliance and Enforcement: The purpose of getting the person under supervision to comply with the requirements of the sentence of the Court, including what we now call Community Payback, and to take Enforcement action should they fail to comply—this *'ensuring that the individual serves their sentence'* is a purpose in its own right, and with care it can be measured as such.

Second, Likelihood of Re-offending: The practitioner should engage with the individual who has offended and get them in turn to engage with a range of *constructive* work—this enables the individual to become **measurably less likely to offend again in future**.

And third: Risk of Harm to others: The practitioner needs to monitor the behaviour of the individual, and, using what we call *restrictive* interventions where necessary, take all reasonable action in order to **minimise that person's Risk of Harm to others**. The Probation Inspectorate has established a way of measuring that too."

Bridges also remarks that

"[W]e have penal hawks that say prison is the only real answer to crime, because it deters the individual and others, and also protects the public; and we have penal doves who say that this only makes people worse and stores up more trouble for the future, and that we should always focus on helping people instead."

I agree with that statement because we are dealing with complex issues which require "both/and" rather than "either/or" approaches. I am sure that he and Faulkner have more in common than they have irreconcilable differences. How is it then that they articulate such different approaches? And does it matter?

This part of this essay has explored the post-war development of probation and social work. Both contributed to the creation of the welfare state and both seemed to have values, knowledge and key skills in common but probation never fully "bought in" to the notion of a social work profession. It became more and more exasperated with what it saw as the failures in training (though it could never adequately answer how these came about since every course with a probation setting had a say in the development and teaching of the curriculum and half the training took place under probation practice tutors) and with the demise of CCETSW seized the chance to become independent. This left it nowhere to go except the Home Office. I suppose I would be showing my bias if I said that what we have now is a sophisticated version of Rainer House. Social work has its own troubles but it does have the structures in place to develop a more independent profession.

Another factor is that probation has one employer — the Home Office (as later superseded in this regard by the Ministry of Justice) via NOMS — and so is susceptible to influence and direction with no countervailing forces. Social work is the responsibility of the Department of Health which has to negotiate with many employers and take note of the requirements of the GSC.

Thus, when Lord Carter suggested that there should be an "end-to-end" management of sentences it was but a short step to setting up an organization — NOMS — to achieve this. It was a bureaucratic solution which ignored the profoundly different histories, values and organization of the Prison Service and Probation Service. Probation officers have become "offender managers". Concealed within that phrase is a Utopian belief that "if only" things were properly organized and staff were properly deployed, then we could crack the problem of re-offending. Like all Utopias it has already become Dystopian.

So. Should I Be Writing This?

Probably not. What is someone, retired for more than a decade, doing, writing about the future of the Probation Service? I'm only too aware that I'm not in touch with day-to-day practice. Yet a recent account in the *Guardian* of the work undertaken by probation officers shows that painstaking, value-driven, co-operative casework, mindful of public safety, is taking place, probably the norm rather than the exception. At the same time, at a recent lunch for Association of Retired Chief Officers and Inspectors of Probation (ARCOIP) members, a number of people expressed their dismay at the pressures now placed on staff and the low regard in which the service seems to be held in the media and public discussion. We wondered how we might give them some backing. After all, it does seem a pity, no, rather strange, that people with long experience and having had the chance to reflect on that experience, do not make some suggestions as to the contribution the service does make to, not just public safety and the reduction of crime, but also to showing how it can be done in a humane and effective way. This is all the more important since, in the words of Wikipedia, "A separate and distinct voice for probation has … been lost given the demise of the National Probation Directorate and the passing of the Association of Chief Officers of Probation". The formation of the Probation Chiefs Association (PCA) marks a point at which a fundamental review of the responsibilities and the resources required to undertake them could be influential. What follows is an outline of an ambition for the service which would make it even more central to the criminal justice system than it already is.

Reports

In any one year, probation officers will prepare around 200,000 pre-sentence reports and will be supervising around 200,000 people. About three-quarters of the reports are for magistrates' courts and about a quarter for the Crown Court. Fast delivery PSRs make up nearly 40 per cent of all such reports, a proportion that has grown rapidly. This is crazy. It is, nevertheless, a consequence of the history of PSRs which, for most of the life of the service, were prepared by the local probation officer who would, for the most part, supervise the offender if he or she decided they could offer something to prevent further re-offending. In essence—and this is not meant to be belittling—it was, "I have a hunch I can get on with/influence/offer some practical help and advice to this person". Over time, it became more sophisticated, but at bottom it was still dependent on the judgment of a single probation officer. Psychological research suggests that most of us, most of the time, make up our minds about any new person we meet in about 20-minutes. If that's the case, why is a three-week remand necessary, unless further opinions are brought to bear? So this procedure was a clear candidate for speeding-up the court process and making it less costly. Which duly happened.

It is crazy for three reasons.

First, it undervalues what the probation officer does. He or she is the only person in the court process charged with trying to understand why the offender has reached the point at which he now stands and to work out ways in which he or she might take responsibility for making amends and, in the longer term, for changing his or her behaviour. It also has the effect of demonstrating to the offender that no-one is taking his or her predicament seriously; he or she is caught up in a process from which he or she can gain nothing—no incentive, no insight, no help or, in rather more archaic language, no advice, no assistance, no friendship. He or she is faced with no challenge to his or her assumptions or patterns of behaviour.

Second, a court appearance is a life crisis for the offender whatever the bravado with which some of them confront it. We know that a life crisis is a key moment when change—behavioural change—is more possible than at any other time. It is a moment, lasting no more than six weeks at the most. We squander the potential of that moment at our cost.

Third, we know that a probation officer's caseload is, in the main, made up of young men who are persistently committing relatively serious offences.

"There is substantial evidence that offenders as a group are significantly atypical of the general population in terms of the constellation of personal difficulties that they face. Commonly they will have a range of associated psychosocial problems such as unemployment, housing difficulties, poor educational achievement, disruptive family arrangements and mental health problems; a substantial minority will have attempted suicide, or misused drugs and alcohol. For a substantial sub-group of offenders, their difficulties have been lifelong; almost a third have been in care as children and they show significantly more disrupted and difficult behaviour and problems than those who have not been in care" (Ford, Pritchard and Cox, 1997).

In addition, they are more likely to be heavy smokers and to be more accident prone than the general population.

This cohort of young men not only causes a great deal of damage and loss through their offending but they are also a charge on Health Service and social security budgets. Making contact with these young men is a major task for the Health Service but one which they find extremely difficult, let alone providing them with health education and treatment. Much the same is true of further education and skills training. The question therefore arises of whether it is possible to use the crisis of the court appearance as an opportunity to enable access to these other services.

It will not have gone unnoticed that these ideas are contained in the government Green Paper *Engaging Communities in Criminal Justice*, where community courts are perceived as problem-solving forums which engage a wide range of professionals as well as local community contacts. The Government seems to have stepped back from the cost of providing purpose-built centres. Instead, it proposes to test other models, based on existing magistrates' courts, involving multi-agency working and "virtual problem-solving teams". Repeat offenders would go before the same judge, or magistrates, who would review their progress. Perhaps we are on the brink of constructing a new "narrative" about the rôle of the probation officer and the links that should embed the service in the local community.

I don't want to downgrade the importance of "hunches"; indeed I think they are vital especially in the assessment of risk where the prickling of the hairs on the back of the neck tells us something is going on even if we are not quite sure what. But I want to suggest that it should be only a part of a much more extended assessment. That assessment would take place in a probation centre which would:

- include amongst its staff a psychologist and a nurse
- an employment adviser
- rapid referral to psychiatric services
- have formal arrangements with the local college of further education for entry into appropriate courses.

Everyone would:

- see a nurse to check on their general level of health, with reference to diet and fitness and including their use of drugs, alcohol and tobacco

- undertake tests to determine their levels of literacy and numeracy a personal history and risk-assessment as well as their current housing.

The probation officer should be responsible for drawing all the information together and discussing it with the defendant. If in doubt about the implications of the findings, he or she should convene a case conference at which the defendant should normally be present. This should always happen when the offence has been a violent one or there seems to be a substantial risk of violence.

Taking Responsibility

Now for the key point. It may have appeared that the collection of a far wider range of information is the major change I am seeking and, clearly, I do see that as being of great importance. The greater change I am arguing for is a change in the ownership of the information. *It belongs to the defendant.* He or she has provided it and it is for him or her to decide what use he or she makes of it. In a technical and bureaucratic sense, it no doubt belongs to the court or the Probation Service. But in a personal, emotional and motivational way, it belongs to the person who provided the information. No doubt, he or she will need a lot of encouragement and "motivational" interviewing, to enable him or her to make use of it. No doubt, the probation officer will have to overcome a good deal of cynicism on the defendant's part as he or she will have often been through many such processes before. In those cases, it is usually the authority that uses the information in order to decide what they should do with or to the defendant. This is with the best intentions but there will be a tendency to view the defendant as the object of an investigation not the main actor who has to make decisions about what use he or she is going to make of what has learned (Consider how affronted we feel when we sense that a colleague is "case-working" us). This tendency has been strengthened by the abolition of "consent" to any order that might be made. The abolition of consent has not been seen to be important. Many probation officers saw it as a charade since the risks of refusing an order were far too high; and courts found it peculiar to be dependent on the consent of the offender for any order they wanted to make.

It is instructive to go back to the 1907 Probation of Offenders Act. The defendant was not asked to give his or her consent but to "enter into a recognizance". It is a significant change from the passive to the active mood. In the assessment process I envisage, the defendant would present to the court a short, signed, document with three elements:

- I take responsibility for what I have done
- I will make amends as far as I can
- I will undertake the following activities to improve myself.

This would be accompanied by the probation officer's report which would give the evidence on the sincerity of the defendant's offer, the background that had led to it and, of course, relating it to the seriousness of the offence and public safety. The probation officer serves the court in providing an independent, impartial account as happens at the moment. Having helped the defendant to prepare a life-plan, he or she has to stand back and make a judgement on whether it will work. So much social work is on this edge of "helpful distrust", of advocacy and scrutiny. It seems an impossible dream but probation officers know it is possible and that disasters happen when the work gets too far away from that edge.

Having said that, it may be the case that it is practically and emotionally too onerous and confusing for one person to combine befriending and therapy with the scepticism required of checking—in both senses of investigating and stopping. This is an area that needs more exploration.

The Process of Supervision

There is a wide recognition that the Probation Service should have a lot of links into other statutory and voluntary agencies and that much of the work of rehabilitation should be undertaken by them. This is very positive but in all the talk of commissioning, partnership, inter-agency co-operation it sometimes feels that there is a hole where the defendant should be. In truth, probation officers know that effective change only takes place when they engage with the offender, that is to say, consent is gained although it is not articulated. However, it is preferable to use positive words such as engagement, contracting, "entering into a recognizance".

For most offenders, a cognitive behavioural group would be an essential part of their rehabilitation. They should be required to attend two sessions a week starting after no more than four working days; if they miss a session, then they would re-enter the course at the point at which they left, not the group in which they were. It is a step in the learning process which has to be recovered, not a detention. This puts the emphasis on learning all the necessary social skills. When the content of these groups is boiled down, they focus on genuineness, empathy and non-possessive warmth, that famous therapeutic trinity (Truax and Carkhuff) which are in fact the essence of living together in a civilised way. In other words, knowing and being able to control oneself; being able to get into another person's world and imagine how they feel; and expressing oneself in an open and non-defensive way. Such groups also enable them to challenge each other which, again, we know that participants find both helpful and authentic.

In addition, other activities would be undertaken to remedy the conditions highlighted in the assessment. This is why assessment-based, as it is currently on self-report is so inadequate. Home, employment and social (peer group) network contact is surely imperative in knowing about the problems to be resolved and why a single supervisor is no longer a viable or valid model. The task of the probation officer is to ensure that the offender carries out his part of the contract but also, and crucially, to help the offender make sense of the various experiences he is going through.

This is not the place to go into the managerial issues of this suggested change except to say that the logistics must be very carefully worked out. The organization will be different in different areas. For example, Dorset came in the middle in terms of caseload and we found that we needed to take referrals from every court in the county to justify the concentration of staff required and the number of offenders who needed to be introduced into groups. There is also the important issue of making provision for women. It is not fair for a single woman to be parachuted into an otherwise all-male group; special arrangements have to be made. There are all sorts of logistical problems to be overcome. In Dorset it meant collating all the public transport routes and connections and pick-up points for the service's vans. This will be much easier in urban areas and perhaps impossible in some rural ones. The concept that has to be grasped is that we are introducing people into a programme, tailored to individual needs, and not, primarily, into a relationship. The model is an educational rather than a therapeutic one. In doing so, we can have the paradoxical effect of increasing contact time probably five times or more than in the conventional reporting model.

There's no point in glossing over the fact that it is hard to get alienated young men motivated enough to participate. We do need to take breach action and to have an understanding with the courts that such action is disciplinary rather than punitive and that it is an unavoidable element of the change process. These young people have deeply ingrained patterns of behaviour which to us seem self-destructive but which for them have held many rewards, not least of companionship and release from depression.

The Sainsbury Centre for Mental Health has just reported that up to 80 per cent of crime in the UK is committed by people who had behavioural problems as children and teenagers, costing as much as £60 billion a year. Only one child in 20 has a conduct disorder but they go on to commit 30 per cent of crime at a cost to society of more than £22 billion a year. A lifetime of crime committed by a single prolific offending person's behaviour can cost up to £1.5 million. Another 45 per cent of children have mild or moderate behaviour problems, and go on to commit half of all crime at a cost of £37 billion a year. The report maintains that early intervention programmes can significantly reduce crime levels (*Guardian,* 23 November 2009).

Other research has shown that two-thirds of crime is committed by around six to seven per cent of all offenders — namely those prolific offenders identified in the previous paragraph. At some point they will all be on the probation caseload. They are those same children which the Sainsbury Report has identified, only by the time they reach the Probation Service their behaviour will have become much more damaging and their attitudes more deeply embedded. Even so, some two-thirds of those questioned while in prison expressed the wish to change—they recognise the desolation of their lives but lack the skills to ameliorate it. A vibrant, relevant probation centre offers an opportunity to gain just those skills and the support to help them through the rough times. The probation officer/Probation Service/centre must always focus on the need of those in trouble to get into wider community networks as soon as ever possible. That's where the voluntary agencies could be most help.

The Sainsbury Report emphasises how much support the parents of children with conduct disorders need. We should not forget that many of the young men coming onto the probation caseload are already parents or soon will be. Part of the groupwork undertaken at the centre should be intensive parenting tuition. Their own experience has been of inconsistent and unloving parenting. A volunteer ran a parenting group in a YOI and recalled teaching these 18-year-olds how to sing the traditional nursery rhymes. It is hard to imagine a more poignant image.

Once they have completed the intensive part of their rehabilitation, they will need continuing support in consolidating their progress. In some cases, this will mean help in getting work or decent housing; in others, a shoulder to lean on, a helping hand in getting into new, non-criminal leisure activities, a sponsor. We should aim to interest various kinds of clubs to take one or two ex-offenders as members and within those clubs to have volunteers willing to introduce and integrate them. Recruiting volunteers seems to be getting more difficult and the service will have to give some thought on how this might be overcome. It does seem to me that if the service runs the kind of intensive, crisis driven, citizenship courses that I have suggested, then it follows that we need to give them support as they make a re-entry into society. Beyond that, we must try to involve the community as a whole in this enterprise. The service would need to invest in traditional community work; many of the communities from which offenders come are themselves lacking in investment. Helping those communities to achieve a robust kind of self-help would enable them to re-integrate ex-offenders without harm to themselves. The prize is very great. Sainsbury suggests that preventing one child in 25 from entering a life of crime would be cost-effective. I think we can do better than that.

A probation officer would of course still be responsible for each case. The aim is not to replace him or her with "cheap labour" but to work with individual volunteers and community groups in a genuine crime prevention project.

Establishing the same kind of network would apply to high-risk offenders though a probation officer would work directly with the ex-offender with all the continuing assessment and close contact that that implies. Vocabulary is important; we need to have a convention whereby the criminal moves from defendant and offender to ex-offender and, hopefully, fellow citizen.

The service should capitalise on the meetings with magistrates who oversee the supervision that is taking place. Such meetings underline the seriousness with which the offender's behaviour is taken; but it also provides an opportunity for community representatives to reward the offender for the progress he or she is making—a novel and meaningful experience for most of them. It could also provide them with an opportunity to re-negotiate the deal.

Resettlement

This is a major part of the work. I doubt that it can be much improved without a major re-casting of the penal system, along the lines set out by the Commission on English Prisons of the Howard League. They suggest a radical localisation with local authorities taking responsibility for prisons. Most crime is committed by local offenders who will return to the same area. Once local authorities begin to see the large, and largely ineffective, budgets now commanded by the National Offender Management Service, there will be immediate and powerful pressure to use community sentences.

In the meantime, prisons should be accountable to the local Probation Service for preparing a plan of activity within the prison that matches the assessment of what is necessary to prevent re-offending. Under the scheme I am putting forward, many of the people sent to prison will have gone through the assessment process. That should be the basis of the plan to be followed.

Ex-prisoners released on licence should follow the same path as those offenders who have been placed under supervision—assessment if necessary, taking part in targeted courses and activities and community support.

Training

Training is undergoing a yet further review. Recruitment itself seems to have been suspended until decisions have been reached about how training should in future be organized. On a cursory reading of the consultation paper, it seems more of a re-casting of current training, with the commendable aims of ensuring that the qualification for probation officers should be at honours degree level and of providing training for probation services officers.

Just as the recent scandals have brought home the complexity and often frightening nature of the interventions that social workers are required to carry out, so the same is true of probation officers who deal with the most damaged and destructive members of society. The importance and difficulty of the work they do needs the kind of recognition that now seems to be going to be given to social work. The social work profession seems to have found a champion in the Minister for Children, Ed Balls, who is calling for better training, extra pay to keep experienced practitioners at the front-line and the setting-up of a Royal College of Social Work. Who will do the same for probation?

Leadership

Though it will have complex responsibilities, duties and tasks, the Probation Service need not be a complex organization. Naturally, managerial skills are required and they should be of a high order. But the key requirement is to keep an unwavering focus on the quality of the interventions carried out by staff. The interventions are complicated and demanding. Dealing with damage, destructiveness and depression all the time, it is not surprising that sometimes the probation officer protects himself or herself by not looking too closely at what is happening. To ensure good practice requires sympathetic and incisive supervision. Furthermore, there must be absolute clarity about who is responsible for what — senior staff must carry responsibility as well as front-line staff. That is a question of professional leadership.

Let me quote from an article in *Times Higher Education*:

> "If an organization is playing at the highest level. it needs to be led by someone who understands the business at the highest level…

> Top architectural, legal and consultancy firms are invariably — and rightly — run by people with a first-class professional record, and not by outsiders claiming generic management or leadership skills. We can see a similar phenomenon in sport — star basketball players 20-years down the line, prove to be the best coaches (This also applies to leading universities). The better the scholar … the better the university does" (Goodall, *Times Higher Education*, 15 October, 2009).

Nuff said.

Conclusion

These are some of the ideas that have been rattling around the back of my brain without trying to give them any coherent expression. I don't expect I am alone.

It may well be that I am too out of touch to make a useful contribution. But I've written them down to see whether they key into Roger Statham's note in an edition of the *ARCOIP Newsletter*:

> "Within ARCOIP there is a general sense of frustration with the state of politics and in particular with criminal justice and social policy. There is also a quiet anger about the way in which probation is being run. Culturally and organizationally probation simply does not fit with prisons.
>
> With an election and public sector cuts on the agenda there may be the opportunity to inject a probation perspective into the agenda. I don't believe that we are passé, or that the probation ideal is no longer relevant. After all fashions come round and the present punishment-orientated approach is having a profoundly negative impact on social attitudes generally."

It does seem to me that the debate now taking place in respect of social work, the decision to revise probation training and the creation of the Probation Chiefs Association (PCA) may be a moment to publicise what probation officers do and how we might improve the effectiveness of the criminal justice system. To do so requires that we bring to bear a coherent philosophy. If you look up "community sentences" on the NOMS website you will find that in nearly every case the offender "is required" or "is ordered". This essay takes a different stance, namely, that they should take responsibility for what they have done. The probation officer's task is to help them in facing-up to what that means and giving them the skills to help them change their behaviour. We have a lot in common with Sure Start and with youth justice teams, each working at different points of the spectrum but focusing on the effects of disadvantage. There are important charities such as Nacro, the Prison Reform Trust and Howard League who would join us in formulating such a coherent philosophy. Philosophy is not the right word because the point is not to understand the system but to change it.

Can we create a movement, forge alliances, engage with the political system to promote the kind of approach outlined here?

A Note on "So"

"'So' operates as an expression that obliterates all previous discourse and narrative and at the same time functions as an exclamation calling for immediate attention. (Seamus Heaney on translating the first word of Beowolf)."

I acknowledge and am grateful for the critical help given by Gordon Read.

Malcolm Lacey, Probation officer, London, 1960s; Chief Probation Officer, Dorset, 1982–1997.

13. From Wales to Durham and Back: My Probation Experience

Martin Jones

In the 1960s, probation training, whether through the Home Office or university, usually required two practical placements, with a probation officer acting as tutor. For the probation qualified tutor these were additional duties and did not bestow any extra remuneration. Equally other serving officers within the same office would also be supportive to the trainees and so too would be court staff, magistrates and the police. This was my experience both in Bristol and Cardiff. Bristol had a training unit linked to the university. All staff, including students, were given a free briefcase and expected to wear a suit. Saturday morning work was also a commonplace occurrence throughout the service. I soon realised that there were excellent support systems within the Probation Service and the close bonds, which existed at all levels, were qualities that lasted throughout my whole career.

Following qualification I was appointed to work in Cardiff City. This was a busy office, centrally-based and serving a wide area. Some 20 probation officers were supported by a single senior probation officer and a principal probation officer who at that time was Arthur Haswell. Lack of managers did not seem to detract from the ability of staff to perform at a high level of competence and I learnt a great deal from working alongside many of them. Morale was good, as many staff functions testified, especially on rugby international days. I could never understand when Home Office inspectors' visits seemed to occur on days preceding matches and they always appeared to have a ticket! Cardiff was an excellent centre for learning to cope under pressure and the local service was in the vanguard of developments and new initiatives—a fact recognised nationally.

Due to family reasons, after three years, I transferred to work for the Norfolk Probation Service based in Kings Lynn. The principal probation officer was Bill Dale. This was quite a culture shock. Located with a small team (no senior PO) in a busy market town where there were Quarter

Sessions, magistrates' courts which met frequently and three rural courts which met weekly, the large geographical area meant that there was a lot of home visiting and late-night working. My predecessor had at one time been a police court missionary. He was well respected in the area and was a hard act to follow. The court clerks and magistrates deferred to his suggestions on many things which did occasionally have some advantages. However his links with local organizations, groups and retail businesses was excellent and I greatly benefited from this. A form of community service seemed already to exist in part of the area long before its statutory introduction. Apparently, my predecessor took advantage of some young offenders by getting them to do gardening or washing cars for them and, they were either paid or given a meal. I found it most irregular at the time although I have to say some offenders and magistrates benefited from getting to know each other a little better.

In this sort of location one was more isolated and had to use ones own initiative to cope with day-to-day matters. The magistrates were extremely supportive and applauded new initiatives. I was able to establish a Marriage Guidance Council service in the area, and a Prisoners' Wives Group. Towards the end of my four year stay a senior probation officer was appointed although his large geographical remit extended to cover Thetford too, which was 40-miles away. Significantly there was an established close link with Kings Lynn Town Council and this was of mutual benefit in dealing with problems of crime and social deprivation. Altogether, I found the working experience quite pleasant and was able to get some satisfaction from the positive responses both in dealing with offenders and their families and the support systems within the local authority.

I eventually moved to work as a senior probation officer in Durham County based in Hartlepool. The industrial town had just seen the local steel works close and the fishing fleet was already drastically depleted. Unemployment was high and a degree of despair pervaded the area. Crime was also of concern and parts of the community were severely socially deprived. Some 12-probation officers were coping with a heavy workload and because of staff sickness I found myself managing two teams for almost a year. Some staff were newly out of training. However a good spirit existed amongst enthusiastic team members and the adjacent areas volunteered to assist in the early days of coping with some of our problems. Another example of the good spirit within the service generally. We also had support from the headquarters team in Durham headed at that time by George Rees. I witnessed the opening of the new court complex and oversaw the establishing of a purpose-built probation office during my time in charge. This boosted morale although it was about to be further tested by the Government's plans for Hartlepool, which was to be absorbed into the newly defined County of Cleveland, later to become Teesside yet again.

The boundary change coincided with my promotion to assistant chief probation officer based in the Durham headquarters. Durham had also been subject to other boundary changes which saw part of its northern enclave being lost to the newly formed Northumbria Probation Service. Under the leadership of Peter Warburton and with my ACPO colleague Charles Hocking we set about defining new structures and tasks. I took on responsibilities for half the fieldwork teams and organized staff seconded to five penal establishments in the area. At any one time 18-staff were on secondment and we set up a programme whereby Teesside and Northumbria shared the workload. I considered this to be a quite necessary part of the work in helping the process of rehabilitation and giving prison staff more insight into the community and family issues of prisoners generally. Durham had a knowledgeable and progressive probation committee and they were extremely supportive to all staff. Durham became one of the pilot areas for setting up statutory community service and it proved successful. I also had responsibility for opening a substantial "working in" hostel for these sent by courts from a wide geographical area. The project comprised a large house in its own grounds with workshops and a market garden industry. My five years in Durham saw many additional areas of work being taken on by the Probation Service nationally and locally in what was one of the most productive times in its development.

In the 1980s, I became chief probation officer of West Glamorgan. It was for me a sort of homecoming as my family are Welsh and I did my first training placement in Swansea Prison. The appointment for me proved quite a shock. The service had gone through unhappy times and I soon discovered staff morale was low. A few years earlier there had been boundary changes and three court areas had been grafted onto Swansea Borough (soon to become a city) from the former Glamorgan area. It had not been a happy marriage and this was reflected in the attitude of some magistrates particularly those outside Swansea. The probation committee did not appear to function well and was dominated by a forceful county chief executive who initially had been charged with getting the Probation Service off the ground. Significantly my predecessor had not found things easy.

The staff office accommodation was dire in parts of the county with two teams housed in condemned buildings. This accommodation had been provided by the new local authority as a stop-gap measure. The local service had not applied the normal conditions of service relating to car purchase schemes, mileage rates, etc. As a consequence there was much disenchantment amongst staff about these issues and, I also discovered that trade union advice was not to apply for jobs in the area.

Against this backdrop I set about trying to improve matters, recognising that it would not be easy and would take time. I built a relationship with the local authority chief executive and had frequent contact with the Home Office lobbying for resources. Some of these were hard-hitting meetings and I felt that the civil servants had little concept or understanding of local political machinations. The probation inspectorate were not able to help beyond commiserating about the quality of the chair of the probation committee. However things improved with the appointment of a new chair who had a good understanding of the ethos of the service and was a first class organizer. We developed a good working relationship which helped consolidate the improvements I had begun.

A modern building to accommodate all the city teams, a new day centre, a community service facility and a bail hostel were all realised. A new Crown Court building provided space which also helped us set up a specialist Family Court Team. These developments led to an improvement in staff morale which was further cemented by restructuring and refocusing the middle management group. This step-change together with the loyalty and support at ACPO level helped me move the service forward.

I also valued the ready contact and support from many chief officers, particularly at difficult times, through the structure provided by the Association of Chief Officers of Probation. This was an example of the probation family at work, which also enabled me to make contributions to the service nationally whilst chairing two major committees. In addition, I was able to represent at international conferences and served on the Parole Board.

From a personal perspective in my last year it was pleasing that the inspectorate confirmed that the local service was a viable healthy organization with work of a good standard. Morale was now good and a perceptive probation committee was playing a full part in developing the service. On this high note I opted for early retirement, nearing the age of 62 and after 13-years at the helm. A decision helped by further impending boundary changes that had bedevilled my 32-year career.

All of us are but mere custodians of our time, but I hope that my modest contributions helped make the world a happier and safer place in which future generations are able to flourish. As for probation where will it be in ten, 20 or even 50-years, will it exist at all and in what form? It would be good to think that some lessons could be learned from the past and the future used to build on these experiences.

Martin Jones, Probation officer, Cardiff City Probation Service, March 1965; Chief Probation Officer, West Glamorgan, 1981–1995.

14. From San Francisco to Jordan: A Probation Journey

Mary Anne McFarlane

"How about probation?" Tim suggested in 1971. He had considered it but went into law, more money. "What's that?" I asked. I had decided after six months with the Gray's Inn firm that law was too structured and tedious for me. I was shortly due to work in San Francisco as an au pair and took some advice to do a bit of volunteer probation work. In Marin County I befriended female shoplifters, observed ground-breaking groupwork with juveniles, heard about links between diet and offending and watched my link probation officer bawl out his offenders for non-reporting. In the city I visited young black prostitutes, not understanding most of what they said and not seeing any financial alternative for them. However they loved the accent and seemed to enjoy talking to me. My ex-burglar volunteer colleague Clarence was sadly killed while I was there, because he wouldn't agree to participate in further crime. I was 21 and this looked like an interesting way to make a living.

On my return I applied for over 50-jobs and was interviewed in Maidstone for a temporary probation officer post. I asked them if I could think about their offer over lunch which rather startled them. Over a pie and a pint looking at the swirling Medway I realised this was a life-changing decision and that I would take it.

"That your car?" asked Peter Ralphs (deputy chief) nodding at an elderly Wolseley 1500 in the car park whose bonnet was secured with a lot of wire, courtesy of a gallant lorry driver after it blew up in my face *en route* on the M4. "You might want to buy another one with your new salary" (£1,000 a year).

I felt completely at home in my new team. The two seniors symbolised the service then. Flo was a perceptive old-fashioned social worker and David was introducing community service (we got Green Shield stamps for each new order secured in court) and activity-based supervision. Happy days on the

Macklin on the Medway, taking offenders for working cruises and opening their eyes. My borstal boy Bob failed to report and I drove all the way to West Malling to shout at him, like the Marin County probation officer. He never failed again. These early days taught me the value of giving offenders the chance to experience some positive and different activities, reasonable rôle models and succeed in something.

Social policy training at Bristol completely transformed the way I looked at society, with Tony Hall, David Bull and other fine minds to challenge us. Social work was clearly set then within the context of economic, social and political decisions, with radical non-intervention on the one hand, though there was plenty of family therapy and individual-based intervention at the other. Then to Southampton for a Certificate of Qualification in Social Work (CQSW) and seven-years as a main grade officer. Those entry groups of 1975/6 were innovative, courageous, diverse, though all white, hard-drinking and fun. Many went on to lead the service. Although we lacked the evidence for most of our interventions there was a real engagement with and investment in offenders and their ability to make changes, which has since been found to be a key feature in effective working. We ran a day centre, the best time of my professional career. Christmas Day with magistrates bearing soup, power cuts and gifts from a local cigarette factory. Later after it was closed I would meet the guys down town, bemoaning its demise. There was something about the lack of structure but clear behavioural boundaries and a warm welcome that kept many of our destitute, lonely and often crazy clients in touch and reasonably safe. When I left, my secretary kept my case-load reporting without fail to her for three-months while they awaited my replacement; the offenders having a great deal of respect for her.

Probation was a terrific career for a woman. I was able to cover all aspects of the work, run groups, had a lot of professional freedom and never felt oppressed by the outstanding group of seniors. I also gained new skills and confidence through Napo, the trade union and professional association. Through Napo I learned to promote equal opportunities, chair committees and speak to a large audience. "How do you do it?" I asked Maggie, deputy leader. "I just concentrate on which way I'll fall when I pass out!" she told me. Good advice.

I was the first senior probation officer to take maternity leave in Hampshire, giving them a bit of a quandary and they sort of filled in my post, much better done the second time round. Another more structured day centre at Havant built on local partnerships (drug-workers, employment links and volunteers) which have remained my passion throughout the years. We began to implement National Standards, worked with offenders in structured groups and introduced them to computers. But I wasn't seeing enough of my daughter.

So onto five-years at HM Prison Parkhurst when it was still a top security prison. The regular hours were useful with young children, as was the crèche over the road. I hadn't expected to enjoy the work as much as I did, ending up doing an MPhil on prison probation work and gaining huge respect from some, not all, of my prison officer colleagues. We set up a visitors centre and shared working with the prison staff. I covered C-Wing which housed the most serious mentally-disturbed prisoners, but with a multi-disciplinary team that produced some progress. Even with truly weird folk there is the possibility of change and moving forward with most of them, though sudden conversions to religion could pose as many problems as they resolved. The IRA in the Special Secure Unit mostly wanted things to be different for their children. By the time I left women officers had been appointed, proving to be generally much fitter and more able to defuse situations than their male colleagues.

After a camping holiday at Compton Bay in the pouring rain for three-weeks, I went back to work early (never happened before or since) and applied for two assistant chief officer jobs, mainly due to the weather. Then to West Sussex with two fantastic years in senior management. Such innovative partnership working with local community groups and strategic thinking I had not encountered before. I lapped it up. But I wasn't seeing enough of the kids so with regret at leaving Sussex, two-years later moved back to Hampshire.

Steve Murphy was the best boss I ever had, he led from behind and got the most out of his team, fantastically bright and principled. I think it was a tragedy that he didn't lead the Probation Service nationally for longer. Steve supported me in undertaking a year's exchange with a senior manager in Washington State for a year. The probation service was starting to engage with "What Works" and accredited programmes and Washington State was running them, so a good combination. I had the privilege of accompanying Ed Latessa as he undertook the Correctional Programme Assessment

Inventory at a juvenile prison, and learned about how to properly evaluate programmes. We had a wonderful year. Cheryl, my counterpart, made my seniors more self-sufficient and I persuaded hers to meet with me once a quarter and share a bit! When I walked into my office overlooking the Olympic Mountains and the Puget Sound I thought I had died and gone to heaven. Cheryl had a view of the car park in Winchester but still relished the city and the experience. A year later we gave a talk to the American Probation and Parole Association in Tennessee, reflecting that we had spent very little time together but knew each other's lives very well. We just beat a hurricane back to Nashville having gone on a visit to the Jack Daniels distillery. We are still in touch.

Not long after my return to the UK, I was asked go on another second-ment to be a member of the Criminal Justice and Court Services Bill Team at the Home Office. This team, mainly made up of civil servants, supported ministers through Parliament and the legislative process. Shami Chakrabati (now director of Liberty) was part of the legal advisor team that worked with us and I remember her as clear, compassionate and fearless. The Act, passed in 2000, was to transform our profession into the National Probation Service for England and Wales. The experience of seeing how probation was cynically and negatively viewed by many politicians and civil servants was salutary and showed me clearly how determined leaders have to be to drive though evidence-based policies and practice. This was a difficult experience domes-tically for me but as often for women leaders my husband made it possible.

Although the restructure made the service vulnerable to later changes through the 2000 Act, it did achieve better consistency, reduced costs in due course, more women at the top and a national programme of assessment and interventions that was internationally ground-breaking. The mistake in my view was to abandon this direction later that decade, combine with the Prison Service under the banner of offender management and sacrifice the national probation influence that had been gained. Because of the nature of the caseload with most offenders on community orders, we have always had more joint work with police and local authorities than with the Prison Service. Personalities and some bad judgements however got in the way.

In 2001 we moved for my chief's job, amalgamating the former Devon and Cornwall services. For me there is an optimal size for an effective personal service like probation, and Hampshire/Devon and Cornwall were reasonable sizes. Being a chief was absolutely the hardest thing I have ever done. Being able to set the strategic direction and make critical choices, building a new team and engaging with my board were exhilarating experiences, as were the national meetings with so many able women at the helm and diversity being so prominent an issue.

But our public services are complex, far more so than many private enterprises, and the juggling of the interests of key stakeholders, including of course the offenders, the victims and the staff was as much if not more than I could handle. As always the team was crucial to success and support. I am proud that we developed local partnerships extensively and worked policies together with other agencies, in particular those on domestic abuse with the police, local authorities and the voluntary sector. Budget and disciplinary issues always dominated though and at times I was very impatient with the self-indulgence of one or two individuals, at the expense of the organization. The amount of projection that a leader attracts is extreme and wearing but I was lucky enough to have the counter-balance of two great kids, my husband and several animals, so not much time for wallowing.

By 2007, when we were receiving Excellence Awards I thought it was time to move on. I had no wish to return to London and the kids were approaching university. I applied successfully to be in the national pool for residential twinning advisors who lead projects for the European Union. I also became a member of the CEP Board (the European Probation organization). The latter gave me a unique view of Probation Services across Europe and a new set of colleagues in many different countries. I was then asked to head an EU project in Turkey with the newly created Probation Service there. Our son always says that we deprived him of the big step of leaving home as we left it almost as soon as he did.

Living and working in Turkey was amazing, though not without its challenges, particularly as a woman working with the judiciary. It was so refreshing to have one's experience and knowledge valued and used, compared with the recent relentless market approach and contestability activities in the UK. Our project developed probation services for juvenile offenders and for adult victims of crime. We had 60 experts from seven countries working over 900 days in Turkey and wrote nearly 30 policy, practice, training and programme manuals. It was our first experience living in a Muslim country and we made many new Turkish friends, learning some of the language and travelling all over the country. Developing new probation services in another language sends you right back to basic principles. You need to be quite sure why you want to do something, what the theoretical base is and how it can be best carried out. All but one or two experts found it an enriching if challenging experience and 22 of us have written about the experience in *Crossing Cultures: Transferring Policy and Practice—A Case Study from Turkey,* edited by Rob Canton and myself.[1] We understand that at least some of our work has been widely used and sustained in Turkey and other projects are continuing there.

At the end of the two years I took retirement, as it is not a good plan to go back in life. But retirement for me simply means not being bound to full-time employment. I have been lucky enough to continue working abroad, in Palestine, Croatia and currently in Jordan where I have been developing a new Probation Service with colleagues. In some ways I have come full circle as we used the same methodology for consultation that I used in Parkhurst Prison for my research with long-term prisoners. This stakeholder evaluation enables the material to come directly from the participants and we believe we have built a model that is appropriate for Jordan, rather than being superimposed. An article in *Eurovista* gives more detail. As a member of the European Society of Criminology, and of CEP, I am constantly aware of the critical relationship between policy, practice and research, as outlined in an Association of Chief Officers of Probation lecture by Jenny Roberts many years ago.

Working in the Middle-East at the moment is pretty interesting, rather as working in Marin County after the Angela Davis shootout was in the early 1970s. Offenders are the same really, usually poor, ill-educated, with health problems, often abused, but mostly trying to get to a position where they can work and have a family, like the rest of us. I have worked with the really bad guys, and even among that group only a few were truly irredeemable. We have articulated the core values of probation in the Jordanian strategy; a punishment served in the community which enables work and family life to continue, belief in change, respect for individuals, primacy of the victim,

---

1.   Forthcoming, Palgrave Macmillan.

society's responsibility to support rehabilitation, and the notion of restitution and community payback as a win-win formula. I have learned that rehabilitation is an integral part of Islam. And it has been humbling to see so many Muslim colleagues and friends cope with and demolish the stereotyping and prejudice that is globally present. In both Turkey and Jordan it is very hard to make progress as a woman, but not impossible, and those individuals and organizations that are combating violence and oppression need our support.

I don't miss the pressure of UK probation work but I do miss the people. Working with a range of other local, national and international organizations I am struck by the quality of working relationships and managerial quality that I took for granted in probation. We are good at facing difficult issues, thinking them through and finding options with the help of others.

I am an optimist so, however distressing this current process is for our profession, I believe that eventually some powerful local partnerships will emerge. It will simply not be possible to make a huge profit out of community corrections and the risks will be too great for it to be 100 per cent controlled by the private sector. I haven't a problem with the voluntary and private sector contributing to interventions and programmes, they have always done that. But it is wrong to give away state responsibility for services which affect court decisions and carry out the oversight of offenders on behalf of the courts. And the fragmentation of delivery will eventually, sadly, come to its own demise with reports on what went wrong and further efforts in the future to redress the damage.

It takes a special person to work with offenders, not everyone wants to do it, but those that do are by and large generous of spirit, independent and hard-working. These people are to be found all over the world and I have met them in Turkey and Jordan. It is they who will take the essence of probation forward and good luck to them.

Mary Anne McFarlane, Probation officer, Hampshire Probation Service, 1970s; Chief Executive Officer, Devon and Cornwall, 2001–2010.

15. The Road From Wigan Pier

Mike Worthington

I have often been asked why I decided to be a probation officer. Well, there is no clear answer to the question. However, family background, the non-conformist church I attended, running junior youth clubs in downtown Wigan and a late-1950s and the TV drama series *Probation Officer* were contributory factors, for sure. What is clear is that I decided that this is what I wanted to be when I was in the sixth form at grammar school.

My aspirations sadly fell on deaf ears in post-war, industrial Wigan, more particularly at its somewhat snobby grammar school. In the town, I'd done well by passing my "scholarship", at school I was earmarked to read geography at a redbrick university. True to my non-conformist ideals, I did not do what was expected of me. I left school after my A-Levels, cleared off to Butlins for the summer, returning in September to sell newspapers, cigarettes, etc. at the town's bus station kiosk. So began three years of various jobs — shop, labouring, office — whilst attempting to get some sensible advice on how to join the Probation Service. In my darker moments, even now, I think I missed out on the chance of going to university at 18, but, on the other hand, I gained invaluable experience from my three years of bumming around in the "real" world.

At some point in those three years, the *Daily Herald* (yes, the *Daily Herald*)[1] featured an article highlighting the lack of suitable applicants for the Probation Service. In my first letter to be published in a national newspaper (a copy of which a cousin of mine gave me recently), I responded by stating that I wanted to join the Probation Service but had been unsuccessful in being accepted. What should I do? This caused merriment amongst my friends who pointed out that "suitable" might be the operative word here!

With the help of a number of good people, I was finally interviewed at the Home Office in 1963 (and took great exception to their questioning of

1.   The *Daily Herald* was a UK daily newspaper published from 1912 to 1964 (and a forerunner of *The Sun*).

my then religious beliefs!) and, in the autumn of that year, started pre-professional training on the two year Certificate in Social Science course at Liverpool University, paid for by the Home Office. My time in Liverpool was a revelation. Members of staff in the department included Professor T S Simey, Penelope Hall, Dorothy Deeds, J B Mays and Olive Keidan. I was an innocent abroad and only in hindsight did I recognise how fortunate I was to be given the opportunity to learn in this environment.

I also encountered, for the first time, the real world of probation. I undertook a six months, two-days-a-week "observational" placement in the Garston office of the then Liverpool Probation Service. The office patch included the Toxteth district of the city. A mixture of the poverty and community spirit of Liverpool 8 at that time made a big impression on me, as did the culture, commitment and humour of the Garston team. It confirmed for me that this is what I wanted to do in life.

From Liverpool University, my professional training was on the one year Home Office Rainer House course. After the Liverpool experience, I did not rate the three months spent studying there, but enjoyed enormously the long placements I did in first Leeds and later Lancaster Probation Offices. During that year, I met probation officers with whom I kept in touch throughout my career. I was beginning to feel part of the family of probation.

What did I gain from those three years training? Well, it was of its time. Father Biestek's seven casework principles taught me, amongst other things, to start where the client is, be non-judgmental, recognise the importance of the relationship between worker and client and to "stay with" the client, in spite of setbacks. J B Mays taught me the importance of sociological influences on offending behaviour and Penny Hall confirmed for me the importance of essential and comprehensive state services in a civilised society — the now derided welfare state. My probation placements taught me that I was an officer of the court, that a probation order was an alternative to a sentence and that, as a probation officer, I was accountable locally. All of the above stood me in good stead throughout my probation career and beyond.

Although Lancashire North offered me a job when I successfully achieved my Home Office Letter of Recognition, I opted to join the Lancashire South East Service, for personal reasons. Let me make it clear that it was not any outstanding qualities of mine which led to the Lancashire Services competing for my appointment. Anyone with a qualification was greatly sought after in what I soon realised was an era of significant direct entry to the service. And as most qualified entrants were second-career people, graduate entrants, like me, were a prized appointment!

Thus began six happy years in the Bolton Probation Office, learning my trade, feeling a mix of satisfaction, pride and frustration in what I was doing and being part of a good, supportive team. Or rather, two teams, for we had Bolton borough and county teams in those pre-1974 days. I had great rôle models and mentors in these early years. My patch was initially the Urban District of Farnworth, later covering Kearsley and Little Lever, as I became more experienced. An average caseload of 70 throughout those years, all male, aged ten to 65 plus, 150 social enquiry reports for court each year, two evening report centres and two evenings home visiting every week, court and office duties (including Saturdays), case committees, team meetings—this was my life and I loved it!

On my patch in those years, I developed good relationships with other statutory agencies—notably the court, police, Children's Department, health visitors—employers, landlords and other sources of accommodation, secondary modern schools and youth clubs. I was a regular visitor to Risley Remand Centre, Strangeways Prison, Buckley Hall Detention Centre and various approved schools and borstals. I should say that the Probation Service took over responsibility for the after-care of prisoners from the National Association of Discharged Prisoners Aid Societies (NADPAS) (later the National Association for the Care and Resttlement of Offenders and nowadays Nacro) the year I joined the service, which in retrospect, significantly changed the face of it..

Within two years of starting in Bolton, I was supervising students and training direct entrants to the service. This made a big impression on me, more of which later. I was involved in innovative developments, notably the S E Lancashire Community Work Group, which later became the Selcare Trust—the charitable arm of the service and the first of many care trusts established in England and Wales. To cope with the volume of voluntary after-care work, for which the service was never properly resourced, we established a group of volunteers at the office, selected, trained and supported by the team. And annually, we had the famous (or infamous) probation summer camp, where a group of six probation officers from the area took 36 juveniles, under supervision from different Lancashire towns, on a week's camp. Suffice it to say that a book could be written on the escapades at these outings — the beaver pit at Chester zoo and the sewage sluice gates on the Wirral are still painful memories!

On joining the Bolton Office, I was told that it was expected that I join the National Association of Probation Officers (Napo), attend branch meetings and the annual national conference. My first Napo conference was in Scarborough in 1967 and my next in St Andrews, the last to be held in Scotland, before probation there became part of the new Social Services Department — a route successfully resisted in England and Wales a couple of years later I became involved in branch activities, memorably seconding a motion, proposed by David Finch, that we refuse to supervise the first parolees on April 1st, 1968 — for reasons that I cannot now remember! It did bring our principal probation officer, Jack Marsh, to a branch meeting, to see for himself what these revolutionaries were plotting. In the early 1970s, I was elected chair of the East Lancashire Branch of Napo and two years later, David Finch and I were elected the first Nationjal Executive Committee representatives for the North West, in a new regional structure for Napo. In 1979, by then an assistant chief probation officer, I was elected as a national vice-chair of Napo. My (unsuccessful) campaign was to retain Napo as an all-grade professional association. My fellow vice-chair, Bill Beaumont, was a new radical and successfully led the Napo Action Group to transform the association into, effectively, a "main grade" trade union, was the last chief officer grade to hold national office.

I never had any ambitions for promotion. I was happy in my rôle as a probation officer. Then in the early-1970s, a particular colleague was appointed senior probation officer, an appointment which surprised and shocked everyone. Not only did I start to think, "I could do a better job than him," but other colleagues started to say this to me as well. So, in 1972, I was appointed senior probation officer in the Oldham County team and thus began another very happy and fulfilling five years. Once again, I led a good team and the culture of the Oldham office — borough and county teams — was positive, innovative and inclusive. I was fortunate when I started in Oldham, in having two experienced SPOs — Phil Weetman and Ron

Tench — to lean on, whilst I learned the ropes.

Whilst I was in Oldham, the Selcare Trust became established as a thriving charity and we opened two bed-sit units in the town, one for males (A-Wing Strangeways in the community!) and one for women and an evening centre (forerunner to day centres, but clients were employed back then!). Again, we had a strong group of volunteers attached to the office and good relationships with many other agencies.

In the mid-1970s, I found myself being approved by the Home Office to apply for ACPO posts and shortly afterwards, being appointed ACPO in the Stockport/Trafford Division of what was now Greater Manchester. Looking back, it feels as though this process was inexorable, almost inevitable, and one that I did not carefully think through, as I normally do. Fortunately, it proved to be a positive move. It was a time, shortly after the creation of the large metropolitan counties, when in a new management structure, the rôle of the ACPO was still unclear. Was it a "super senior" rôle, or was the ACPO the chief's representative on earth? I enjoyed being a bit of both and perhaps, unwittingly, helping to form the rôle into something more coherent. The Greater Manchester Management Group of which I was a member was a team of all talents and big personalities. It was a privilege to be part of a group which I believe played a significant part in shaping the development of the very professional Probation Service of the 1980s.

After three years in Stockport/Trafford, a post was created in Greater Manchester which was the inevitable next move for me — ACPO (Training). My own experience of pre-entry training, together with the early experiences of supervising students and training direct entrants, led me to have strong views about the importance of relevant, high quality qualifying training and post-qualification professional development. When I was elected to the Napo National Executive Council in 1974, I was also appointed chair of the Napo Training Committee. For much of the next 25-years, I chaired first Napo and later, ACOP Training Committees.

In 1974, as chair of Napo Training Committee, I played a part in convincing the Home Office to include a requirement in Probation Rules that anyone appointed as a probation officer in England and Wales should hold a recognised professional qualification. This requirement was written into the rules in 1975 and remained in place for the next 20-years ("The

Golden Age of Probation"?). Sadly, in 1995, as chair of the ACOP Training Committee, I sat in a House of Commons Committee with Helen Schofield (Napo) and Rodney Carroll (CPC) and listened whilst this requirement was removed. Undaunted, the service united in refusing to return to the appointment of direct entrants and with the false dawn of New Labour in 1997, Jack Straw, the new Home Secretary, accepted the need for a qualification for probation officers, providing it was not social-work based. A group of us, academics and representatives of the probation organizations, worked hard and quickly to establish a new qualification, based in higher education and independently validated. At my retirement, in May 1999, the Home Office presented me with the first copy of the new Diploma in Probation Studies.

As ACPO (Training) in Greater Manchester, I developed a comprehensive in-service training programme for all staff, complementary to the northern Regional Staff Development Unit programme. The northern RSD Unit still gets a mixed press with those around when it existed (it closed in 1992) but for me, the opportunity to meet with staff from other areas in the north on a residential course, exploring some aspect of probation practice and sharing ideas, was invaluable. The opportunity to be a member of an RSD staff team, and later to be a course director, undoubtedly enhanced my professional development and confidence.

In the early 1980s, Len Yates, then deputy chief probation officer (personnel) in Merseyside, let it be known that he was planning to retire and started to say that I would be his successor! And so it came to pass! In 1984, I was appointed DCPO (personnel) in the Merseyside Service. Why make this move? Well, as training ACPO in Greater Manchester, I was accountable to Anne Roberts, also DCPO (personnel), who I admired and who knocked me into shape as a senior manager! So moving to this post in another area seemed like a logical and welcome move for me. It also enabled me to return to the scene of my pre-professional training.

So I left my comfort zone of Greater Manchester, after more than 18-years. Merseyside proved to be a shock to my system. Its culture was very different to the one I was familiar with, just down the East Lancs road. It was more aggressive, negative and inward-looking. On my first day in post, my secretary greeted me with "So you're the Woolyback"—a scouse term of "endearment" for Lancastrians. The tone was set! The management group I joined was

male-dominated, with most of its members having been internal appointments. In 1985, Liverpool was politically-wracked by a Labour administration
which had been hi-jacked by the Militant Tendency and the impact on the
public sector was disastrous and a city in decline was now in turmoil.

In this climate, I began a war of attrition, particularly with the Merseyside
Branches of Napo and the National Association of Local Government Officers
(NALGO), to try and wrest some semblance of control of the Merseyside
Service for the employers and management. We had a good head office
management team of David Mathieson, Roy Adams and Marlyn Minto and
an excellent chair of the probation committee in Jean Wotherspoon. I like
to believe we made some progress in restoring balance, order and accountability in the three-and–a-half years I was in Merseyside. But I would say
that, wouldn't I?! For my part, I grew up professionally during my time in
Merseyside—and still retain many friends there.

Whilst I was in Merseyside, rumours began to reach me from sections
of the Greater Manchester Service that some people believed that Cedric
Fullwood, who returned to the area with acclamation when appointed CPO
in 1982, would soon be moving on to greater things and that I had moved to
Merseyside to get senior management experience in another area, in order to
return as Cedric's successor. This came as a complete surprise to me—and
I'm pretty sure Cedric was unaware of the rumours! The thought had not
crossed my mind. I had gone to Merseyside to do a job I very much wanted
to do and had not planned beyond that. However, people then started asking
me, "When are you applying for chiefs' jobs?" and I found myself responding
with, "It would have to be a metropolitan county in the north".

Thus, in 1988, two such vacancies occurred and I applied for both. John
Hicks was rightly appointed in South Yorkshire and shortly afterwards, I was
appointed in Northumbria. Probation staff in the North West were shocked
at my decision to move to the North-East and knowing my proud Lancashire
roots, kept telling me that commuting to Newcastle would be difficult! For
my part, it always felt the right move for me, one that I have always been
comfortable with—and grateful for. I knew a lot of staff in the Northumbria
area, from Napo, RSD courses and ACOP and I always liked what I saw.

My eleven years as CPO in Northumbria can be divided into two distinct
halves. The first five years were a time of innovation and growth. With two

redoubtable Tory Home Secretaries, Willie Whitelaw and Douglas Hurd, keeping at bay the reactionary hordes of Thatcher, the Probation Service prospered in the build-up to, and immediate aftermath of the 1991 Criminal Justice Act. The Act was designed to reserve imprisonment for only serious and violent offenders and initially, succeeded spectacularly, with a fall in the prison population of over 10,000 in the year after its implementation.

In Northumbria, we took full advantage of the momentum created by the Act, with the opening of two purpose-built hostels, three day centres and a training and staff development centre. We pioneered the development of bail information (with the establishment of the first pre-trial services team in the country), victim liaison (with the setting up of possibly the first Victim Liaison Unit), the first Sex Offender Unit in the Service, a partnership with the Artists Agency to locate artists in residence with the service (a scheme which lasted for ten years, with different artists in day centres, hostels, probation and community service teams) and formalised a first partnership plan with the voluntary sector, through which seven per cent of our annual budget was committed to partnership work. We appointed specialist staff for accommodation development; education, training and employment; addictions; mental health; race issues; debts and benefits and car crime. We pioneered the development of IT, with our system being selected by the Home Office for roll out nationally—with disastrous results! I was fortunate in having a succession of wonderful, supportive committee chairs and a talented colleague, Sue Winfield, as my deputy. Heady days indeed…

The second half of my time as CPO was heralded by Home Secretary Michael Howard ending the post-war political consensus on criminal justice, declaring instead that "prison works", rapidly doubling the prison population and waging war on the Probation Service—by cutting resources, stopping non-statutory work and removing our professional qualification. Life in probation became a battle for survival. The false dawn of New Labour soon evaporated and the climate under the new administration became even more punitive, with "tough" measures the only ones to be seen to have merit in the "war against crime".

Fortunately, in Northumbria, under the charismatic leadership of Chief Constable John Stevens, we continued to develop imaginative and effective policy and practice. We established an effective inter-agency Community

Safety Strategy and in the 1990s, crime in the Northumbria area reduced by 46 per cent — the largest reduction anywhere in the western world at that time. This included New York, where "zero tolerance" attracted world-wide attention. Two facets of our work at that time were enshrined in the 1998 Crime and Disorder Act — the new requirement that local authorities set up Community Safety Partnerships and the establishment of a Youth Justice Strategy for England and Wales, which mirrored developments in Northumbria and Thames Valley.

In spite of these victories against the tide of the time, in 1999, I decided it was time to retire. After eleven years as chief in Northumbria, most of my reasons for leaving were positive. However, I could see the way the political wind was blowing for probation and I felt I could no longer give the 100 per cent commitment I had given throughout my career. I was not alone in this view and sadly, subsequent events have more than borne out what we felt, as we have watched the Probation Service we knew being gradually dismantled.

Fortunately, both my rôle and experience in the Probation Service proved to be the springboard for a wide-ranging and fulfilling life after probation, nationally, regionally and locally. Some of my activities have been directly or indirectly related to criminal justice, many have not. All have been exciting, demanding and satisfying and I have the Probation Service to thank for the platform it provided for a rich and rewarding 15-year post retirement "career". That story is however for another day.

Mike Worthington, Probation officer, South East Lancashire Probation Service, August 1966; Chief Probation Officer, Northumbria, 1988–1999.

16. A Probation Journey within Teesside 1975–2005: Never Far from Home, Forever Striving

Peter Hadfield

For the person who has never ventured to Teesside (and there are many!) a quick Cook's tour (that would be a thing!) of the geographical and demographical make up of the area. Teesside now consists of four unitary authorities, Redcar and Cleveland, Middlesbrough, Stockton-on-Tees and Hartlepool. The River Tees, originally the border between Yorkshire and Durham, separates Redcar and Cleveland and Middlesbrough from Stockton and Hartlepool. In effect we have the throwing together of Yorkshire folk (Middlesbrough's Acklam Park was on out ground where Yorkshire County Cricket Club played county cricket. Durham CCC, in its early years played county cricket in Stockton and Hartlepool. Uneasy bedfellows indeed and an ill-fated attempt to weld them together as Cleveland County was abandoned on the early-1990s resulting in a return to old rivalries and "tribalism".

This was and will be for the foreseeable future a tough area to live and work in. There are huge swathes of deprivation with second, third and fourth generations of unemployed people. Industry came to Teesside in the 19th-century, iron and steel works, engineering, shipbuilding, chemical works, and a lot of money was made for the shareholders and owners; but just as quickly heavy industry departed, leaving the population high and dry with little current inward investment. I once took umbrage when I heard that Teesside was part of "The Rust Belt" but truth be told it is.

So the reader will quickly deduce that Teesside had many associated social problems and that the Probation Service would be kept busy — and during my tenure (1975-2005) it was certainly that. This said, most of the "busyness" emanated not from the offenders who could be a joy to work with and the *raison d'etre* for getting out of bed. No, most of the grinding hard work came from a continual political and administrative interference in the work of the service which eventually created one which became so uncertain of itself that its own eventual demise became inevitable (2014 almost there!).

I get ahead of myself, let me say where I come from, who I am, what I do (or did), when I did it and how (any Probation Service reader will quickly recognise this analysis method!). I was born in Middlesbrough (North Ormesby) a tough area, though we soon moved to Thorntree a socially-deprived council estate in East Middlesbrough. Dad was a bricklayer (often unemployed) and mum permanently wore a leg calliper as a result of childhood polio. My parents were Methodist (primitivish!) and I was brought up with all those associated values. Fortunately, I was blessed with a reasonable brain. I passed the eleven-plus and went to Middlesbrough High School. This excellent and much missed grammar school system still had its class system and social divisions. On sober reflection I have concluded that my accent, parental occupation, and council estate domicile meant I inhabited the C-stream throughout!

Leaving school I went to work as a technical apprentice (steelworks chemist) with Dorman Long Steel Ltd., which is now defunct. I completed my apprenticeship at 21 then lured by the prospect of £1,000 a year at 23, I left for ICI Nylon Chemical Works again now defunct for another ten years. I think of my final couple of years with ICI as my "Age of Reason". Did I want to stay here, a decent salary, a good pension? Should I spend the rest of my working life surrounded by intelligent people, but risk becoming depressed by their lack of drive, or showing much evidence of any social conscience or interest beyond their immediate selves? The answer was no, but what to do? Somewhere in my past I had heard a Probation Officer address my Methodist youth club and a latent fascination came back into my mind. As a consequence in 1975 I walked into my local probation office, in Middlesbrough, and asked how I could become a probation officer. Thus my probation journey commenced.

My Journey Chronology
- Volunteer and trainee probation officer 1975-1978
- Probation officer Middlesbrough West 1978-1980
- Court liaison probation officer 1980-1981
- Probation officer Middlesbrough West 1981-1983
- Probation officer Redcar 1983-1985
- Senior probation officer Resource Unit 1985-1988

- Senior probation officer Middlesbrough West 1988-1991
- Assistant chief probation officer HQ. 1991-2005.

I was interviewed as a prospective volunteer by Vic Barnes a senior probation officer (SPO) in Guisborough Probation Office, now long gone. Vic
was a Baptist local preacher, and he must have thought I was suitable volunteer material as he sent me off to the Redcar Office for me to work from
there. That meeting with Vic was the first time in my journey that I met a
committed Christian member of the Probation Service. I gradually discovered
there was a not an insignificant number of Christian probation staff working
in the service (local preachers, ex-priests, even an ex-monk!). Perhaps this
was a remnant, a throwback, to those early Christian values of the founding
temperance movement. However, by 1975 secularism was displacing any overt
spiritual values in probation and one's beliefs could never be openly used
as the basis for one's motivation. Nevertheless reflecting on my own values
then perhaps my Methodist upbringing had played a part in me beginning
my journey, and certainly Methodism is a part of my life now.

Derek Horner was a probation officer in Redcar. He was Home Office
trained and an ex-police constable. He always seemed to me to be a wise
probation officer. He quickly told me that I had to be an exceptional volunteer or not to bother at all as he didn't want an extra case (me!), rather that
I was there to support his work with his caseload. Furthermore he did not
want any of his caseload (note ownership) being let down by any volunteer
who might be only half-hearted and not totally-committed. Over the years
I applied this yardstick to all probation volunteers, i.e. "Be exceptional or
don't bother"!

Suitably "counselled" by Derek I commenced my work as a volunteer. My
very first case was Stephen L a 15-year-old boy with learning difficulties. He
lived with his mum on a tough run down estate — Dormanstown. Dad had
disappeared years ago and now mum was struggling with this simple but
difficult adolescent. Many times I used to pick-up Stephen on my motorbike
and we would go to the breakwater at Teesmouth. We would watch ships
come and go and talk about where they were going or where they were from.
At the very least this gave mum a break and I like to think Stephen had a
bit of welcome avuncular attention. It didn't last. Stephen was remanded in

custody for his part in some thefts and he was given a hospital order — this was of course 1975. The last time I saw Stephen was in an old grey asylum at Winterton, Sedgefield (now demolished). I was really upset. This was not right, it was unkind! I was all the more determined to become a PO to try to make a difference. I often wonder if Stephen even now remembers those times when we watched the ships and if he knows that someone was interested in him and that he had value. Probation has always been a long game, and the positive memories of being valued as a person can influence behaviours years and years into the future.

Whist still volunteering, in 1976 I was accepted on the Certificate of Qualification in Social Work (CQSW) course at my local Teesside Polytechnic. For the purpose of learning I was employed for two years as a trainee probation officer by the Home office at £2,184 a year. The day before I started, I worked my last two-by-ten shift in ten years at ICI and walked away without a backward glance. It is easy to say now, but I had two sons aged six and eight, a wife and a mortgage to pay and, I had just dropped 80 per cent of my income. I cashed in ten years' worth of pension and fixed up a part time taxi job (Saturday/Sunday nights 10 pm to 6 am) to fit in with the CQSW course and to make ends meet. Probation was a vocation for me. I was single-minded, and determined to qualify and get a job as a probation officer.

I found academia remarkably easy. After 15-years in local industry I was amazed at the slow, easy pace of the staff and students on the course. I was enthralled by the notions within social work values, but always struggled to fit them into a real world context. I loved my practice placements, at the North Yorkshire Probation Office in Northallerton, Richmond Approved School and finally back to Redcar Probation Office to link-up with my inspirational Derek, who was now my student supervisor. Together with my taxi work and placements I think I learned more about being a successful probation officer than through the slow "lotus eaters" life at the poly.

Derek gave me a mixed caseload, everything was fine until I was waiting in my cab for a fare outside the local Starlight nightclub in Redcar at 2.30 am. The "fare" was Julie one of my caseload! A quick chat with Julie served as a contact and went into the "Part C" of my records! She had been reasonable enough as a taxi fare but I felt that we both had a bit to explain next time she reported.

The CQSW came to an end following exams and assessments. I had applied and was appointed as a pre-confirmed probation officer to commence 1st July, 1978 at the Middlesbrough West Probation Office at 160 Albert Rd. The Middlesbrough West team covered the half of the town including the famous St Hilda's area, which was known locally as "over the border", i.e. south of the railway line and definitely the wrong side of the tracks. It was a really tough area with many notorious characters, but who welcomed me, the probation officer, into their front rooms. We were the one part of the criminal justice system which seemed to be accepted in this setting. These home visits provided real opportunities to understand the context surrounding offending and to "advise, assist and befriend". My old Austin 1300 was often "guarded" outside by the local kids who recognised me as their older brother's or parents' probation officer. I worked as the liaison officer to the Church Army Hostel in St Hilda's — 80-cellular rooms for homeless men. If the hostel had a bed (and sometimes if they didn't) no-one was refused. I remember thinking how Dickensian it all was. The hostel was eventually replaced by a smart clean new building with about 40-beds and clever assessment procedures resulting in some homeless people failing the assessment and being refused a bed ... progress?

Early in my career the wind of change was starting to blow strongly in probation. In order to create greater efficiency a new specialist court liaison team was established which included me. The Teesside courts had 15 magistrates' courts and three Crown Courts and the team was set up to service all of them in a more efficient way, and to an extent it did. However it also meant that we saw the start of the generic field probation officer becoming detached from courts, as they no longer presented their own reports or conducted their own breaches. This was only the start of erosion of the generic rôle which would in my view eventually de-skill probation officers in aspects of their core work. However there was little doubt that the Probation Service was grossly inefficient and change was both possible and necessary. As a recent entrant from industry I could see this need for change and I welcomed and embraced it, and as long as I could clearly detect the humanity and care were part of it I was happy to promote it.

Of course change and indeed cultural change can be slow and painful but it seemed to me fairly early in my career that the status quo was not desirable or indeed sustainable.

Whilst in the court team, I signed up to do a part time LLB at Teesside Poly. I did two years which gave me enough insight to realise the poor service some of our clients were getting from some the legal profession. It gave me added confidence to intervene in courts and address the bench directly … great sport and happy days although not always well-received by benches and solicitors … hey ho!

I left the court team and after a short spell once again in Middlesbrough West I arrived back in Redcar now as a confirmed and qualified main grade field probation officer. Vic Barnes was still the SPO and of course Derek Horner was there and was now a colleague team member. The Redcar team really was set in its ways and I remember the obstacles put in my way when together with Doug West, a colleague, we set up a motorbike group in the cellar of the building. This was an innovative development, and we were using the group in order to reach out to some pretty inarticulate youths. I had a large urban/rural caseload and all seemed to be well.

I then heard about a new assistant chief probation officer at HQ in Middlesbrough, one Roger Statham! My colleagues in Middlesbrough told me to watch out as this man wanted to talk more about managerialism than offenders! Now I had already begun to notice how some probation officers were certainly not committed or driven by any missionary zeal, altruism or the slightest notion of vocation. Indeed it seemed to me that many colleagues had adopted an ostrich-like stance and were determined to resist any form of accountability or performance management. They were happy to occupy what many saw as a rôle which by and large was unreservedly respected by the public. This suited some staff and they were determined to maintain an autonomous rôle. Quite frankly the organizational hierarchy seemed acquiescent, powerless and to an extent were merely collusive hand-wringers, content to accept the status quo when faced with the prospect of managerialism being seriously introduced into the Probation Service

Sadly, in all of this the National Association of Probation Officers (now Napo) was unwilling or unable to see the way the future was shaping up, a pity that this campaigning trade union was not more progressive in those early days of profound change. I was to resign from Napo when I became an SPO and they began to promote the concept of senior-less teams.

Having had a background in industry and seeing the overly laid back autonomous stance of some of my colleagues, I was intrigued by the reports of this new assistant chief probation officer's (ACPO's) views and after checking out his real aspirations I decided that I wanted to play a part in the changes. I felt strongly that performance and accountability of probation officers were not mutually exclusive to care, some compassion and support for offenders. I felt I could make sense of my experiences in the world of industry coupled with my drive to "make a difference" for some of the disadvantaged folk I had known and knew in my community of Teesside. It was just about thinking differently about the way the service approached the tackling of the same problems.

After a failed application to become a senior probation officer I asked to speak to Roger Statham. He came to see me in Redcar. Vic, my SPO, told me that it was a first visit to the Redcar office by an ACPO in ten years! It was for me a seminal moment. I applied for the next SPO post and in 1985 was appointed as SPO in the Statutory Resource Centre which was a new unit in the old drop-in day centre. Between us Roger and I closed this day centre. This had been an institution and its closure caused some ructions but it was now the start of a new dawn. The year previously the Home Office had issued its Statement of National Objectives and Priorities (SNOP). This was the first real manifestation of the gathering storm of increased centralised control over all the then 56-probation areas. A key measure in the document was for probation areas to provide clear alternatives to custody. I set about designing some of this provision.

About this time, I was much taken with the offending behaviour work of Priestly and Maguire.[1] It capitalised on Schedule 11 of the 1982 Criminal Justice Act which allowed a condition in a probation order requiring the offender to attend a specified place and undertake specific activities to address their offending and thereby reducing the risk of further offending. The Bale Risk of Custody Scale[2] at referral ensured we were demonstrably providing

1. *Social Skills and Personal Problem Solving: A Handbook of Methods* (1978), Priestley, P, McGuire, J, Hemsley, V, Flegg, D and Welham D, London: Tavistock Publications.
2. "The Cambridge Risk of Custody Scale" (1986), Bale D, Cambridge: Cambridge Probation Service.

an "alternative to custody". The programme was thus marketed and sold to the courts as an alternative to custody. The programme supported by the attendant probation order used groupwork offending behaviour techniques espoused by Priestly and Maguire but also wove in my own local knowledge in respect of some of the practical needs of Teesside offenders. The programme was entitled "Change Your Ways in 30 Days" (CYW30D).

So here it was, care, compassion practical education and offending behaviour work in one package, it epitomised for me the possibilities, and it was successful. So much so that it was studied and evaluated by Professor Colin Roberts from Oxford University. I was flattered. This was about the time that the "What Works" evidence-based practice movement was afoot (driven by the chief inspector of probation the late-Graham Smith). Sadly, in my view, the principles and practice of CYW30D was taken by academics and psychologists who reworked it and re-badged it as cognitive behavioural therapy led to inflexibility and structure became more important than the current and pressing needs of the offender. The balance shifted too far.

I was sad but glad in the circumstances to let CYW30D go. I was drafted back into a recalcitrant field team in 1987, in my old stamping ground of Middlesbrough West. It had become a difficult and dysfunctional team under a benign SPO. It was made up almost wholly of the type of sceptical POs described earlier in this essay. It was a tough experience but I enjoyed the challenge. I introduced some performance measures and a caseload index system which illuminated considerable differences in performance and exposed who was actually doing the work as opposed to those who merely "talked a good fight". This open process enabled all the team to see the importance of being honest about what was really being achieved in the work that we did, but some aspects of the old negative culture still found it difficult to accept the reality of a changing world.

The work at the heart of cultural change continued in my middle-manager rôle and eventually at the second time of applying in 1991 I was appointed assistant chief probation officer. I was told I had to think "strategically", in truth I wasn't too certain what that meant at the time. My first job on my first day was to shave £40K off our hostel refurbishment plans. Part of my responsibilities were our two approved hostels and we were in process of refurbishing one and rebuilding the other. Unexpectedly I was cast into a morass of public indignation, anger and naked nimbyism. It was quite scary when during a site visit to the refurbishment project a large piece of concrete was thrown (I'm convinced by a neighbour) through a window just missing me and the SPO. This event preceded an arson attack on the building. Suddenly the pressures of a caseload and a recalcitrant team paled into insignificance! Difficult meetings with local residents eventually calmed things and inviting them into the hostel and ongoing liaison ensured peaceful co-existence.

Nationally there were by now increasing signals that we had to be more accountable, more efficient, and our work had to be demonstrably effective. In Teesside we had seen what was coming and had introduced our own practice guidance setting out levels of contact, etc. I re-hashed the standard case record so that SPOs more systematically monitored performance measures. From a local perspective we were ahead of the game as it were and it was frustrating to feel that other areas seemed slower to respond. The publication in1992 of National Standards (many redolent of our own practice guidelines) started to pull other areas into line. It was clear to me in my contacts with other areas that the service as a whole was dragging its heels and allowing the agenda to be set nationally. The Association of Chief Officers of Probation (ACOP) did not really provide the leadership required, indeed they could not as they represented 56-areas who never really spoke with one strong voice.

As part of my ACPO induction in 1992 I had been sent to Henley Business School on the Strategic Management Course. I spent six weeks there. My colleagues on the course were from the private sector, banking, oil, logistics, import/export. I was the only public sector manager there. After the continual pressure from Home Office, and Her Majesty's Inspectorate of Probation, which led to at times doubting ones managerial ability, it was nice to compare public sector manager's ability with private sector high fliers. I did not feel myself wanting in any respect, maybe apart from comparison my out-of-pocket allowances!

I covered almost all of the senior management rôles over the next few years, helping manage the tensions of the internal changing world of probation in juxtaposition with the changing local external world. Teesside Probation Service, formerly known as Cleveland was coterminous with the old Cleveland County. The old single local authority structure had certain advantages, just one social services department and one education department.

In 1996, Cleveland County was abolished and the four unitary authorities described at the start above were established. As a result we had new and multiple sets of relationships to build: there were four sets of community safety partnerships, four youth justice teams and so on. The functional/ geographical portfolios of my four ACPO colleagues created challenges, but I enjoyed my rôle in all of this and it was possible to be responsive to local issues. I also thought that being a native Teessider gave me advantages in making productive working relationships with other agencies.

By 1998 we were desperately short of probation officers, typical of an unattractive area competing for staff. The Home Secretary, Michael Howard unhelpfully had abolished the social work training of POs and this left a vacuum. Typically also because of formula funding we were also short of money. Always innovative and bold, Teesside Probation Service concep- tualised and then recruited offender supervisors to do just that, supervise offenders, but importantly not those at high-risk. Probation officers, the best trained staff would continue supervision of these offenders but those assessed as low-risk would be supervised by offender supervisors who would be properly trained. All cases would be overseen by a middle-manager who had responsibility for all case allocation. Offender management training was set up with a local further education college, and used the National Vocational Qualification (NVQ) structure that lead to access on a proba- tion officer training course. Thus the innovative scheme was educationally sound and it gave career opportunities to the old probation ancillary workers.

Sadly despite real attempts to find common ground, Napo took excep- tion the scheme and gained an injunction, which was served on the chair of the probation committee personally, against the use of offender supervi- sors, despite ancillaries and hostel staff being used for years and pending a judicial review. Roger Statham, who wrote the submissions, and I went to the Royal Courts of Justice for the presentation of evidence in August 1998.

Mr Justice Collins found for us, noting that the CPO's evidence had been prepared without the help of lawyers and calling Napo's evidence opaque. Just a brilliant experience justifying the faith we had in doing the right things as we saw them. It was a highlight in my career as the outcome was so vital to our running of the service on Teesside, which as an unattractive area always had to rely on home grown talent. This was a seminal moment with far-reaching consequences, in securing a proper training and development structure for our probation staff and it had far reaching consequences. At the time both ACOP and the Home Office seemed unaware of the significance of events and had left Teesside with the risks and costs of an action that we did not want, however because of the court findings costs did not fall on the local service.

Of course the relentless central pressure for greater efficiencies went on. Here in Teesside, we worked hard at it all and tried, successfully, to be good performers in terms of innovation and service to the courts while still delivering value for money. An HMIP performance inspection in 1999 of the North East region's three services, County Durham, Northumbria, and Teesside, found that "Teesside appeared to represent the best VFM in relative terms by showing above average performance and below average cost". So we were doing something right!

During 1998-2000 I studied for an MBA at Teesside University. My dissertation published in May 2000 discussed the new rigorous enforcement regime in the supervision of offenders. My research demonstrated that enforcement did not necessarily promote the likelihood of compliance and the relationship between supervisor and offender remained a key ingredient in the supervision process. I graduated from Teesside University with a distinction.

The National Offender Management Service (NOMS) had reared its head in 2000. We were to become a national service. Many chief probation officers took the opportunity to accept redundancy terms and leave and at a stroke in 2001, a huge amount of experience departed. My CPO, Roger Statham, was one of them. I felt pretty low, Roger had been such an asset to probation, he had battled locally and nationally taking and using any platform he could to try to move things forward. I too applied for redundancy but the chair of Teesside Probation Board declined my request. I thought I had a case because my rôle changed from assistant chief probation officer to assistant chief officer of probation, really not that unsubtle and certainly more than just semantic.

I thought I still had things to offer particularly now that I had the academic qualifications to match my experience and I applied for the vacant chief's job. Although I was successful at the assessment centre I was not offered the job in my preferred areas of Teesside or North Yorkshire and was disappointed.

The writing was on the wall.

My journey continued over the next few years but the joy and previous *esprit de corps* of the senior management team had gone. The cold hand of centralisation which requisitioned ownership of our buildings, which stilted innovation and imposed schemes and financial measures not to Teesside's advantage made my personal journey from industry to probation feel less and less valuable. Any lingering sense of vocation was rapidly being crushed. Probation work should be straightforward. Just to "advise, assist and befriend" offenders which may still be a good starting point!

By 2005, I had had enough and I retired early on health grounds. Although this was my probation journey over, it was never going to be the end of the journey for me. The contacts and relationships made through the years assisted me to become a non executive director of a primary care trust, now abolished in favour of clinical commissioning groups, and an independent member of Cleveland Police Authority, now abolished in favour of police and crime commissioners. So the journey goes on, I have recently befriended a man on prison licence as an unofficial volunteer in some community work. What goes round comes round, perhaps we will go and watch the ships at Teesmouth!

Peter Hadfield, Probation officer, Teesside Probation Service, July 1978; Assistant Chief Probation Officer there, 1991-2005.

17.   My Probation Journey

Peter Warburton

At first, my ambition was to be a youth leader/administrator, after enjoying voluntary youth work and scouting at the local Methodist Church. On applying for training to Westhill College, Birmingham, I was referred for interview the same day to Birmingham University, and accepted on a B Soc Sc (Hons) course, from 1954–57, under the tutelage of Dr Winifred Cavanagh JP—author of the then standard text on *Juvenile Delinquency*. This course kindled my interest in criminal justice work and, during my studies, I heard a local senior probation officer speak about his work at the Social Studies Association, it was then that I recognised where my future career lay.

In those days it was understood that to enter the Probation Service a post-graduate qualification was needed (which I could not afford to take), so I applied to be a housemaster at an approved school instead. Just before taking up my appointment, posts for direct entry probation officers in County Durham were advertised, and in an interview with the whole probation committee I was appointed to serve at Gateshead, in a Service then led by Bill (later Sir William) Pearce.

At that time, a typical 80-85 "caseload" comprised a majority of juvenile probationers, some adults under supervision, eight to ten reports per week for magistrates' courts and higher courts; together with a variety of other work involving matrimonial counselling and reconciliation, adoption enquiries, fine supervision and a miscellany of "kindred social work", covering such matters as neighbours' quarrels, debt advice, and the aftermath of attempted suicides. Whilst the working days began at 9 am, it is hardly surprising that they often ended about 8 to 9 pm.

Social enquiry reports for the court were expected to cover an offender's background, family situation, school and work performance, sporting/social interests and outlook; and a respectful recommendation for probation (possibly with added conditions) could be included if considered appropriate. Officers frequently attended court to present reports personally.

Supervision was based on "social casework" (or "deep casework"), whereby in serialised discussion with the offender, he or she was helped to learn from previous mistakes in his or her life experience, and make improvements in the future. Stress was laid upon the relationship forged between officer and client as a key means of effecting positive change, and how a wide range of community contacts could help the process (e.g. home/school visits; help to obtain work or accommodation) together with regular office reporting on progress. Local magistrates took an ongoing interest through (monthly) case committees with probation staff, sometimes providing practical ideas and useful contacts, support for "breach" action where needed, and backing for early-discharge of orders when rehabilitative work was judged to have been successfully completed. All an officer's activities were regularly inspected by local senior staff, and Home Office inspectors.

Senior probation officers were central to Probation Service work, and when I gained promotion in Birmingham (1964), and later in Consett (1966), and Sunderland, County Durham (1968) I became responsible for the leadership and guidance of a local team of six-to-eight officers; the link between court and team, and the representative of the CPO locally. In Birmingham, I was also liaison probation officer to the then Assize Court, when sitting.

In 1970, I was appointed to be one of three assistant chief probation officers based in Durham City. In addition to oversight of a geographical share of this large combined area which stretched from the Tyne to the Tees, each ACPO had an allocated interest in a specialist sector of work (for example after-care, training, and in my own case, community service).

ACPOs advised as well as represented the CPO, supported SPOs, ensured county policy was implemented, and engaged in problem-solving generally. The county office was a close-knit team, but ACPOs and CPOs also had their respective valued support forums at regional and national levels.

In 1974 I was selected as the CPO for the new Durham Probation Service following local government re-organization, and the ethos of probation began to change, becoming more managerial in style, and focussed on "targets" and "punishment in the community" rather than on the rehabilitation of offenders. The Probation Service had been governed hitherto by a committee formed of magistrate representatives from each constituent court (augmented latterly by "community members") and was administered by local government staff appointed by the county council—to act as secretary, treasurer, legal adviser, etc. Funding came from the Home Office (80 per cent) and local authority (20 per cent)—and diplomatic as well as casework skills were required by the CPO in gaining the best "deal" for the service—but broadly speaking in my period of office (1974/94) it was a time of slow, hard-won but steady growth.

Durham Probation Service had a reputation for pioneering initiatives, and I remember our teamwork together in this challenging period through its highlights:

- Community service—one of the six "pilot" areas, which managed the rapid initial expansion of community service orders.
- Ancillary workers (now probation service officers), pilot area, first ancillary appointment in the UK.
- Throughcare—following assimilation of after-care work into mainstream probation in 1966, Durham seconded probation staff to each of its prisons, and formulated practice guidelines adopted by each NE Probation Area; together with agreements set out and signed with each prison Governor.
- Probation hostels—premises were found and the new hostel regime established.
- Partnerships—imaginative joint projects were negotiated, set up and run with voluntary and other groups—which broadened the base of probation work, giving access to significant additional funds, and enhancing support for clients. We also recognised the importance of the rôle of administrative and clerical staff, introducing training and conferences to help meet their development needs.
- The potential of volunteers to contribute to work with offenders was also grasped and a programme of recruitment and training was implemented. Volunteers played an important part in mentoring offenders when day centres were developed as part of probation's work.

Beyond county boundaries, I was proud during my "journey" to contribute to the vigorous NE regional CPO group, and the national CPO conference, through its Development Sub-Committee, and Salaries Committee. In addition, I enjoyed the stimulation and responsibility of nearly ten-years spent as a member of the Parole Board.

The thing that gives me most satisfaction is the part played in staff development and the realisation that no fewer than five members of the Durham staff went on to become CPOs in London and other parts of the country.

Peter Warburton, Probation officer, Durham Combined Area Probation Service, 1957; Chief Probation Officer, County Durham, 1974–1994.

18.   From Stoke to Middlesbrough: A Probation Journey Through Industrial and Political Wastelands

Roger Statham

It was Arnold Bennett who used the soubriquet The Five Towns for The Potteries when in fact Stoke on Trent was made up of six towns. Ironically from a probation point of view the one that Arnold Bennett missed out was Fenton which by 1968 housed the magistrates' courts for the area. For a young probation officer in December of that year Fenton and its courts was to become the hub of a very busy life.

The Stoke on Trent Probation and After-care Service was one of the smallest in England and Wales and its staff were housed in just two offices, Hanley and Longton. Hanley Town Hall was also the home of the Quarter Sessions. I joined the team of Ken Buckle, senior probation officer covering the northern part of the city, Burslem and Tunstall and their surrounding areas. This was home to some of the many pot banks, the artistic delights of Wedgwood, Doulton, Meakins, Wade, Adams, Spode and Moorcroft and Clarice Cliff were here. But its buildings were blackened with smoke and lungs filled with the dust of industry. Stoke was a typical industrial landscape, its industry was slowly dying, and with it the disappearance of the bottle ovens, that had baked some of the most beautiful china and earthenware the world has seen, and had added to a unique skyline.

Crime for adults was often linked to alcohol, be it theft or violence, and for youngsters part of the daring of their acquisitive adventures. Housing, if it was not in the rows of terraced houses, was on the pre-war and post-war estates we know as social housing. One such estate was Chell Heath home to most of the offenders on the team's caseload. A proportion of the houses were of a two storey prefabricated type already beyond their projected lifespans. If the houses were lasting longer than was expected, the lives of the people certainly were not. Industrial disease and premature death were accepted with the resignation of over familiarisation. These were the houses that we visited routinely as probation officers and each provided a unique cameo of despair.

On one of my first home visits I was met at the door by Mum wearing a hat and was shown through the front room of the terraced house to the living-room, where a Gollum-like figure with a yellowing face sat by the winter fire. A lifetime of potteries dust and Wild Woodbines had become a wrecking team. These parents had had their son a bit late in life and could not understand why he had got into trouble. Why did Geoffrey behave the way he did? Why did he break into the shop with his friends? Why did he want to fight his dad who was so ill? Why did he not do as his mum told him; his mum who went to chapel on Sundays and whose only pleasure was a visit to bingo on Friday nights? Oh yes and why did he go drinking when he wasn't 18 yet? Suddenly the job I had taken on seemed enormous.

I had inherited my caseload from a Home Office student, who was finishing his placement and, the rest of my team who had had caseloads of over 50 each. The ages ranged from ten to over 50, all men as it was not permitted for male probation officers to supervise women, a local rule maybe? From the team, a mentor, Norman Webb was appointed to provide me with ready help and guidance, and to make sure my social enquiry reports would stand up in court. The mentoring and weekly team meetings led by our senior provided an immersion into probation culture. We were working within the guidelines provided by the law and the many Home Office circulars and with the help of Jarvis's *Probation Officers Manual*.

Team meetings also provided the means for allocating work, usually in the form of requests for reports for the courts, magistrates, Quarter Sessions or Assizes (as they were before the Crown Court), but mostly magistrates. Taking on a request for a court report was often the introduction into a new case, but sometimes it was a current client who had committed another offence and omitted to tell you at the last office visit. These same team meetings were a source for both learning and of lateral support, which was also provided by colleagues outside the team particularly the kindly John Mood. Case discussions could help analyse the personality of an offender the dynamics of a family or the significance of an offence. Being part of this ongoing process provided reassurance, a route to linking theory with practice and much needed personal support when things got rough.

Just how rough could things get? Being a probation officer was not an emotionally neutral experience, the ability to get alongside people, to empathise with them to support them and to try to help put in boundaries for behaviour required personal resilience. Whatever people thought about probation, and the criticism was that we were on the side of the offender, offending was never condoned; in fact there was a very real aspiration that clients did not re-offend. When they did so under supervision there was genuine disappointment and indeed a sense of failure for the supervisor. I remember when someone on my caseload was arrested for attempted murder. He was a 17-year-old who dressed like a biker and had been involved in mods and rockers skirmishes. Only on this occasion he had taken his mum's carving knife from the kitchen drawer and stuck it in someone.

His dad was a postman, and his mum, a dinner lady, doted on her three sons. Terry the nearly-murderer was the youngest; he was on probation for a previous internecine scuffle and personality-wise was an exquisite mixture of arrogance and diffidence. He worked on the pots and having spent more than a year taking clay to the makers had his sights set on being a caster—using liquid slip to make cups and jugs. He also liked the music of Carly Simon.

To say the least he fitted the crazy young fool label. Behind the tough image he was in an internal rage and could not express himself. He hid his inadequacy behind his hard rocker costume and long hair. His time inside was shorter because the knife had not been longer and his victim young and physically resilient. Custody was salutary but not wholly so and he emerged truculent still.

After release, getting a job quickly helped and, sessions on office visits challenging his attitudes were assisted by the common ground of Carly Simon and his musical interests. This empathetic casework relationship gave me influence with him and slowly he began to develop insight into himself, albeit in microscopic measures. He began to be able to look at his own attitudes to things in his life and to reflect on them. Other things in his life began to fall into place too; he prospered at work and then found a girlfriend. He did not re-offend.

Elsewhere with Geoffrey, well I visited his parents during the time until his father's death and I tried to explain to them that their son still had value. To dad in particular I hoped that I conveyed to him that Geoffrey might seem to be cruel but maybe Geoffrey just wanted a well dad with whom he could play fight. It was also important that dad did not die thinking badly of his son. As far as he was able, Geoffrey talked when he came to see me on office visits, and I tried to help him express his sadness about his dad. To what extent one might be successful with this or any other strategy was never clear, part of the resilience required to do the job was that you never got feedback, and anyway there was always the next crisis to deal with.

For many offenders the next court appearance would be the next crisis. It was in this setting that a probation officer's job would become a broker between the offender and society with the courts being the arbiters of the sentence. Social enquiry reports were the vehicle for translating the attitudes and social milieu into coherent arguments about appropriate sentences. Seriousness of offence, social circumstances and personal attitudes had to be weighed against the likely response to the sentence. For the probation officer there would usually be an ongoing commitment to supervision whether it was a custodial or non-custodial sentence. However there might be some key issue or event that made a supervision order a critical opportunity at the time. Not being able to convince the sentencers of the validity of an argument and losing someone to custody felt like a failure. The probation officer, as servant of the court, with a full social enquiry report, later to be sacrificed by short cut mechanisms designed to speed up the courts, was a key part of ensuring that criminal justice system had an element of social justice.

The above is just a glimpse of what life as a probation officer in Stoke was like at the end of the 1960s and into the 1970s. Organizational issues seemed remote, George Chesters the principal probation officer for Stoke seemed to preside over the service in a low key way, as well as handling much of the divorce court welfare work. Funds were provided through the local authority and the clerk to the justices was secretary to the probation committee. As for our employers, well we met them to account for our work at case committees and were invited for tea after meetings of the probation committee itself. This was full of rather benign and kindly local people, largely either business people or trade unionists. They seemed rather sympathetic to the needs of offenders and were supportive of the job that we were doing. They also seemed to understand that going into the homes of offenders was not an easy job but nevertheless saw it as essential recognising that social circumstances played a part in attitudes and offending.

In 1974, Stoke amalgamated with the Staffordshire Probation Service just at the time community service was being introduced as a measure nationally, after the success of the six pilot areas. That year being appointed as the first community service organizer for Staffordshire, created profoundly different challenges, both for me personally and organizationally. It meant transferring all my cases, including one I had supervised the whole time, to colleagues and beginning the task of creating an organization within an organization complete with its own budget.

Community service was controversial, it was a punishment in the community with reparative and rehabilitative elements; it was also to be used as an alternative to custody. As a result sentencers wanted hard physical graft and probation officers bridled at the idea of punishment. This simplistic overview has within it some of the dynamic tensions that bedevilled the Probation Service over future decades. These tensions were philosophical, political and financial too as community service schemes with a finite capacity and ring-fenced costs could be easily measured. Soon everything was to be measured.

Probation had now shed its client centred image and its brokerage rôle in the courts and had been extended into promoting the use of work in the community as a kind of recompense for offending. Organizationally, CS was budgeted and costed in a more open way than had previously been the case in probation, it also created a new dynamic in managing the staff and their workload. Ultimately this financial awakening was helpful and was to inform future challenges particularly in the imminent world of cash limits, but it led to painful choices.

After four years in CS and two years as a fieldwork team senior, there was a move to managing the Rainbow Day Centre in Hanley. Day centres were a 1980s development which in Stoke built on the "drop-in office" innovation in Shelton. From a national perspective, each day centre could be said to have had its own characteristics, the Hanley centre was truly drop-in and, it had probation clients alongside anyone else who wanted to use the facilities. It was innovative as it also combined a youth training scheme in another part of the building. In reality most of those who used the Rainbow were offenders and all might be described as on the fringes of law-abiding society. Many were dysfunctional, lonely and isolated.

The old labour exchange building provided a warm and largely safe haven where a cup of tea and a warm meal could be purchased for very modest sums. The day centre regime was expanded to include a pool table, table tennis, cards, dominoes, film shows, art classes, and basic healthcare. All human misery was here on a daily basis and for the hardworking staff crisis management was ongoing. It is fair to say that the centre regime did sustain many of the users, and essentially counselling was an inherent part of every conversation and activity. A game of table tennis or pool might be an exercise in anger management. When specific anger management classes were started, the vehicle used was how to take back to a shop a pair of trainers that were found to be faulty. It was not long before swearing and threats were part of the rôle play. Nevertheless it was possible to help individuals develop coping mechanisms, and in many ways the staff were rôle playing reasonable behaviour to people who had seen very little of it in their daily lives.

Day centres came at an interesting point in probation developments and might be seen as a metaphor for what was happening to political attitudes to social disadvantage. There was no doubt that they were doing a good job with the people that they served but as the users were not all on current probation caseloads it was difficult to demonstrate the benefits empirically. In contrast the youth training scheme at the Rainbow, part of a government initiative to confront a huge rise in unemployment in the 1970s, as traditional industries died, was capable of measurement. Trainees did acquire skills and get into jobs. Interestingly it was also an early example of partnership/joint funding being used, and was to influence the strategy to increase partnership working between probation and other bodies that led to a change in funding rules.

As public expenditure came under greater scrutiny post-1979, financial pressure increased on probation and anything that was not mainstream was under threat. The Statement of National Objectives and Priorities (SNOP) of 1984 was a watershed and refocused probation funding significantly. This was at the point when I moved as ACPO to Cleveland (later Teesside), and one of the first jobs I did was to close the day centre in Middlesbrough. Like the one in Hanley it was doing a good job and had hardworking innovative staff. Whilst this may have been seen as a wholly negative move there was a very real and positive aspiration to use the group working skills gained through experience in day centres to enhance the supervision process for offenders by adding programmes. Anger management was to become a statutory part of supervision.

By 1989, now in the rôle of CPO, the job was very different to the one I had started in Stoke in 1968. Teesside had a similar social profile to the Potteries in that levels of poverty, unemployment, poor health, early death and high crime rates were endemic; but the service I went to was fragmented and poorly-led. The pockets of good practice had to be built on and individual performance was in the spotlight. This was uncomfortable for probation officers who had hitherto had a good deal of professional freedom and inevitably there was reaction against it. It was a difficult period not helped by a trade union, the National Association of Probation Officers (now Napo), which was anti-pathetic to the idea of management and was increasingly anti-Government. But it was clear that the wolves were at the door and would not be going away.

Chief probation officers at the end of the 1980s and throughout the 1990s were not only having to manage their own services, which were under increasing scrutiny and financial pressure, but also having to do the same concerning the political fallout from the unpopularity of the service with the political classes. This was to reach its peak with the political vindictiveness of Michael Howard when he was Home Secretary, for him prison worked. The political pre-occupations with punishment and personal responsibility were a long way from the compassion and social awareness of the 1960s; however within probation itself humane values were still alive. All the work done on Teesside and other areas through the nineties and into the new century still had at its core the aspiration to rehabilitate offenders and treat them with respect. Programmes were designed to re-skill individuals, not only in attempting to re-equip them for any opportunity in an ever-challenging job market, but also in terms of their own social functioning. For example when we discovered that many young men going to young offender institutions were already fathers, we ran parenting classes. The service was still able to demonstrate a capacity for principled pragmatism.

However in its interface with the political world, largely through the Association of Chief Officers of Probation (ACOP) and Home Office officials, chief officers were struggling to create a unified voice and to manage the dynamics of financial restriction. The 1997 general election saw a new Government, but, with no change of attitude to probation, the service was in difficulty. It was alleged that the incoming Prime Minister had said that chief probation officers had been drinking in the last chance saloon.

When New Labour was elected in 1997 the North East was populated with the party elite. Most notably the dark art of media-spinning was taken to new heights by some of them. In contrast one of my Teesside MPs was Mo Mowlam who despite personal and political challenges never lost touch with the people. She never lost the capacity to talk straight and it was Mo who would knock on the door and take a box of biscuits into the bail hostel at Christmas. It was just one example of her never losing sight of what life was really like in the community she served (When a new bail hostel was built on Teesside it was called Mowlam House).

However the kindness and humanity of one member of Government could not mask the political reality and there was even a move to change the probation name. The survival of probation in what was clearly going to continue to be a market-driven world was now in doubt. When the Probation Service was nationalised in 2001 half the chief probation officers left. It was to herald a period of organizational tinkering that continues.

How is it possible to assess the changes over the 45-years from 1968 and what is the legacy of probation? It does seem important to recognise that there has been a shift in public attitudes and indeed in collective perceptions of what we mean by society and social attitudes. The welfare state is now the nanny state, and successive governments have seen the market as the answer to providing public services. Whilst the election of 1979 might have been a pivotal point in the shifting of attitudes the election of 1997 was even more fundamental. Electors found that there had been little change in Government philosophy and indeed that there was no longer an alternative to Conservatism in the political landscape.

For the last three decades, probation just like health and education has been caught up in the dynamics and mechanisms of creating pseudo-markets to deliver public services. The underlying philosophy might appear to be simply to get the cost of these things off the government's balance sheet but the structures created to do this are not transparent enough for a real assessment to be made of the true financial costs. At the same time organizational targets and protocols have helped stifle initiative and even the capacity to care. Some of the disclosures from the Mid-Staffs Health experience suggest that we cannot trust our carers to care. Worryingly, the likely response is to create even more regulation, so that staff will be supervised or inspected to personal breaking-point.

What is being lost is the culture of caring and the recognition that people need to be nurtured in order to grow, develop, heal or survive. Quite simply we have an ethical crisis in modern Britain, and neither the media nor politicians want to talk about it. Self-interest rules and the scandalous growing social divides do not seem to matter.

So where does this leave probation and its legacy? The simple answer is, under threat. Caring for offenders is what the probation service was about, caring for those who were at the bottom of the pecking order in society, the most undeserving. With a government hell bent on privatising the challenge will be to ensure that the emerging structure has humane values at its heart, this is essential. It is also critical that the performance of private companies must not be hidden behind commercial confidentiality. Already there are enough issues here to make this a fundamental cause for concern.

More optimistically there are still examples of good practice and caring people in all public sector services. These are the people who hold the ring who keep the cultural aspirations for fairness and humanity alive. Even amongst politicians there are those who manage to hold on to values.

In whatever form probation emerges from this latest assault it will be important that humane values can still influence our criminal justice system. Some things are not for profit and as a nation we will be diminished if we do not hold to this.

Postscript

As the other scripts for this book began to come in I reflected on this journey piece and resisted changing it as it was in a sense of the moment that it was written. Later I was struck by how different it might have been and how much more there is to tell. There could be stories about courts, experience as a member of the Parole Board, political stories, memories of *Newsnight* live from Middlesbrough, and the Cleveland Child Abuse Scandal. These are just a few that spring to mind. I could have written at length of all the highs and lows of a lengthy career in probation and some of the invidious decisions one had to take. However one thing has struck me and that is how sustaining are the recollections of all the people I have worked with over the years, as are those expressed by the contributors to this book. Probation was very special and there was almost a sense of it being a family when I first started in Stoke. But probation was not just about probation officers; there were many talented and committed people in support rôles, secretaries and admin staff, and later finance and personnel staff too. Each has played a part in maintaining the operation of probation, and it is easy to overlook their valuable contribution.

I have been lucky in that from the outset I had a super secretary who could remember all my cases, track appointments and generally help me not forget. My last secretary when I was a busy CPO was simply brilliant, ensured that I always had the right papers for meetings and had superb diplomacy skills. Helpful others were invaluable too, handling tricky front of house services with difficult and aggressive clients, particularly in the Rainbow Day Centre in Hanley. All their rôles were defined by their responsibilities of the time, but the thing that they had in common was commitment. What talented people there were, significantly amongst treasury and personnel staff when services grew and took these services in-house from local authorities.

In an earlier age the work of those in support rôles, for me, will always be defined by Peggy Walford who was the secretary to George Chesters the principal probation officer for Stoke mentioned above. She was also the one person admin system, who did everything from ordering the toilet paper to ensuring Home Office returns were completed. She also ensured that we were paid at the end of the month by Stoke-on-Trent Borough Council who handled finances on behalf of the probation committee. Peggy set up a system so that meal allowances, claimed when working late, were actually paid in cash at the end of the month, as she thought that as young impoverished probation officers we needed a bit of pocket money. To say that she was thrifty with the service's money was an understatement, one had to virtually return an old biro to get a new one. She was absolutely committed to probation throughout her lengthy career. Her devotion to probation continued after retirement when she came to be a volunteer at the Rainbow Day Centre making cups of tea and providing a little oasis of serenity behind the coffee bar.

This book would not be complete without taking a little space to record the value and sheer commitment of all of probations support staff over time.

Whimsically as a final thought I wondered about a soundtrack for the golden age of probation. As a probation officer driving around the grimy Potteries streets in my VW Beetle, I listened to a crackly radio playing T Rex, Gerry Rafferty, Rod Stewart, Cat Stevens, Van Morrison and many more. Their songs provided escape and sustenance between the often painful dynamics of home visits, and the weary drive home after working many late nights. Everyone will have their own playlist, but what about an anthem? What might be a defining song to capture something of the era? Dexys Midnight Runners, *Come on Eileen* was definitely the anthem of the Rainbow Centre in 1982, but *Melting Pot* by Blue Mink seems to say something of what we have been trying to capture.

Roger Statham, Probation officer, Stoke-on-Trent Probation Service, December 1968; Chief Probation Officer, Teesside, 1989–2001.

Roger is co-author of:

Managing the Probation Service: Issues for the 1990s (1992),

Statham R and Whitehead P, London: Longman.

The History of Probation: Politics, Power and Cultural Change 1876–2005 (2006),

Whitehead P and Statham R, London: Shaw & Sons.

19. One Journey Across Four Decades of Probation: 1972–2010

Steve Collett

"… a small island of decency and humanity in the criminal justice system …"[1]

"For much of the 20th-century, probation was a core institution of criminal justice. Extensively used, in the vanguard of penal progress, it was often regarded as the exemplary instance of the penal-welfare approach to crime control. In today's criminal justice world, probation occupies a position that is more conflicted and much less secure. Over the last 30 years, probation has had to struggle to maintain its credibility, as the ideals upon which it was based have been discredited and displaced. Under pressure from government it has tightened its procedures, highlighted its supervisory capacities, downplayed its social work affiliations, intensified its controls, and represented itself as a community punishment" (David Garland, 2001: 177).

"**8 November, Leeds.** Walking along Wellington Street towards City Square I pass the offices of the probation service, now plastered with protest leaflets and posters from Napo against the selling off of the service, protests that in my view are wholly justified. The notion that probation, which is intended to help and support those who have fallen foul of the law, should make a profit for shareholders seems beyond satire. As indeed is the proposal to take the East Coast line out of what is virtually public ownership and reprivatise it for the likes of the expatriate Branson. I never used to bother about capitalism. It was just a word. Not now" (Alan Bennett, 2014).

---

1. This phrase is taken from *Redemption, Rehabilitation and Risk Management: A History of Probation* (2011), Mair G and Burke L, London: Routledge.

Campaigning and Delivering

I've used the Garland quote above a number of times in talks and other articles, because it seems to me to be a brief but superbly accurate description of probation up to the millennium. It captures the reason why I became a probation ancillary worker in 1974 but it also highlights those strands of penal policy which were to become counter-productive not only for probation but as I shall argue, for wider society.

First of all a word about the term—*probation*—so much has been written about the Probation Service and the concept of probation but it never ceases to amaze me how it can be used in so many contexts to convey so many meanings. In the above quote from Alan Bennett's 2013 diary, he specifically mentions the *probation service* but he also refers to *probation*. It is not clear whether he is using the latter term as shorthand for the Probation Service or as a reference to the concept of probation—of putting someone on test to behave better in the future—or indeed as a reference to supervision under the guise of a probation order. *Probation* is a wonderfully ambiguous but inclusive term and when used in conversation or print it can be left to the audience or reader to interpret whether it is referring to specific organizational and bureaucratic features, a concept and a set of values for conducting offender supervision or indeed as a (now defunct) sentence of the court.

Terms like offender management, risk management, assessment, control and surveillance have slipped into the official discourse to describe the work of the Probation Service but we still default to using probation as an umbrella for the rehabilitative endeavour—of committed professional work on the personal and bureaucratic level to deliver rehabilitation—to give individuals the opportunity to lead crime-free productive lives that have meaning to themselves, their families, their victims and the wider community (see Burke and Collett forthcoming, 2015).

I didn't understand all that, of course, as a raw and inexperienced 19-year-old recruit to the Liverpool Simon Community[2] in 1971. I had read Tony Parker's *The Unknown Citizen* (Parker, 1963) before I started at the Simon Community and was now beginning to experience living in the a residential community with women and men whose poverty and exposure to

---

2. A number of Simon Communities were set up across the country during the 1960s to provide
    accommodation and support primarily for single homeless men and women.

homelessness, sometimes complex needs and the destructive impact of short prison sentences meant that they were well-known to the local criminal justice system. In probation terms, they were often categorised as voluntary after-care (VAC) cases. This seemed to me to be a brilliant notion — that the engagement of the ex-prisoner was voluntary but the response of probation was statutory — I guess a significant and practical expression of *penal-welfarism*! These VAC responsibilities then brought me into contact with probation and what struck me about the probation officers that I met then was their authority as officers of the court but also their humanity and realism about what they could achieve without giving up on a sense of hope for the future. They conveyed a sense that, despite the inequities of society and the often brutal use of imprisonment for petty offenders, these men and women were worthy of probation help (to *advise, assist and befriend*) within *the here and now.* This was what Bill McWilliams referred some 16-years later as the *personalist* approach to probation work (McWilliams, 1987). It was also no coincidence that the Simon Community was founded by a probation officer (see Wallich-Clifford, 1974, 1976), who would complete a day's work at Bow Street Magistrates' Court and then at night share the bomb sites and skippers of skid row with homeless men and women in order to try and understand the range of responses needed to reach those on the very limits of society.

Although I didn't fully understand it at the time, the 1960s and early-1970s reflected a *Butskellite*[3] consensus around penal policy and the treatment of offenders. In other words, there was a consensus across the political parties that the relatively liberal approach (penal-welfarism) to offenders should not be subject to the vagaries of party politics. This consensus also reflected a belief in the efficacy of the worker as a professional and a concomitant belief in the importance of the emerging criminal justice and social work professions. During this period, the Probation Service was often lauded for its work but it remained a *Cinderella* service in terms of money and influence. It was also a period in which there was significant social and political action to try and rectify the deficiencies in the welfare state. In 1966, *Cathy Come Home*, a seminal drama directed by Ken Loach about family break-up and homelessness shocked a nation into understanding that poverty and

---

3.   The term conflates the names of R A Butler of the Conservative Party and Hugh Gaitskell, leader of the Labour Party.

homelessness had not disappeared and it was also during this period that the great campaigning charities Shelter, Child Poverty Action Group (CPAG) and the Campaign for Homeless and Rootless (CHAR), for example, came into being.

At the local level, probation was part of that mix and for those of us who entered the service in the early-1970s, there was a tolerance, even an expectation, that we would contribute to the development of wider partnerships and social provision as a reflection of our concern to rehabilitate offenders and our understanding of the wider social and economic causes of crime. For me, the dire state of accommodation in Liverpool common lodging houses for single homeless men and the lack of access to primary healthcare was an abiding concern that maintained my involvement in campaigning issues as well as working in a city centre homeless offenders team.[4]

This is how Garland summarises the period:

> "In the middle decades of the last century, the criminal justice system formed part of a broader solidarity project. Its programmatic response to crime was part of the welfare state's programmatic response to poverty and destitution. Criminal justice was shaped by the politics of social democracy, and its ideals were the re-integrative ideals of an inclusive welfare state society. And if its actual practices fell far short of these ideals, as they typically did, they could at least be criticised by reference to these ideals, and reformed in ways that lessened the gap." (2001: 199)

Drifting From Community to Corrections

The pace of change was never quick enough for those of us who wanted greater social and economic equality but it felt like probation could still operate as a force for change. The urban disturbances in 1981 in places as different as Brixton, Handsworth and Toxteth also demonstrated a continuing connection between probation and the communities it served, albeit in much harsher socio-economic and political times as the great neo-liberal enterprise gathered momentum. In Liverpool, the disturbances occurred

---

4. The service fully supported my engagement in local campaigning work to establish better facilities for single homeless men and women providing it was not party political. See Collett, S J and Stenham, R (1977), *Primary Medical Care and the Single Homeless*, Liverpool: Liverpool Community Health Council.

at the beginning of July 1981 and centred on the Toxteth area of the city. The historical legacy of slavery in terms of the depth of disadvantage and discrimination in housing, health, employment, education and training coupled with outright racist policing of Liverpool's black population was such that an agency like probation, of itself, could not tackle, let alone solve, these institutionalised disadvantages by its own efforts. However, the service was, in a number of important respects, geared up to make an important impact — it was community-based in the sense that it was not only used to operating in the homes and neighbourhoods of offenders, but it was intertwined with local partner agencies outside as well as within the criminal justice system (see Collett, 2013). Probation had begun to develop community-based or detached services which were co-located with other agencies in, for example, tenement flats (Simpson and Crawley, 1985; Broad, 1991). Ironically probation's relationship with the police was virtually non-existent but in the aftermath of disturbances, the service's credibility within the local community was such that it could operate as an honest broker between community representatives and local agencies, including the police. As the 1988 Gifford Inquiry outlined the situation:

> "...the service sponsored an employment scheme under the government's Community Programme. The scheme brought in a number of Black employees to probation offices in Liverpool 8. It provided job opportunities, as well as learning experience for the probation office staff. Black workers became involved in the probation service, victim support, youth work and voluntary agencies and some were recruited into the probation service as a career" (Gifford, Brown and Bundey, 1989: 203).

The response to inner-city dereliction was completely inadequate, but the point was that probation as a community-based service with a vision wider than a narrowly correctional one was able to build on what few resources were made available. It was also able to influence future patterns of service delivery.

Things would change pretty quickly though as probation became more and more constrained within a narrow correctional focus and a decade later, Mike Worthington, then chief probation officer of Northumbria, after local disturbances on Tyneside during September 1991, was making a passionate plea for probation to restore a greater partnership-based community focus to its work (Worthington, 1992) and the need to return to a compassionate society rather than one simply espousing punishment and survival of the fittest (Worthington, 1991).The report he had commissioned on those disturbances provided a picture, most probably replicated throughout the service nationally, of local service delivery becoming increasingly office-bound and "withdrawn from the community focus which at one time used to characterise its work" (Northumbria Probation Service, 1992:10).

Rising to the Challenge of Racism within the Criminal Justice System

Whilst probation's correctional drift was gaining momentum during the 1980s, it was also the case that race relations began to challenge probation to respond constructively in a way that seemed to be ignored by other criminal justice agencies. Evidence was emerging that whilst there was little variation in the level of crime generated by black and white communities, black men and women appeared to be caught up in a system where decision-making from the street to the court ultimately propelled them disproportionately into our prisons. On 30th June 1989, our prisons held some 48,532 individuals. Both black men and women were significantly over-represented compared to their proportion within the general population (by a factor of three and fiv respectively). The explanations were complex and a broad range of research was beginning to show the relevance of differences between Black and Asian communities, the impact of age and the double discrimination experienced by black women. Practitioners and managers within probation were trying to make sense of their search to better understand the processes (indirect and institutional) that were resulting in over-representation within custodial institutions and under-representation on community alternatives.

Like some other probation areas, Merseyside committed itself to a comprehensive anti-racism training strategy as one mechanism for tackling these complex organizational and institutional problems. It is fascinating to look back to what we would now see as the duty to promote racial equality under the Race Relations (Amendment) Act 2000. A backward glance also provides a timely reminder of the expectations that were being placed on the service in advance of the implementation of the1991 Criminal Justice Act. David Mathieson, Merseyside's then chief probation officer summed it up in the Foreword to *Managing and Developing Anti-Racist Practice within Probation* (1992):

> "This is a time when the Probation Service is being urged to move centre-stage in the criminal and civil justice systems. Of all the agencies involved, the Probation Service ought to be able to give a clear lead in respect of anti-racist practice in view of our traditional social work values which emphasis respect for people without discrimination" (Kett, *et al* 1992).

I believe the Merseyside strategy represented a key strand in developing anti-racist practice and what is striking was the argument that racism could only be understood in terms of its institutional nature. It took the murder of Stephen Lawrence and, in 1999, the MacPherson Inquiry to get full ownership of this view across all the agencies. MacPherson defined institutional racism in terms of unwitting *behaviours*. In our strategy, we stressed the *impact* of our behaviours rather than the *intentions* as the key. We also eschewed the *saris and samosas* approach which emphasised better understanding of cultural diversity. Within our strategy, the political use of the term *Black* was to denote the fact that skin colour rather than cultural differences was the important factor in understanding discrimination.

The training strategy included every member of staff and took two years to complete. In retrospect, some of our approaches were mechanistic. Promoting an understanding of racism in the context of skin colour to the exclusion of cultural differences may also have been shortsighted. However, it was just months after the main training for staff was completed that Steven Lawrence was murdered on the 22nd April1993 and why—essentially because he was a black youngster.

I'm not sure that probation ever got the recognition it deserved for tackling institutional racism. The service learnt that humanitarian values alone were insufficient to confront discrimination but these early attempts to tackle racism were ultimately about the aspiration of delivering justice to all offenders and all victims as well as tackling prejudice (see Collett, 2008 for a fuller discussion).

Optimism dashed

For me there was a buoyancy and optimism about probation in the early-1990s despite the ever-darkening storm clouds of Thatcherite social and economic policy. Not only was the 1991 Criminal Justice Act a seminal piece of constructive legislation but, in its implementation, the Government had allowed for significant joint training with the magistracy and judiciary (see Burke and Collett, forthcoming, 2015, Chapter 3). The early signs for moving away from the use of imprisonment were positive even before the sentencing framework became operational in October 1992. A slow but fairly constant rise in the post-Second World War prison population was halted and between January 1992 and January 1993, it had fallen by some 4,000 to approximately 44,000 (Home Office, 2003: 6). From an operational and practitioner perspective, the provisions of the act were beginning to make sense and it provided for a more rational and constructive exchange between probation and sentencers. To the disinterested observer, these two factors alone might be taken as evidence of the successful implementation of a significant and complicated piece of legislation for once achieving its policy and operational aims.

Indeed, insofar as the 1991 Act was based on *just deserts*, its provisions were seen as supporting such a liberal approach to sentencing that it was soon to be emasculated and key provisions repealed. Downes and Morgan (2002: 296) succinctly captured the politics of the period following implementation:

> "Alarmed by their deteriorating position in public opinion polls, both in general and on crime, the Conservatives rapidly cast their previous and long-germinated penal policy to the winds and sought to regain lost terrain. First Kenneth Clarke, then Michael Howard, as new Conservative Home Secretaries after 1992, quickly dropped the key reforming clauses of the 1991 Act: unit fines (which linked the level of fines to disposable income) and the need normally to disregard previous convictions in sentencing. Michael Howard's notorious 'prison works' speech to the Tory Party Conference in 1993 was the climax to this somewhat panic-stricken shift" (Quoted in Mair and Burke, 2012: 153).

In a number of important ways, probation now had to face up to the realities of its continued existence as the rehabilitative arm of the correctional services, tentatively positioned on the centre of a stage that was being dragged ingloriously to the right with every public utterance from Conservatives — soon to be joined in that chorus by New Labour. A creeping realisation that the service needed to modernise to survive was quickly replaced by disillusionment and concern that dancing to the politician's tune made very little difference to the long-term authority and standing of probation

In retrospect, the 1991 Act can be seen almost as an aberration by a Government who realised their mistake and quickly went about making amends. In the wake of the murder of James Bulger and before his killers were brought to trial, the then Prime Minister, John Major, utilised all his skill for political opportunism by uttering his view that we should *understand a little less and condemn a little more* (See Collett 1993). Major followed that up with a comment in a 1994 speech that *crime is a decision not a disease* (quoted in Garland, 2001: 198). The gloves were off and amongst practitioners, at the time, there was a clear awareness of the accelerating demise of penal-welfarism. With the higher political and media profile given to crime, law and order during the last decade of the 20th–century, punitive crime control policies were increasingly viewed as a mechanism for securing electoral support for political parties beyond the actual instrumental intent of the proposals — it all seemed to set the mood music for hardening social and economic policy .

In this context then, Prime Minister Tony Blair's often repeated *tough on crime, tough on the causes of crime* (1993) can be viewed as a very clever mechanism for introducing ambiguity into public understanding of criminal justice policy approaches to rehabilitation. Although often quoted or referred to, the title of the article is rarely mentioned — in fact it appeared in the *New Statesman* under the heading "Why crime is a socialist issue". Whilst most certainly *Old Labour language*, the phrase itself reflected Labour's concern with law and order and found its way four years later into a party's manifesto that was significantly New Labour.

A Brief Respite Before Disaster
Notwithstanding these worrying uncertainties about probation's future, the creation of the National Probation Service in 2001 and a burgeoning

evidence-based practice or w*hat works* strategy offered some hope and it was certainly the case that probation was funded as never before. As a chief officer from 2001, I welcomed many of the early initiatives both within probation and across the criminal justice system. What I soon found to be a major difficulty though was the centre's inability to direct strategically without getting involved in local control, its obsession with targets that were often meaningless at best and self-defeating at worst and the increasing use of prison (twice the level following the implementation of the 1991 Criminal Justice Act) as a knee-jerk to its ever-toughening law and order stance.

The relationship between New Labour and probation became up close and personal and if one set of circumstances highlights the tension between the efficacy of professionally developed services and political interests it is the *volte face* that Home Secretary John Reid delivered in relation to the carefully developed rôle of approved premises in accommodating dangerous offenders including those who had committed offences against children. Approved premises offered a supervision lifeline to local agencies, particularly through multi-agency public protection arrangements (MAPPAs) for the initial management of dangerous offenders before longer-term plans could be put in place. Reid, however, was unable to support the policy of his own department and of his own officials. As a highly placed official within the NPD said to Jon Silverman:

> "The *News of the World* told the Home Secretary that it had obtained details of the
> locations of bail hostels and was prepared to publish them unless he took action
> to remove sex offenders. The NPD view was: 'Let them go ahead and publish'.
> It might result in a few bricks through windows but that happens anyway in the
> normal course of events. We were sure we could handle the fallout. But there was
> no appetite on the political side to stand up to the paper. Of course John Reid
> dressed this up by saying 'we've taken a principled stand on this'—but you can
> draw your own conclusions" (2012: 36 interview with author, 4 September 2008).

Reid's decision to cave in to the *News of the World* represented a serious threat to public protection measures at the local level and put local services on the back foot, many of whom had spent inordinate time convincing both local authorities and local communities that it was in their interests to support this specialised rôle for approved premises. Probation services felt let down and unsupported particularly when perceived mistakes in their supervision of dangerous offenders were, quite rightly, subjected to intimate scrutiny and review.

These kinds of decisions motivated by personal and party gain were being taken, however, within the context of New Labour's neo-liberal intent to restructure and privatise as much of the welfare state as they could get away with. Judy McKnight, the retiring general secretary of the National Association of Probation Officers (Napo) captured the nonsense of organizational change within the National Offender Management Service (NOMS) brilliantly in her 2008 Bill McWilliams lecture (see McKnight, 2009) but behind all the manoeuvrings and politics of NOMS was the ideological commitment to ultimately break up probation and hand over the seemingly profitable parts to the private sector. The Coalition simply took over where New Labour left off.

Over to the Masters of the Universe

The question I ask myself is why New Labour and now the Coalition Government have been intent on destroying probation as an integrated public sector service. I've come to the conclusion that it's not simply because sometimes we get it wrong or we could deliver more effectively or even that neo-liberalism demands profits for its friends and cronies. It must be destroyed because in its historical mission, held by staff of all political persuasions, probation held to the belief that those who offend are not inherently bad or even different to the rest of us and that they can, with skilled professional help and support, be reintegrated into mainstream society and lead good lives. This is an antiquated and irrelevant view for those who must believe that they are superior to those who fail. As Danny Dorling comments in *Injustice: Why Social Inequality Persists:*

> "...the rich talk of the laziness, laxness, fecklessness and general uselessness of the poor in contrast to their perceptions of themselves as great risk takers and great labourers, as highly efficient, intelligent and sensitive people. What they really have is a very highly developed sense of personal self-worth. It is difficult not to think like this if you are affluent, and it is how most affluent people think;

if you are rich and admit to being only human too, well, how do you excuse your riches" (2013: 220).

If the neo-liberal mind-set of the current political elite is so convinced that the culture of the Probation Service is dangerous then the corollary must be that the service's *dénouement* under Justice Secretary Chris Grayling's *Transforming Rehabilitation* represents a real opportunity to further punish and control the poor and marginalised. I have no doubt that probation staff within the newly formed National Probation Service or any one of the 21 community rehabilitation companies will valiantly try and uphold the best of probation's values and beliefs in their supervision of individual offenders. How long this will be possible within a burgeoning culture of control, punishment, surveillance, risk identification and management at one extreme and the commodification of individuals for profit at the other extreme is difficult to assess. All I know is that we will all be losers—individuals in trouble, staff who engage in the rehabilitative endeavour and the wider community.

This account of my journey has been partial and idiosyncratic in that it has attempted to capture moments that were important to me but also, hopefully, symptomatic of a public service that has had such a proud and distinguished history and one that has tackled problems other criminal justice agencies were often complacent about. A final comment to complete my journey—Whilst I retired from the service at the end of 2010, I notice that I still refer to *us* in the above commentary! I still feel part of the Probation Service but for how much longer? What the Coalition has achieved on the foundations provided by New Labour is—as Alan Bennett has so eloquently caught it—*beyond satire*.

Steve Collett, Probation Officer, Merseyside Probation Service, September 1974; Chief Officer, Cheshire Probation Service, 2001-2010.

References

Bennett, A (2014), "Diary: What I Did in 2013", *London Review of Books,* 36(1), 9th January, downloaded at http://www.lrb.co.uk/v36/no1/alan-bennett/diary accessed 13th January 2014.

Blair, T (1993), "Why Crime is a Socialist Issue", *New Statesman,* 29(2): 27–29.

Broad, B (1991) *Punishment under Pressure: The Probation Service in the Inner City,* London: Kingsley.

Burke, L and Collett, S (forthcoming 2015), *Delivering Rehabilitation: The Politics, Governance and Control of Probation,* London: Routledge.

Collett, S (1993), "Beyond Reason and Understanding: The Everyday Understanding of Crime", *Probation Journal,* 40(4): 184–187.

(2008), "Tackling Anti-Racism in the 1980s", in *Moments in Probation* compiled by Paul Senior, Crayford: Shaw & Sons: 25-26.

(2013), "Riots, Revolution and Rehabilitation: The Future of Probation", *Howard Journal,* 52(2): 163-188.

Dorling, D (2013), *Injustice: Why Social Inequality Persists,* Bristol: Policy Press.

Garland, D (2001) *The Culture of Control,* Oxford: Oxford University Press.

Gifford, L, Brown, W and Bundey, R (2009), *Loosen The Shackles: First Report of the Liverpool 8 Inquiry into Race Relations in Liverpool,* London: Karia Press.

Home Office (2003), *Prison Statistics England and Wales 2002,* London Home Office.

Kett, J, Collett, S J, Barron, C, Hill, I and Metherell, D (1992), *Managing and Developing Anti-Racist Probation Practice: A Resource Pack For Action,* Merseyside Probation Service.

Mair, G and Burke, L (2011), *Redemption, Rehabilitation and Risk Management: A History of Probation,* London: Routledge.

McKnight, J (2009), "Speaking up for probation", *Howard Journal,* 48(4):327–43.

McWilliams, W (1987), "Probation, Pragmatism and Policy, *Howard Journal,* 26(2): 97–121.

Northumbria Probation Service (1992), *The Dog That Finally Barked,* Northumbria Probation Service, March 1992.

Parker, T (1963), *The Unknown Citizen,* London: Hutchinson.

Silverman (2012), *Crime, Policy and the Media: The Shaping of Criminal Justice 1989–2010,* London: Routledge.

Simpson, P and Crawley, P (1985), "Myrtle Gardens: Moving into the Inner
    City", in Scott, D, Stone, N, Simpson, P and Falkingham, P (eds.),
    Going Local in Probation? Case Studies in Community Practice, Norwich/
    Manchester: University of East Anglia Social Work Programme/University
    of Manchester Department of Social Administration.

Wallich-Clifford, A (1974), *No Fixed Abode*, London: Macmillan.

    (1976), *Caring on Skid Row*, Dublin: Veritas Publications.

Worthington, M (1991), "Cause and Effect of City Riots", *Guardian*, 2nd
    December.

    (1992), "Riots Link Suggestion Nonsense", *Newcastle Journal*, 4th March.

20. Seventies Probation

Sue Winfield

January 1st 1970, my first day and my first job as a probation officer in County Durham, and I didn't have to go to work! In the north-east, January 1st was always taken as a public holiday before it was designated as a national public holiday in 1974. So, it was Friday January 2nd when I reported to Peterlee Probation Office, where I was given a warm welcome by my senior probation officer, Jim Ashton, delighted to have a qualified officer at last, and a woman too! He talked me through the caseload he had selected, a mix mainly of naughty young boys, some very difficult young girls, and adult males and females serving prison sentences. At that time male probation officers were not permitted to supervise women offenders, or clients as we knew them, but female probation officers could supervise male offenders of all ages.

"There's one of your clients I'm going to take you out to meet today," explained Jim. "Her mother's been on the phone and she wants our advice." On the way he explained that Dorothy who was on a probation order and had been living in London for a while and had come home over Christmas with her boyfriend.

"Mrs Miller isn't convinced he's a boy so she wants us to sort it out," he continued. So Dorothy introduced us to Con, we chatted, and found out that they reported to the same office in London. That made our task easier so we reassured Mrs Miller that we would speak to someone at that office on Monday. I did just that and got the confirmation of what Jim and I suspected; Dorothy and Con were female partners, and not just in crime! Qualified I might have been, but as I had discovered so soon—you were always having to deal with the unexpected. Follow-up discussions with Mrs Miller helping her to come to terms with the nature of her daughter's new relationship taught me a lot about family dynamics.

Another unexpected scenario was a telephone call from the headmaster's secretary at one of the secondary schools. "Can you come up to school straightaway—Neil Clark who's under your supervision is causing havoc and as you're his probation officer we need you to get him to stop." I arrived at the school to find that they wanted me to stop Neil running around school going "Hee-haw". His class teacher was a Mr Bray! Why they had to involve me and had not taken hold of the situation before I arrived, located Neil, and escorted him off the premises, which is what I did, baffles me to this day.

I was one of few Certificate of Qualification in Social Work (CQSW) trained officers. After graduating in law, I took an 18-month Diploma in Applied Social Studies at Nottingham University, one of the courses set up in the late-1960s to increase graduate recruitment into the Probation Service. Bill Beaumont and Roger Ford were on my course, and Jenny Roberts (West then) was in the year ahead. John Haines, Nancy Hazel and Geoff Maccabee were our tutors with John and Elizabeth Newson, joint directors of the Child Development Research Unit (and authors at that time of *Four Years Old in an Urban Community*) schooling us in all we needed to know on childhood development and psychology.

Peterlee, named after the celebrated Durham miners' leader Peter Lee, was founded in 1948 to provide housing and employment for those who would no longer have job opportunities in the mines. Our patch was the new town, and a myriad of small mining villages around, as well as a scattered rural community. Alternative employment there was, but mainly in light industry; a number of clothing and food factories provided shift work which became increasingly attractive to women who had never worked before, and not always to the ex-miners. The resultant pressures on the family dynamics frequently surfaced during my home visits!

The team was one senior probation officer, four probation officers, two male, two female and three secretaries. All officers carried a caseload, and had reporting afternoons, on different days so that there was sufficient seating in the waiting room. These would usually run until 7 pm or 8 pm in the evening which meant that after 5 pm I would be on my own in the building with only my reportees to protect me. We all shared the court duties for the magistrates, juvenile and domestic courts, as well as regular office duty, known as kindred social work (KSW). Anyone could be waiting to see the duty officer about debts, housing, difficult children, but by far the greatest number were "marital cases"; no summons could be issued in the matrimonial court, no application could be made by a married woman to go on the housing list without having talked to the probation officer about the prospect of reconciliation. Quite what advice I gave at 22 I now dread to think!

In between the court and office duties we did social enquiry reports involving office interviews, home visits, and visits to remand prisons for those in custody; and there were adoption and *guardian ad litem* reports, frequently time consuming. There were home visits to all on our caseload and the families of those in custody. Regular visits to prisons, borstals and detention centres were undertaken to those who would subsequently be released under supervision. And there was the paperwork. All reports and records were either handwritten or dictated and then transcribed. Court reports were typed, six copies with carbon paper, and asking for any alteration let alone the many I required, certainly developed my negotiating skills.

The courts were central to our activity and there were strong relationships with magistrates, court staff, police and solicitors. The magistrates from the local community were interested and supportive. When out on home visits in one of the colliery villages, I would see the chair of the bench walking to the pit with his bait bag on his shoulder and we would wave as our paths crossed. We attended monthly case committees with the clerk to the court and a small number of the magistrates to discuss the cases on our registers. They would ask for feedback on any cases in which they had a special interest and we would highlight those to be considered for discharge or commendation as well as identifying the ones where breach action was required. Under the terms of supervision orders on juveniles the supervising officer could apply to the court for a summons to bring the supervisee back to court for their own protection. I did this, not often, but on occasion when a youngster was clearly out-of-control and was committing or at-risk of committing offences, often refusing to go home; stopping them for their own good was often the best thing to do. And invariably this would involve a brief time "in custody" in the local remand home before the summons was heard at court. On one occasion when I had taken such action against Sheryl and she was to be taken by the police to Seaham Remand Home, there was no woman police officer on duty, so a predictable request from the police: "Could you possibly act as escort?"; the subsequent journey in the back of the police car gave plenty of time to listen to Sheryl's feelings about what I'd done to her.

As a young inexperienced officer bursting with enthusiasm and bright ideas I was nurtured, if not indulged by Jim Ashton. As my SPO he would listen patiently to my latest outburst, problem, bright idea or whatever, offer his perspective, and leave me to get on with it. I cannot remember him ever forbidding me doing anything or getting angry. He did come fairly close to it on one occasion as we walked from the office to the court, and I was so preoccupied telling him about what I was going to say at the case committee, and somehow the office keys dropped right out of my hands, and as luck would have it down a street drain. Not surprising then that I was left to talk to the magistrates on my own.

As well as the strong working relationships Jim nurtured within the criminal justice system, he also created an ethos in the team that we could only truly help our clients if we engaged the support of the community. I gave talks to the magistrates, church groups, even Rotary about the importance of group activities for the young boys I supervised and for which I would need equipment and money for travel. And financial support was forthcoming. So I started with a day trip to Durham hoping that the sanctified atmosphere of the cathedral, the ambience of the castle, and the riverside walks would captivate the young boys and encourage them to better pursuits; it was not the most successful of outings as there was an attempted shoplifting as we passed through the market *en route* to the cathedral. Undeterred I progressed to hikes in Hamsterly Forest and weekend camps in Weardale and in the countryside where there was less temptation.

The ladies of the Womens' Royal Voluntary Service (WRVS)(as it was then) who ran the court canteen kindly gave me some of their takings to support the activities of the Prisoners' Wives Group; this paid for the hire of a room where we ran sewing groups with the off-cuts of materials I had acquired from the local clothing factories and the women could make childrens' clothes and soft furnishings for their homes. We did also manage to fund the occasional girls' night out, and during one such event I was introduced to a new wine experience—"*Mate Us Rose!*"

Once I had established the links with the factories, it was not too difficult to persuade the personnel manager that she might like to interview a young girl on my caseload, very carefully selected of course, and eminently suitable (in my opinion) to be given a trial for a job. The food factories were often responsive to my approaches for job opportunities for adults. However when seeking job opportunities for clients, my star was Sergeant Paddy Fox, the Army recruiting officer. There were several young men, many of them strong applicants, but also quite a few who were not, but Paddy was always willing to see them and give them a chance.

There was a different sort of community which was very important in the early days of my career: the wider probation community. In Durham County there were many stars: Bill Pearce was principal probation officer although he left in late-1970 for London, Graham Smith was senior probation officer in Durham City (and he followed Bill a couple of years later) and Anne Mace was a probation officer in Sunderland. Each went on to highly successful careers. Napo Northern Branch was a strong and lively forum which drew together colleagues of all grades across the North-East, and through which my sense of the wider probation family grew. Our annual conferences held at Shap Wells Hotel, and subsequently at Otterburn Hall attracted speakers and probation colleagues from all over the country and in the early-1970s we were often joined by colleagues from Northern Ireland.

Another significant development in establishing the concept of an extended probation family, in my mind at least, was the establishment of regional staff development in 1970. Bill Bayley was the first regional staff development officer (RSDO) with George Best as his deputy. I started with a pre-confirmation course, followed the next year by a post-confirmation course, and on these would meet colleagues from across the north and establish friendships some of which would continue throughout my career. One of the hallmarks of these courses was that they were a week long; much enjoyed by the attendees, but possibly considered an indulgence now. A second feature was the interesting venues for these residential courses; Burton Manor in Cheshire, Lytham St Annes, but the most notable was the Diocesan Retreat House at Crawshawbooth, or more particularly the amenities in the village including the dog cemetery, the local pub, and what we were told was the last remaining coal-fired fish and chip shop in the country.

After the relevant RSD course in student supervision, no doubt at one of the above venues, I was able to take students, and for the next three or four years there was a regular flow of them to our office from Newcastle and York Universities; they had to work hard because it was such a busy office, but we had fun too, and longstanding relationships were formed. I was also the university liaison officer for Durham University; I understood that the post was to encourage graduate recruitment into the Probation Service. The careers officer would identify those expressing an interest, and I would talk to them and arrange observation placements for those wishing to take it further. Presumably there were others filling this rôle at other universities, but I never met them, and I have no idea whether graduate recruitment increased.

In 1975, I was appointed community service organizer. Durham County was one of six pilot areas for this new sentence and I took over from Fred Phipps who had set up the scheme; my task was to consolidate it.

Community service was a wonderful addition to the courts' sentencing powers. It had varying appeal. To some it was a punishment, to others a let off, a route to rehabilitation for others. In reality it is all of these. And the key to a successful order was good assessment of the offender and then appropriate placement in the community. Those assessed as suitable for individual placement would be matched against available projects in their local community; youth clubs, luncheon clubs, old people's homes, community associations, riding for the disabled. Durham County Council introduced a policy to take community service offenders into their residential homes, and when there was a possible candidate I would submit a detailed application to the assistant director of social services so he could assess the offender, including their risks, their skills and decide on suitability; ability to play the piano was often crucial in the decision.

In addition to individual placements we also required a range of community activities which could accommodate a group of three-to-four offenders supervised by a Probation Service ancillary. We had some exciting projects: archaeological digs at Piercebridge and Binchester Fort under the supervision of eminent Durham University archaeologists, Peter Scott and Professor Rosemary Cramp. Another was developing a range of environmental sites for Durham Wildlife Trust at Joe's Pond and Hawthorn Dene. Beamish Museum was in its early days and with little financial support at that time. The director, Frank Atkinson (a member of the probation committee) was more than happy to provide endless activities for community service offenders, usually clearing the land around the coal mine or renovating buildings such as the miners' cottages, the bandstand and the farm.

And whilst these exciting and imaginative projects were often just regarded by those serving their sentence as "somewhere to work-off my hours", every now and again there would be a star: the young man who progressed to train as a youth leader or the person who became a keen archaeologist after successful completion of his order. I say young men, and of course they were the majority, but there were women too on community service. One was a real star: Brenda was placed at a hospital for the severely sub-normal and progressed to working on a ward as a voluntary ancillary worker.

It did not always turn out so positively; those who were reluctant to attend sometimes had to be dug out of bed, not the sort of Sunday morning activity I would choose, and pigeon racing was not an acceptable excuse for absence. There was plenty of court work, usually prosecutions for breaching the order following three unacceptable absences. It was essential to enforce the orders, not only to ensure good compliance from offenders, but also to maintain confidence in the scheme amongst courts and the community.

There were plenty of opportunities to promote the sentence more widely. As a pilot area for community service orders, it was important to provide regular feedback to sentencers, the Home Office and their researchers as well as to the wide range of organizations supporting the scheme by providing placements. And when the scheme went national there was a call for many more speaking engagements as others prepared to implement this new sentence. There were talks to magistrates, training seminars, proba-tion seminars, and even talks to procurators fiscal as Scotland prepared for implementation. The most prestigious of all these was the University of Cambridge's Institute of Criminology conference at Trinity Hall on the subject of "The Community Service Order". Jenny West, who had led the pilot in Nottinghamshire, and I both spoke about our respective experiences and, in the odd spare moment in the ten days of the conference, we were able to enjoy a few of the delights of Cambridge in that long hot summer of 1976.

I loved my job in those early years as a probation officer and then as community service organizer. I would not go so far as to say that I loved the offenders, but I have vivid memories of many of them; I can recall their names and addresses, see their faces and picture talking to them and their families in their homes. My strongest recollections with community service is of the organizations, and more particularly the outputs from their projects; those refurbished miners' cottages at Beamish, the new woodland paths and steps at Hawthorn Dene, the newly painted youth centre. And in those early days I learned about the importance of identifying and nurturing the potential of the individual, but also that if the individual was to develop that potential fully, then the community had to be engaged, actively and symbolically.

Probation in the 1970s was about supervising offenders in the community, with the community and for the community. As officers of the court we were accountable to the court but we had their support to work with offenders as individuals to rehabilitate them within their community. With many cases we had the active support of the community too, essential for the full rehabilitation of the offender. Almost half a century later as new organizations emerge to undertake the work of the community rehabilitation companies (CRCs) it is my hope that they will develop a vision for re-integrating offenders into the community which requires the active engagement of the community.

Sue Winfield, Probation officer, County Durham January 1970; Deputy Chief Probation Officer, Northumbria, 1988–2002.

Index

Abel Smith, Brian *80*

accountability *10, 14, 18, 64, 128, 161, 174*
  Ministers to *14*
accredited programmes *155*
activities *140, 141, 153*
  non-criminal activities *143*
Acton *123*
Adams, Roy *166*
addiction *57, 108, 167*
administrative interference *169*
adoption *12, 104, 126, 181, 212*
adults *22, 99, 131, 181, 185*
Advanced Social Work Course *81*
"advise, assist and befriend" *34, 89, 95, 103,
    117, 173*
Advisory Council on the Penal System *65*
Advisory Council on the Treatment of
    Offenders *41, 64*
advocacy *74, 140*
affinity *89*
after-care *12, 27, 41, 58, 64, 162, 182*
  Central After-Care Association *37, 65*
  voluntary after-care *58, 162, 198*
aggression *103*
alcohol *12, 61, 90, 101, 116, 137, 185*
Alderson, John *110*
alienation *142*
Allen, Dudley *35*
All-Party Penal Affairs Group *53*
all-purpose court officer *103*
alternatives to custody/prison *46, 54, 91,
    111, 175, 189*
altruism *12, 89, 174*
amalgamation *43, 156*
ambiguity *204*
ambition *15, 136, 163, 181*
amends *137, 140, 204*
American Probation and Parole Association
    156
Amherst, Massachusetts *84*

amphetamines *108*
Amsterdam *122*
ancillary workers *97, 183, 197, 215*
anger *146, 190*
  anger management *33, 190*
Anthony, John *84–85*
apprenticeships *26, 170*
approved school *126, 162, 181*
archaeology *215*
Archer, Colin *56–63*
Armitage, Simon *55*
Army recruits *214*
Artists Agency *167*
Asha Centre *62*
Ashridge *62*
Ashton, Jim *210, 213*
Ashworth, Andrew *50*
Ashworth Hospital *53*
Asians *201*
aspirations *11–20, 160, 175, 187, 202*
assessment *29, 100, 112, 132, 138, 156, 197, 215*
asset stripping *14*
Assizes *182, 186*
Association of Black Probation Officers
    27, 52
Association of Chief Officers of Probation
    *18, 48, 51, 53, 66, 86, 111, 122, 136,
    151, 191*
Association of Chief Police Officers *51*
Association of Retired Chief Officers and
    Inspectors of Probation *vi, viii, 11,
    136, 146*
Atkinson, Frank *215*
attitude *12, 66, 133, 146, 187, 188*
  public attitude *19*
  revengeful attitude *34*
Audit Commission *49, 52*
Auld, Mr Justice *50*
autonomy *31, 34, 64, 126–128, 174*
bail *111, 151, 167, 192*

"bail bandits" *51*
bail hostels *110*
bail information *51, 67*
Bailey, Royston *84, 109, 120*
Baker, Kenneth *18*
Bale Risk of Custody Scale *175*
Balls, Ed *145*
Baptists *171*
Barking *94*
Barley, Diana *109*
Barnes, Vic *171, 174*
Barnett House *62*
Barratt, Paddy *21*
Barrow, Arnold *59*
Basingstoke *112*
Bayley, Bill *84, 214*
Beaconsfield *56*
Beamish Museum *215*
Beatrix Potter *40*
Beaumont, Bill *163, 211*
bed and breakfast *91*
Bedford Prison *116*
Beeston *108*
befriending *30, 44, 74, 85, 140, 153, 180*
begging *99, 101*
behaviour *15*
  behaviourists *116*
benefits
  benefits of scale *43*
  benefits to communities *128*
  welfare benefits *74, 167*
Bennett, Alan *vi, vii, 19, 196–197*
Bennett, Arnold *185*
Berinsfield *118*
Bermondsey *79*
Best, George *214*
Biestek, Father *161*
Binchester Fort *215*
Birmingham *89, 110*
  Birmingham University *181*
  Birmingham Wheels Project *111*
Blackbird Leys *118*
black people *27, 28, 94, 111, 153, 200*
Blair, Tony *204*

blameworthiness *72, 76*
Bolton *162*
Borehamwood *57*
borstal *32, 38, 58, 59, 102, 154, 162, 212*
  Borstal After-Care Association *61*
  "neighbourhood borstals" *65*
Boston (USA) *110*
boundary changes *150*
Bow Street *198*
Bradford *42*
Bradford University *42*
Brady, Ian *41*
Brathay Hall *41*
bravado *137*
breach *103, 113, 128, 142, 173, 216*
Bridgeman, Barrie *21–24*
Bridges, Andrew *133*
Briggs, Asa *46*
bright ideas *212*
Brighton *27*
Bristol *27, 105, 148, 154*
  Bristol University *28, 35, 107, 112, 132, 148*
British Association of Social Workers *130*
Brixton *99*
  Brixton Prison *82*
Broadmoor Hospital *53, 108*
brokerage role *188, 189*
Brown, Chris *60, 80, 107*
Buckingham, Bob *22*
Buckinghamshire *107*
Buckle, Ken *185*
Buckley Hall Detention Centre *162*
Bulger, James *204*
Bull, David *154*
Burbidge, John *33, 35*
bureaucracy *43*
Burslem *185*
Burton Manor *214*
"Bus Boycott" (Bristol) *27*
Calderbank, Liz *49*
Callaghan, Jim *46*
camaraderie *40, 117*
Camberwell *99, 119*
Cambridge *68, 216*

Cambridge Criminology Course *62*

Cambridge Institute of Criminology *44,*
216

Campaign for Homeless and Rootless *199*

Cannings, Jim *86, 97–106*

Canton, Rob *158*

capital punishment *86, 102, 124*

Cardiff *45, 148*

care *25, 57, 137, 173, 175, 193*
care and control *25, 66*
care of the elderly *16*
childcare *16*
journey in caring *25–29, 34*

Carlisle, Lord *50*

Carnegie Trust *44*

Carroll, Rodney *165*

Carter, Lord *53, 135*

case committees *31, 41, 124, 182, 188, 212*

case conference *139*

caseload *21, 31, 40, 42, 99, 108, 117, 137, 141,*
156, 162, 181, 186, 212

casework *80, 91, 92, 116, 136, 161*
"deep casework" *182*
one-to-one casework *70, 77*

cash limits *66*

Cathy Come Home *116, 198*

causes *76*

cautions *108*

Cavadino, Paul *53*

Cavanagh, Winifred *181*

Centenary Celebration *54*

Central Council for Education and
Training in Social Work *130*

Central Council of Probation Committees
86

centralisation
cold hand of centralisation *180*

centre-stage *202*

CEP *157*

Certificate in Social Science *161*

Certificate of Qualification in Social Work
121, 154, 172, 211

Chakrabati, Shami *156*

change *78, 103, 140, 146, 154, 158, 173, 182*

"Change Your Ways in 30 Days" *176*
changing behaviour *12, 137*

charisma *102, 110, 120, 167*

charity *14, 164*

Chell Heath *185*

Cheshire *43, 53, 214*

Cheshunt *57*

Chesters, George *188, 194*

Chetham's School of Music *52*

children *104, 109, 125, 129, 162, 211*
child abuse *42*
childcare *16*
Child Development Research Unit *211*
Childen and Family Court Advisory and
Support Service *131*
Child Poverty Action Group *199*
child protection *85*

Children and Young Persons Act 1969 *131*

Childs, Geoff *82*

Christianity *89, 171*

Christie, Nils *44*

church *28, 42, 61*

citizenship courses *143*

civil aspects
civilised culture *16*
civil riots *12*

civil servants *47, 49, 52, 96, 97, 128, 151, 156*

Clarke, Kenneth *49, 203*

class *75, 98, 108, 170*

Cleveland *150, 169, 190*

"**clients**" *21, 26, 34, 64, 95, 117, 124*
"favourite" clients *32*
"staying with" *161*

Coalition *11, 206*

Coates, Les *83*

cognitive behavioural methods *132, 140, 176*

Collett, Steve *53, 196–209*

Collins, Mr Justice *178*

commendation *212*

commercial confidentiality *193*

Commission for Racial Equality *45, 50*

commissioning *140*

Commission on English Prisons *144*

commitment *78, 194*

"common sense" *69*, *107*

community *10*

 community centres *48*

 community courts *138*

 community networks *142*

 community payback *134*, *159*

 community probation officers *48*

 community rehabilitation companies *10*,
  14, *207*, *217*

 community resources *109*

 Community Safety Strategy *167*

 community service *12*, *43*, *44*, *65*, *84*, *91*, *97*,
  104, *128*, *149*, *183*, *189*, *215*

  first order *109*

 community spirit *161*

 troubled communities *48*

companionship *142*

compassion *12*, *16*, *175*, *191*

competence *119*, *148*

competition *13*

complacency *207*

complexity *73*, *198*, *201*

compliance *132*, *134*, *179*, *216*

computer training *155*

conciliation *84*

condemnation *51*, *74*, *204*

conduct disorders *143*

confidence *58*, *74*, *119*, *120*, *154*, *216*

confidentiality *85*

consent *86*, *139*

 consent to marry *104*

Conservatism *54*, *66*, *192*, *203*

Consett *182*

consistency *156*

contact *70*, *85*, *141*, *172*

 close contact *143*

contestability *157*

contracting *140*

control *197*, *207*

 control of behaviour *74*

 out-of-control *212*

 social control *35*, *78*, *132*

Cook, John *112*

co-operation *50*, *85*

Cooper, Frank *107*

Cooper, Joan *44*, *45*

Copenhagen *46*

coping *190*

Cornwall

 Devon and Cornwall *156*

corporal punishment *86*

corrections *52*, *131*, *199*

 correctional drift *201*

 Correctional Programme Assessment
  Inventory *155*

Cotton, Bill *98*

Coulsfield, Lord *54*

councillors *43*

counselling *71*, *96*, *190*

 family counselling *77*

courage *12*

courts *58*, *71*, *100*, *113*, *117*, *126*, *148*

 Crown Court *118*

 higher courts *104*, *181*

 officers of the court *93*

 presence in court *22*

Coventry *21*, *111*

Cowley *118*

Cowperthwaite, David *46*

Cramp, Rosemary *215*

Crawforth, John *49*

Crawshawbooth Diocesan Retreat *214*

"crazy young fools" *187*

creativity *67*, *80*, *84*, *120*

credibility *68*, *196*, *200*

cricket *33*

crime *27*, *129*, *185*

 Crime Concern *110*

 crime control *196*

 crime prevention *110*, *117*

 crime reduction *66*, *68*, *136*

 high crime areas *191*

 "war against crime" *167*

Crime and Disorder Act 1998 *48*, *168*

criminal

 criminal classes *11*

 criminality *133*

 Criminal Justice Conferences *50*

Criminal Justice Consultative Council 49, 52

Criminal Justice Act 1948 38, 86

Criminal Justice Act 1982 175

Criminal Justice Act 1991 18, 48–51, 86, 132, 167, 202, 203

criminology 39, 44, 74

crisis 188

crisis management 190

Croatia 158

Cropwood Conferences 44

Crossing Cultures 158

Crown Court 136, 151, 173

culpability 73

complex culpability 76

culture 11, 13, 15, 193

cultural identity 15

Cumberland Lodge 56

Cumbria 111

cynicism 139

Dale, Bill 148

damage 145

dangerous offenders 85, 107, 205

Davies, Martin 43

Davis, Angela 158

day centres 12, 43, 61, 66, 67, 77, 84, 93, 111, 151, 154, 167, 175, 183, 190

Day, Michael 36, 45, 80, 82, 110

Deane, Rosemary 82

debate

lack of 17

debt 181, 211

decarceration 113

decency 196

dedication *vii*

Deeds, Dorothy 161

deep-end offenders 112

democracy

need to rediscover 13

Department for Work and Pensions 80

Department of Health, etc. 53, 77, 135

depression 142, 145

deprivation 14, 35, 94, 116, 149, 169, 170

desolation 142

despair 186

destructiveness 145

self-destructiveness 142

detention centres 33, 58, 212

deterence 134

development 119, 164

deviance 30

Devon 84, 109, 117, 118, 120

Devon and Cornwall 156

Dholakia, Navnit 50

diagnosis 71

dual diagnosis 107

diet 153

difference 15, 17, 48, 201

making a difference 55, 96, 172, 175

dilemmas 15

Diploma in Applied Social Studies 211

Diploma in Probation Studies 165

Diploma in Social Work 121

direct entry 98, 127, 130, 162, 164, 181

Director of Public Prosecutions 51

Directors of Social Service 51

disability 47

disadvantage 11–13, 15, 146, 175, 190, 200

disaffection 26, 77

discharge 212

Discharged Prisoners Aid Societies 65, 162

discipline 114, 120, 131, 142

discretion 58, 87

discrimination 27, 200

double discrimination 201

discussion

lack of nuanced discussion 17

serialised discussion with offenders 182

disease *vii*

disenchantment 151

disillusionment 204

Disney, Miss and Walt 40

disorganized individuals 35

disruption 137

disturbances 199

diversion 110

diversity 94, 118, 157

divorce/court welfare *12, 43, 58, 90, 118, 125, 131, 188*

domestic
domestic abuse *157*
domestic courts *125, 211*
domestic disputes *40, 104*

Donnison, David *80*

Dorling, Danny *206*

Dorman Long *170*

Dormanstown *171*

Dorset *141*

Downes, David *50*

dreams *16*

drifting *77*

drink-driving programme *112*

drop-in centres *77, 92, 175*

"drop-in office" *189*

drugs *12, 41, 57, 61, 90, 116, 119, 137, 155*

drunkenness *90, 99*

Dulwich *99*

Durham *109, 148–150, 169, 181, 210*
Durham University *111, 215*
Durham Wildlife Trust *215*

"duty officer" *118*

dynamics *191–193*

dysfunction *189*

early death *191*

East Anglia University *84*

East Barnet *57*

East Midlands *89*

Ecclesfield Grammar School *37*

economic aspects *189, 191, 199, 204*
economic depression *111*

Edinburgh *46, 51*

education *16, 138–140, 158, 176*

Edwards, Fred *45*

effectiveness *50, 68*

efficiency *177, 179*

ego-junkies *17*

elderly *47*

Elephant and Castle *99, 102*

Ellis, Mary *108*

emotion *187*
emotional realities *85*

empathy *141, 187*

"end-to-end" management of sentences *135*

enforcement *130, 134, 179, 216*

engagement *217*
engaging with offenders *140*

enthusiasm *90, 96, 149, 212*

environment *63*

equal opportunities *12, 120, 154*

Esmée Fairbairn Foundation *54*

esoteric knowledge *71*

esprit de corps *180*

ethics *23, 38*
ethical crisis *193*

ethnicity *94*

ethos *182, 213*

Europe *13, 157*
European Excellence Model *96*
European Society of Criminology *158*

evaluation *156*

evening centres *164*

evidence-based approach *67, 93, 95, 112, 113, 156, 176, 205*

evil *41*

Excellence Awards *157*

Exeter *110, 120*
Exeter University *21, 121, 122*

expenditure cuts *13–14*

factories *213*

fairness *193*

Fallon Inquiry *53*

family
Family Court Team *151*
family court welfare role *84*
family dynamics *82, 186, 210*
family proceedings courts *125*
Family Welfare Association *38, 127*

Farmer, Seldon *97*

Farnworth *162*

fatigue *52*

Faulkner, David *49, 50, 64–69, 86, 133*

fears *16*

fecklessness *206*

feedback *188, 216*

Feltham Young Offender Institution *108*

Fenton *185*
Ferguson, John *80*
Fielder, Mary *49*
fieldwork *42, 92, 173, 189*
financial aspects *14, 192*
   Financial Management Initiative *49, 66*
   financial pressure *191*
Finch, David *163*
fines *87*
   unit fines *203*
Fishwick, Colin *107*
Flegg, Deidre *83*
Fletcher-Cooke, Charles *64*
Fletcher, Harry *26*
food vouchers *100*
Ford, Roger *107, 211*
forgiveness *74*
formula funding *178*
Foster, Frank *38*
fostering *113*
Foster, Laurie *84*
Fox, Sgt Paddy *214*
fragmentation *15, 159, 191*
Freud *70*
Frost, Robert *55*
frustration *146, 162*
Fullwood, Cedric *37–55, 166*
Galloway, Burt *110*
Garland, David *196, 199*
Garston *161*
Gateshead *181*
gender *98*
General National Vocational Qualification
   121
General Social Care Council *131*
generic work *173*
Geneva *82*
Germany *45*
Gibbs, Don *114*
Gibson, Bryan *112*
Gifford Inquiry *200*
Gipsy Hill *99*
Gloucestershire *30*
"going straight" *91*

good *34*
   "good guys" of the system *66*
   good practice *145, 191, 193*
Goode, Winifred *64*
Gorton *39*
Grayling, Chris *54, 207*
Gray, Roy *114*
Greater Manchester *46*
Green Forms *61*
Green Shield stamps *153*
Grendon Underwood *41*
Grindrod, Nigel *39, 45*
groups *43*
   group activities *213*
   group dynamics *23, 93*
   groupwork *67, 81, 82, 112, 143, 153, 176*
   group working skills *190*
   women in male groups *141*
Grubb Institute *42, 84–85*
guardian ad litem *58, 104, 118, 126, 212*
guesswork *71*
guidance *131, 177, 182, 186*
guidelines *66, 183*
Guisborough *171*
Hackney *114*
Hadfield, Peter *169–180*
Haines, John *58, 62, 211*
half-way houses *110*
Halliday Review *53*
Hall, Penelope *161*
Hall, Tony *154*
Hambrook, Fred *80*
Hampshire *111, 112, 155–157*
Hanley *185, 189*
hard-drinking *154*
Harding, John *36, 84, 107–115*
hard labour *86*
harm *134*
Harper, John *84, 119*
Harrison, Royden *38*
Hartlepool *149, 169*
Haswell, Arthur *148*
Hattersley *41*
Havant *155*

Havering *94*
Hawthorn Dene *215, 217*
hazards *59*
Hazel, Nancy *211*
health *16, 42, 138–139, 158, 162, 190, 191*
  Health Act 1948 *80*
  health and safety *89*
  healthcare *199*
Heaney, Seamus *147*
help *28, 85, 89, 131, 142*
Henderson Hospital *81*
Henley Business School *177*
Hereford and Worcester *60, 83*
heroin *108*
Hertfordshire *57*
Hewell Grange *65*
Hewlings, David *84, 110*
Heywood, Jane *42*
Hicks, John *166*
High Wycombe *119*
Hilton, Harry *80*
Hindley *65*
Hobsbawm, Eric *69*
Hocking, Charles *150*
Hogan, Mike *44*
Hoggart, Richard *37*
Holland *122*
Hollway, Cath *107*
Holtom, Christopher *35, 107*
Holt, Tom *39*
home circumstances *92*
homelessness *61, 91, 109, 124, 173, 198*
  homeless ex-servicemen *99*
Home Office *11, 21, 42, 48, 56, 62, 64, 89, 97,*
    111, 116, 128, 148, 151, 156, 160, 191, 216
  Probation Unit *48*
  Research Unit *43, 50*
  Trojan horse *128*
Home Secretary *18, 49, 59, 87, 110, 113, 122,*
    165, 178, 191, 205
home visits *32, 58, 91, 118, 125, 149, 162, 173,*
    182, 186, 195, 211
homosexual offences *103*
honesty *176*

Hood, Roger *50*
hope *16, 77, 117*
Horner, Derek *171, 174*
hospital orders *172*
hostage *59*
hostels *23, 43, 62, 66, 83, 84, 99, 104, 150, 167,*
    173, 176, 183, 205
  Salvation Army hostel *77*
House of Commons *54*
House of Lords *54, 66*
housing *116, 143, 162, 185, 211*
  housing associations *111*
Howard League *144, 146*
Howard, Michael *34, 50, 51, 113, 167, 178,*
    191, 203
Howell, Ron *79*
humanity *173, 192, 193, 196, 198*
human rights *120*
Humphreys, John *52*
"hunches" *138*
Hunt, Arthur *112*
Hunt, Lord *43*
Hurd, Douglas *67, 167*
hurt *35*
Hylton, Basil *25–36*
Hyson Green *92*
ICI Nylon Chemical Works *170*
ideas *84*
inadequacy *103*
incentives *16*
incorrigible rogues *101*
independent sector *14*
indeterminate sentence *87*
Indiana *110*
individualism *16, 18*
industry *185, 190*
initiatives *12, 148, 192*
injunction *178*
injustice *12, 117*
  social injustice *28*
innovation *12, 14, 67, 77, 120, 166, 180, 189*
inspection *23, 39, 40, 44, 58, 64, 84, 96, 97,*
    121, 126, 152, 177, 179, 182
  Probation Inspectorate *58*

integrity *12*

intellectual game *70*

inter-agency co-operation *140*

interdisciplinary work *110*

intermediate treatment *33, 41*

international aspects *13, 46, 50, 52, 54, 95, 122, 152, 159*

intervention *71, 156*

interviews *100, 139*

IRA *155*

isolation *189*

Jamaica *25, 26, 35*

James, Jimmy *57*

jargon *71*

Jarvis, Fred *39, 58*

Jehu, Derek *116*

Jephcott, Pearl *38*

"jewel of the system" *ix*

Jews *107*

job satisfaction *15, 16*

"jobsworths" *16*

Joe's Pond *215*

John Lewis mutuality *16*

joint funding *190*

Jones, Beti *45*

Jones, Gordon *56*

Jones, Howard *39*

Jones, John *83*

Jones, Martin *148–152*

Jordan *87, 153, 158*

Judge, Igor *50*

judges *44, 49, 50, 54, 85, 87, 93, 96, 113, 122, 138*

judicial review *178*

Judicial Studies Board *49–50*

judiciary *50, 131*

Jung *107*

just deserts *203*

Justices' Clerks' Society *51*

Justice Secretary *133, 207*

juveniles *12, 22, 33, 99, 104, 108, 112, 153, 157, 181, 211*

Katowice *84*

Kearney, Martha *52*

Kearsley *162*

Keele University *74*

Keidan, Olive *161*

Kennington *97*

Kent *109*

key workers *85*

Kilbrandon, Lord *45, 47*

kindness *192*

"kindred social work" *40, 181, 211*

King's College, London *56*

Kings Lynn *148*

Kingston-upon-Thames *80*

Klein, Melanie *41*

knee-jerk policies *205*

knowledge *127, 135*

labelling *75*

Labour Party *67, 105*

Lacey, Malcolm *57, 59, 68, 83, 124–147*

Lambeth *97*

Laming, Herbert *45, 107*

Lancashire *43, 44, 64, 109, 161*

Lancaster *161*

Langley House Trust *23*

language *71, 94*

late-night working *149*

Latessa, Ed *155*

law *116, 186*

law and order *204, 205*

law degree (LLB) *174*

Lawrence, Stephen *94, 202*

Lazarus, Ernst *56*

leadership *68, 119, 145, 167, 177, 182*

charismatic leadership *69*

learning *29, 141, 182*

Leeds *111, 161*

legacy *87, 192*

Leicester

Vaughan College *23*

Leicestershire *93*

Leicester University *39, 112, 116*

"less eligibility" *80*

Lewis Review *53*

Leyhill Prison *33*

liberal aspects *26*

"liberation theology" 28
licence 144
Lichfield 116
life
  life crisis 137
  "life experience" 40
  life licence 108
  Lifeline 41
  life-plan 140
  lifers 40
limits of society 198
Lincoln 89
listen and nod technique 56
literacy 139
Little Lever 162
Liverpool 39, 197, 199
  Liverpool University 161
Loach, Ken 198
local aspects 10, 13
  local authorities 62, 99, 113, 144, 149, 156, 188
  Local Authorities Association 51
  local service vii
  loss of local accountability 18
locking-up people for longer 19
Lockwood, Howard 89–96, 107
logic 23
London 97
  Inner London Probation Service 80, 106, 113
  London School of Economics 79, 105, 127
  London University 105
  North-East London Probation Service 94
loneliness 189
long game 172
Long Lartin Prison 60, 83
Longton 185
Lowry, Paddy 60
loyalty 151
Luther King, Martin 26
Lytham St Annes 214
Maccabee, Geoff 211
Mace, Anne 214
Macmillan, J J 39

MacPherson Inquiry 94, 202
Macrae, Finlay 64
magistrates 31, 38, 41, 43, 57, 81, 85, 87, 108, 113, 122, 144, 148, 182, 211
  magistrates' courts 22, 39, 97, 100, 136, 138, 149, 173, 181, 185, 198
  stipendiary magistrates 100
Maguire, James 175
Maidstone 153
Maine 110
Major, John 51, 204
management 34, 60, 68, 104, 117, 132, 145, 164, 174, 191
  "tactical management" 65
Manchester 39, 55, 65
  Greater Manchester 43, 48, 164
  Manchester Criminological Society 41
  Manchester Fred 102
  Manchester Statistical Society 51
  Manchester University 42
mandatory sentencing 87
Manpower Services Commission 110, 112
Mapperley Hospital 116
marginalisation 11, 207
Marin County (USA) 153
"marital cases" 211
markets 13, 17
  market-driven world 192
  pseudo-markets 192
Marks & Spencer 46
Marlborough Street 105
marriage
  Marriage Guidance Council 149
  permission to marry 12
Marshall, Richard 112
Marsh, Jack 43, 163
Martinson, Professor 44
Marx, Gerda and Karl 40
Marylebone 82
Massachusetts 108, 113
maternity leave 154
Mathieson, David 166, 202
matrimonial cases 58, 83, 104
  matrimonial counselling 181

matrimonial court reports *31*
matrimonial referrals *40*
Matza, David *75*
Maudling, Reginald *59*
Mays, J B *161*
MBA *179*
McClintock Lecture *51*
McFarlane, Mary Ann *153–159*
McGrath, Dr *108*
McKnight, Judy *206*
McWilliams, Bill *40, 68, 198*
media *17, 52, 87, 109, 136, 192*
letters to *52*
self-interested media *19*
mediation *73, 84, 104, 125, 132*
Mellor, David *67, 111*
Mennonites *110*
mental health *101, 129, 137*
mentally-disturbed prisoners *155*
mentors *82, 87, 96, 120, 162, 183, 186*
mercy *72*
Merseyside *65, 165, 201*
Methodism *89, 92, 170, 181*
meths *101*
Metropolitan Police *114*
Middle-East *158*
Middlesbrough *11, 169, 170, 173–175, 185–190*
Middlesex Quarter Sessions *59*
Midgley, Mary *15*
Midlands *93, 127*
Mid-Staffs Health experience *192*
Mile Oak Approved School *116*
Miles, Ieuan *86*
Militant Tendency *166*
Millard, David *70–78, 83*
Miller, Jerry *112*
mining *211*
Ministers
dealing with *51*
Ministry of Justice *10, 14, 135*
Minto, Marlyn *166*
misfortune *vii*
Mitcham *80*
mods and rockers *187*

money payment supervision *104, 125*
Monger, Mark *116, 124*
monitoring *34*
Mood, John *186*
Moores-Wheedon, Lois *35*
morale *15, 78, 94, 114, 148*
morality *15, 31, 38, 69, 72*
moral complexity *76*
moral conundrums *16*
moral danger *125*
Morell, Eric *107*
Morgan, Rod *50*
Morison Committee *64*
Morrell, D H *75*
Morrell, Les *39*
Morrison, Alan *107*
motivation *16, 33, 77, 85, 139, 171*
motorbike group *174*
Mowlam House *192*
Mowlam, Mo *192*
multi-agency/disciplinary working *138, 155*
**multi-agency public protection arrange-
ments** *85, 205*
multi-tasking *12*
murder *102, 108, 118*
Murphy, Steve *155*
Murray, Andrew *21*
naïvety *12, 90, 97*
nanny state *19, 192*
Napo *17, 154, 214*
narrowness *13*
Nashville *156*
**National Association for the Care and
Resettlement of Offenders** *50, 110,
146, 162*
**National Association of Local Government
Officers** *166*
National Association of Probation Officers
66, 86, 104, 124, 163, 174, 206
National Children's Homes *113*
National Council of Probation Committees
120
National Front *27*
National Institute of Social Work *109*

nationalisation. See *probation: Probation Service: nationalisation*

National Marriage Guidance Council *84*

National Offender Management Service *53, 54, 132, 144, 179, 206*

National Probation Directorate. See under *probation*

National Probation Service. See under *probation*

National Society for the Prevention of Cruelty to Children *42*

National Sports Council *112*

National Standards *113, 155, 177*

National Vocational Qualification *178*

neighbourhood centres/networks *109, 111*

neighbours' quarrels *12, 40, 104, 125, 181*

Nellis, Mike *68*

neo-conservativism *19*

neo-liberalism *19*

Netherlands *122*

Newcastle *166, 214*

Newham *94*

New Labour *10, 52, 87, 165, 167, 192, 204*

News of the World *205*

Newson, John and Elizabeth *211*

New Zealand *87*

Engaging Communities in Criminal Justice *138*

night shelter *61*

nimbyism *177*

non-conformists *160*

non-government organizations *111*

non-judgmental *161*

Norfolk *148*

Norman, Bob *107*

Northallerton *172*

Northampton *49, 116*

North-East Prison After-Care Society *viii*

Northern Ireland *54, 59, 214*

North Ormesby *170*

Northumbria *150, 166, 168, 200*

Norwich *84*

"nothing works" *44, 95*

Nottingham *89, 107, 109*

Nottinghamshire *44, 216*

Nottingham University *97, 211*

Notting Hill *82*

Notting Hill Riots *27*

numeracy *139*

nurturing *193, 217*

objectives *132*

offender

offender supervisors *178*

offenders *95*

offender management *156, 197*

offender managers *135*

office visits *187*

Old Bailey *103*

Oldham *163*

Old Street *80*

on-the-spot reports *100*

Openshaw *39*

oppression *159*

optimism *12*

organizational behaviour *42*

Orton, Geoffrey *98, 106*

Otterburn Hall *214*

outreach *84*

ownership of information *139*

Oxford *56, 62, 119*

Oxfordshire *117*

Oxford University *176*

Palestine *158*

Palmer, Barry *85*

Palmer, Brenda *119*

paperwork *212*

parenting *143, 191*

Parker, Tony *197*

Parkhurst Prison *155, 158*

Parkinson, Geoffrey *80*

parliamentary candidate *105*

parole *27, 41, 58, 65, 97, 129, 163*

Parole Board *43, 83, 152, 184*

partnerships *50, 61, 67, 85, 93, 111, 117, 140, 155, 157, 159, 167, 183, 190, 199*

Paskell, Peter *107, 108*

pathology *118*

Patten, John *18, 49, 67*

Patterson, Alexander *110*
pay *98*
Pearce, Bill *45, 82, 181, 214*
Pease, Ken *43*
Peckham *99*
Penal Affairs Consortium *53*
penal servitude *86*
penal-welfarism *196, 204*
Pendleton, John *68*
Pentonville Prison *82*
Perfect, Mark *52*
performance *14, 68, 96, 174*
　performance indicators *69*
Perrie, Bill *60*
Perrie Lectures *62*
personal change/development *63*
personality *186*
　personality disorder *90*
Peter G *109*
Peterlee *210*
petty offenders *198*
philosophy *15, 72, 74, 76, 116, 146, 192*
Phipps, Fred *215*
Phoenix House *119*
physiology *116*
Piercebridge *215*
placements *38, 119, 127, 148, 172, 215*
　"observational" placement *161*
Pleasance, Geoff *41*
Plymouth *120*
　Plymouth Polytechnic *121*
　Plymouth University *131*
Poland *84*
police *51, 54, 57, 85, 96, 112, 113, 114, 117, 148,*
　　156
　hostile policing *27*
　police court missionaries *39, 63, 133, 149*
　racist policing *200*
political dimensions *37, 46, 59, 65, 86, 95,*
　　113, 116, 132, 146, 166, 169, 185, 191,
　　192, 198, 203
　political aspiration *13, 17*
　political forces *10*
　political ideological demagoguery *14*

political rhetoric *113*
political spin *19*
Pooley, Dick *108*
Poor Law Amendment Act 1834 *80*
Portsmouth *112*
Potteries *185*
Potters Bar *57*
poverty *14, 27, 80, 109, 116, 158, 161, 191, 197,*
　　198
Powell, Enoch *27*
practice *127*
pragmatism *76, 191*
prejudice *13, 72, 159, 202*
pre-sentence reports *22, 108, 117, 136*
　fast delivery PSRs *136*
Preservation of the Rights of Prisoners *108*
pressure *148*
Preston *64*
Preston, Robert *26*
pre-trial services *167*
previous convictions *73, 203*
Priestly, Phillip *175*
prison *34, 134, 144, 150, 183, 212*
　alternatives to prison *41*
　clang of the prison gates *100*
　dispersal sector *83*
　doubling of the prison population *132*
　HM Prison Service *51*
　increasing use *205*
　Prison Commission *64*
　Prison Department *64*
　Prisoners' Wives Groups *149, 213*
　prison officers *96*
　Prison Officers' Association *65*
　prison overcrowding *65, 67*
　Prison Reform Trust *146*
　prison unrest *67*
　Prison Welfare Service *104*
　"prison works" *18, 34, 167, 191*
　recall to prison *129*
　Special Secure Unit *155*
　top security prison *155*
　visitors' centre *83*

privatisation/private sector *14, 17, 54, 95,*
  113, 159, 177, 193, 206
probation *197*
  National Probation Directorate *136*
  probation boards *53*
  Probation Chiefs Association *vi, 55, 136, 146*
  probation committees *43, 58, 64, 132, 188*
  "probation family" *95, 151, 161, 194, 214*
  Probation Institute *10, 88*
  Probation Officer 160
  Probation Officers Manual 186
  Probation of Offenders Act 1907 *44, 140*
  Probation Rules *164*
  Probation Service
      nationalisation *10, 18, 113, 192*
      National Probation Service *14, 53, 95,*
        133, 156, 204, 207
  probation service officers *183*
  probation trusts *131*
  purpose of probation *34*
  purpose of probation officers *34*
problems
  "problem families" *129*
  problem-solving *138, 182*
procurator fiscal *47, 216*
professionalism *107, 126, 164*
  professional independence *66*
profit *vii, 14, 159, 193, 196, 206, 207*
prognosis *71*
prolific offending *142*
propaganda *19*
prosecutors *113, 117, 122*
prostitutes *102, 153*
protection of the public *117*
protocols *16, 192*
psychiatry *44, 81, 107, 108, 116, 138*
psychology *37, 75, 116, 136, 138, 176, 211*
  psycho-babble *72*
  psychologising *70*
psychopathy *90, 108*
public
  public policy *13*
  public protection *205*
  public relations *120*

  public safety *103, 132, 136, 140*
  public sector *193*
punishment *19, 34, 65, 66, 95, 146, 182, 189,*
    196, 207, 215
  punishment in the community *132*
quality assurance *120*
Quarter Sessions *148, 185, 186*
race *26, 28, 62, 94, 200, 201*
  institutional racism *202*
  race riots *111*
  racial discrimination *12*
  racial injustice *66*
Race Relations (Amendment) Act 2000 *201*
radicalism
  radical activism *104*
  radical non-intervention *154*
Radzinowicz, Leon *54*
Rainbow Day Centre *189, 194*
Rainer Foundation/Rainer House *21, 41, 79,*
    82, 97, 127, 135, 161
Ralphs, Peter *153*
Ranby Prison *90*
"rat boys" *51*
Ratcliffe, Stan *80*
rationalisation *86*
Raynor, Peter *68*
Read, Gordon *60, 79–88, 120, 147*
Reading, Lady *41*
realism *198*
reassurance *186*
rebellion *89*
recognizance *140*
recompense *128*
reconciliation *73, 181, 212*
recruitment *64, 98, 116, 132, 144*
Redcar *169, 172, 174*
Redridge *94*
Rees, George *150*
referrals *100, 132, 141*
  rapid referral *138*
reflection *16*
regional staff development *83, 119, 165*
rehabilitation *10, 34, 66, 95, 113, 140, 150, 159,*
    189, 197

"rehabilitation revolution" *65*

transforming rehabilitation *14, 207*

Reid, John *205*

reintegration *10, 125, 143*

Relate *84, 119*

relationships *63, 65, 75, 162, 178, 179*

reciprocity of relationships *76*

religion *39*

remands *112*

re-offending *134, 135, 136, 187*

reparation *73, 189*

repeat offenders *138*

reporting *182*

research *65, 67, 121, 136*

resettlement *83, 144*

resilience *187*

respect *34, 41, 59, 88, 158, 191, 202*

responsibility *16, 87, 89, 133, 137, 139*

restitution *159*

restorative justice *110, 111*

Rethinking Crime and Punishment *54*

retribution *73, 132*

revolution *163*

rewards *78, 144*

Rhodes, Lord *44, 52*

Rhodes Trust *52*

Richardson gang *99*

Richmond Approved School *172*

riots *12, 92, 133*

race riots *111*

risk *134, 138, 207*

at-risk young offenders *112*

high-risk offenders *143, 178*

risk-assessment *12, 16*

risk-management *14, 197*

Risley Remand Centre *162*

Ritson, Bruce *108*

Robb, Gordon *60, 83, 87*

Roberts, Anne *165*

Roberts, Colin *176*

Roberts, Jenny (West) *44, 50, 62, 107, 158, 211, 216*

Robinson, Ray *80*

role models *154*

rôle play *190*

Romania *114*

Rose Hill *118*

Rose, Lord Justice *52*

rough sleepers *101*

Royal College of Social Work (proposed) *145*

Royal Courts of Justice *56, 178*

"rude boys" *26*

Ruskin College *39*

"Rust Belt" *169*

Ruston Bucyrus (Engineering) *89*

Rutherford, Andrew *50, 112*

Rutter, Bill *35*

Sainsbury Centre for Mental Health *142*

Sainsbury, Eric *38*

Sainsbury Report *142*

salaries *59*

Salford *43*

Salvation Army *100*

Samuels, Mollie *89, 105*

Sanders, Hugh *38*

San Francisco *153*

Scandinavia *122*

scapegoating *35*

Scarborough *163*

scepticism *86, 90, 140, 176*

Schmideberg, Melitta *41*

Schofield, Helen *165*

schools *41*

school visits *182*

Scotland *44, 54, 163, 216*

Scottish Office *45*

Scott, Peter *215*

screening *112*

scrutiny *140, 191*

Scunthorpe *89*

Seaham Remand Home *212*

second-career people *162*

Sedgefield *172*

Seebohm Committee *129*

Selcare Trust *44, 162, 164*

self-control *102, 141*

self-worth

highly developed sense of *206*
sentencing *12*
  response to *188*
Sentencing Council *50*
seriousness *73, 117, 118, 188*
  serious offences *133, 137*
  serious offender rehabilitation team *85, 118*
"servants of the court" *50*
sexism *62*
sex offenders *84, 167, 205*
shaming *124*
Shap Wells Hotel *214*
"share sale" *14*
Sheffield *37*
  Sheffield University *38*
Shelter *199*
Shelton *189*
sheriffs *47*
Shropshire *109*
Silverman, Jon *205*
Simey, T S *161*
Simon Community *197*
skills *10, 58, 84, 86, 114, 120, 127, 135, 138, 142,*
    154, 190
"skinheads" *89*
slavery *200*
"slum" clearance *99*
Smith, David *41*
Smith, Graham *86, 176, 214*
social
  social awareness *191*
  social circumstances *188*
  social control *35, 103, 132*
  social discord *12*
  social divides *193*
  social enquiry reports *22, 31, 56, 92, 102, 117,*
    162, 181, 186, 212
  social housing *185*
  social interaction *33*
  social justice/injustice *28, 120, 188*
  socially-damaged people *35*
  social milieu *188*
  social policy *37, 116*
  social security *138*

social services *45*
social stability *33*
social underclass *14*
social unrest *12*
social work *53, 76, 116–118, 127*
  "generic" social work *129*
  Social Work Departments (Scotland) *47*
  social worker *131*
Social Work Scotland Act 1968 *45*
sociology *37, 116*
  sociological influences *161*
soundbites *49*
Southampton *112, 154*
  Southampton University *112*
South Mimms *57*
South Yorkshire *166*
space *77*
special hospitals *53*
specialist reports/staff *43, 117*
Speirs, Bob *39*
spiral of convictions *75*
sports counselling *112*
stability *33*
staff *97, 104, 195*
  staff development *94*
Staffordshire *111, 189*
stakeholders *157, 158*
standards *66*
stand-down reports *102*
St Andrews *163*
state
  reduction in scale *13*
Statement of National Objectives and
    Priorities *34, 67, 175, 190*
Statham, Roger *10–20, 68, 146, 174–175, 178,*
    185–195
statistics *65, 120, 125*
steelworks *170*
stereotyping *159*
Stern, Vivien *50*
Stevens, John *114, 167*
St Hilda's (Middlesborough) *173*
stigma *35, 130, 131*
Stockport *164*

Stockton-on-Tees *169*

Stoke-on-Trent *11, 77, 185*

Stone, Chris *51, 68*

Strangeways Prison *162*

prison riots *48*

Strasbourg *46*

strategy *157, 176, 205*

Straw, Jack *110, 113, 165*

stress *92, 119*

students *105, 117, 119, 164, 214*

student units *105*

succeeding *154*

suicide *137, 181*

suits *148*

Sullivan, Doris *106*

summer camp *163*

Sun *114*

Sunderland *182, 214*

supervision *57, 132, 136, 153, 178, 188, 197*

close supervision *129*

enhanced supervision *112*

process of *140*

supervision orders *33*

support *77, 142, 151, 175*

support groups *12*

Sure Start *146*

surveillance *197, 207*

Swann, Cliff *23, 61*

Swansea Prison *150*

Sweden *122*

Sydenham *99*

talent *16, 194*

"talking a good fight" *176*

targets *14, 16, 69, 88, 94, 182, 192, 205*

accountancy-led targets *16*

Tavistock Clinic/Institute *42, 81*

Taylor, Roy *84*

teamwork *22, 77, 183*

team goals *34*

"Teamwork in Probation" *84*

Teesside *150, 169, 177, 190*

Teesside Polytechnic *172*

Teesside University *179*

temperance movement *171*

Tench, Ron *164*

Tennessee *156*

Tennyson, Alfred *79*

tensions *13, 16, 189*

Thames Valley *168*

Thatcher, Margaret *46, 48, 66, 167, 203*

theology *42*

Department of Theology Conference *51*

theory *127*

therapy *41, 71, 76, 140*

family therapy *154*

Inner London Creative Therapy Unit *119*

therapeutic communities *108*

"therapeutic interventions" *71*

therapeutic trinity *141*

Thetford *149*

thinking differently *175*

Thomas, Jill *51, 86*

Thompson, E P and Dorothy *37*

Thompson, Leslie *27, 82*

Thornborough, Peggy *119*

Thorntree *170*

throughcare *183*

Timms, Noel *42*

Titmuss, Richard *41, 47, 80*

Tooting *81*

Toronto *46*

"toughness" *167, 204*

"tough-love" *25*

tower blocks *99*

Towle, Charlotte *42*

Toxteth *161, 200*

trade unionism *17, 94, 130, 151, 163, 174, 191*

traditions *67*

Trafford *164*

training *43, 62, 64, 84, 86, 92, 97, 108, 116, 120, 127, 130, 144, 148, 164*

youth training *189*

transference *31*

"Transforming Rehabilitation" *14*

"tribalism" *169*

troubled families *69*

truculence *187*

trust *74*

"helpful distrust" *140*
Tuck, Mary *50*
Tunstall *185*
Turkey *87, 157*
turning lives around *15*
twinning *157*
Tyneside *201*
uncertainty *17*
underclass *14*
Underdown, Andrew *49*
understanding *51, 74, 204*
unemployment *12, 77, 138, 169, 191*
Union Jack Club *99*
unit fines *203*
university liaison officer *105*
unpaid work *91*
unruly children *40*
upheaval *43*
urban aid *111*
USA *54, 110, 113, 153*
Utting, William *45*
values *vii, 10, 16, 18, 65, 69, 88, 135, 158, 172,*
    193
  shareholder values *14*
  social work values *66*
Vandy, Miss *40*
Vanstone, Maurice *68*
Vaughan College, Leicester *23*
Vera Institute of Justice *51, 68*
victims *12, 35, 66, 157, 167*
  victim/offender mediation *110*
  Victim Support *62*
Vidal/Hinds, Susan *36*
violence *90, 94, 102, 118, 139, 159, 185*
"virtual problem-solving teams" *138*
vision *10, 65, 68–69, 83, 200*
visitors centre (prison) *155*
Vizard, Michael *84, 116–123*
vocation *174, 180*
voluntary sector *14, 24, 44, 61, 67, 79, 88,*
    101, 109, 113, 142, 153, 157, 183
  Discharged Prisoners Aid Societies *65, 162*
vulnerabilities *119*
Wales *148*

Walford, Peggy *194*
Wallington *80*
Waltham Forest *94*
Walton, David *111*
Walworth *99*
Wandsworth Prison *82*
"war against crime" *167*
Warburton, Peter *150, 181–184*
Ward, David *68*
Ward, Mike *86*
warmth *141*
Warner, Norman *52*
Washington *155*
Wasserman, Sydney *42*
waste *43*
Weardale *213*
Webb, Norman *186*
weekend camps *213*
Weetman, Phil *163*
welfare *80, 91, 103, 126, 129, 135, 161, 192,*
    196, 198
  Prison Welfare Service *104*
  welfare benefits *74, 167*
  welfare state *19, 199, 206*
West *216*
West, Doug *174*
West, Fred *85*
West Glamorgan *150*
Westhill College *181*
West, Jenny (Roberts) *216*
West Kensington *82*
West Malling *154*
West Mercia *61*
West Midlands *45, 62, 65, 110*
Weston, Bill *51, 86*
West Sussex *155*
West Yorkshire *51*
Whatton Detention Centre *89, 91*
"what works" *29, 46, 50, 69, 95, 112, 155, 176,*
    205
Whiskin, Nigel *110*
Whitehead, Philip *68*
Whitelaw, William *67, 167*
Whitfield, Dick *122*

Whiting, Adrian *36*

Wigan *160*

Williams of Mostyn, Lord *18*, *95*

Williams, Raymond *37*

Willson, Michael *120*

Wilson, Harold *42*

Wilson, Richard *51*

Winchester *21*, *156*

Winfield, Sue *167*, *210–217*

Woddis, Mordecai *107*

Wolverhampton *111*

Wolverhampton Crypt Association *111*

women *62*, *65*, *93*, *125*, *141*, *154–157*, *156*, *164*,
      186, *201*, *210*, *216*

Womens' Royal Voluntary Service *213*

Wootton, Barbara *41*

Worcester *59*

Worcestershire *83*

Worthington, Mike *160–168*, *200*

Wotherspoon, Jean *166*

writing *51*, *68*, *78*, *82*, *109*

Yates, Len *165*

York *214*

Yorkshire *169*, *172*

Younger, George *47*

Younger, Kenneth *41*

young men *137*

young offenders *65*, *112*, *131*

young offender institution *65*, *112*, *191*

Young, Priscilla *39*

youth justice *49*, *52*

Youth Justice Board *53*

youth justice/offending teams *53*, *110*, *146*

Youth Justice Strategy for England and
      Wales *168*

zeal *174*

Zehr, Howard *110*

zero-hours contracts *16*, *80*

"zero tolerance" *168*

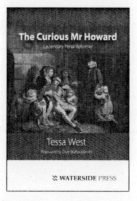

The Curious Mr Howard:
Legendary Prison Reformer

Tessa West — With a Foreword by Clive Stafford-Smith

Wherever he went the perfectionist John Howard brought his influence, genius and reputation to bear seeking to improve prisons and other institutions — and as this book shows he deserves to be remembered as a far greater figure in social history than many people might suspect.

'Impeccably researched and fascinating': *The Howard Journal*

'No-one who reads this wonderful book could dispute that Howard ranks among the most interesting people of his age': *Times Literary Supplement.*

'A brilliant book': Nick Hardwick, Chief Inspector of Prisons

'A riveting account of the great penal reformer, this humane, obsessive, guilt-ridden, lonely dissenter, indeed the "curious Mr Howard"': guardian.co.uk

Hardback & Ebook | ISBN 978-1-904380-73-3 | 2011 | 384 pages

www.WatersidePress.co.uk

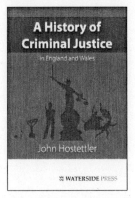

A History of Criminal Justice
in England and Wales
John Hostettler

John Hostettler's work is an ideal introduction. It charts all the main developments of criminal justice, from Anglo-Saxon dooms to the Common Law, struggles for political, legislative and judicial ascendency and the formation of the modern-day Criminal Justice System. Among a wealth of topics the book looks at the Rule of Law, the development of the criminal courts, police forces, the jury, justices of the peace and individual crimes and punishments. It locates all the iconic events of criminal justice history and law reform within a wider background and context - demonstrating a wealth and depth of knowledge.

'Highly recommended': *Choice*

'Every student entering law school should have a copy and read it':
Criminal Law and Justice Weekly

Paperback & Ebook | ISBN 978-1-904380-51-1 | 2009 | 352 pages

www.WatersidePress.co.uk

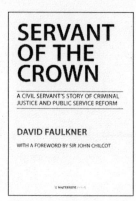

Servant of the Crown:
A Civil Servant's Story of Criminal Justice
and Public Service Reform

David Faulkner — With a Foreword by Sir John Chilcot

Servant of the Crown takes the reader inside Whitehall to see how issues of the day were handled and policies formed as the author progressed to working alongside Home Secretaries and other senior politicians. It includes an explanation of the author's understanding of a civil servant's duty as a servant of the Crown, historically and in a world where public services have become increasingly subject to political intervention.

'Raises crucial questions about ... the proper roles of civil servants and politicians': Professor Rob Canton.

'Enriches our understanding': Professor David Downes.

'Anyone interested in the state and its relationship to citizens should read [this book]': Professor Graham Towl.

'A uniquely rewarding book': John Chilcot.

Paperback & Ebook | ISBN 978-1-909976-02-3 | July 2014 | 208 pages

www.WatersidePress.co.uk